P9-CCZ-837

FREEDOM RIDER DIARY

Carol Ruth Silver

FREEDOM RIDER DIARY

Smuggled Notes from Parchman Prison

University Press of Mississippi / Jackson

Willie Morris Books in Memoir and Biography

www.upress.state.ms.us

The University Press of Mississippi is a member
of the Association of American University Presses.

Manufactured in the United States of America

First printing 2014
∞
Library of Congress Cataloging-in-Publication Data

Silver, Carol Ruth.
Freedom rider diary : smuggled notes from Parchman Prison / Carol Ruth Silver.
pages cm
"Willie Morris Books in Memoir and Biography."
Includes bibliographical references and index.
ISBN 978-1-61703-887-7 (cloth : alk. paper) — ISBN 978-1-61703-888-4 (ebook)
1. Silver, Carol Ruth—Diaries. 2. Freedom Rides, 1961—Diaries. 3. Women civil rights workers—United States—Diaries. 4. African Americans—Civil rights—Southern States—Diaries. 5. African American civil rights workers—Southern States. 6. Civil rights workers—Southern States—Diaries. 7. Civil rights movements—United States—History—20th century. 8. Southern States—Race relations. I. Title.
E185.61.S579 2013
323.1196'0730750904—dc23 2013028811

British Library Cataloging-in-Publication Data available

To Mildred and Nathan Silver,
in whose voices I speak

CONTENTS

ACKNOWLEDGMENTS

Without the help of many people, spanning many years, this book would not have been possible. I am grateful to all of them. My thanks particularly to:

Freedom Rider Claude Albert Liggins, picture editor, my collaborator on the photo essay for this book

Ray Arsenault, including for his definitive history book, *Freedom Riders: 1961 and the Struggle for Racial Justice*

Eric Etheridge, for *Breach of Peace: Portraits of the 1961 Mississippi Freedom Riders*

Craig Gill, University Press of Mississippi, who first suggested to me that this book might be published

Jerry W. Mitchell, investigative reporter for the *Clarion-Ledger*, Jackson, Mississippi, who mentioned this book to Craig Gill after seeing it during the exhibit created by the Mississippi Department of Archives and History for the Jackson celebration of the 50th Anniversary of the Freedom Rides

Jay Wiener, for his encouragement and helpful suggestions

Jane Maxine Silver, my sister, who word processed and corrected the entire manuscript, again, from the manuscript she had helped type on a little pink portable manual typewriter, some fifty years ago, along with other typist volunteers in Los Angeles, in August 1961; without them all, it would never have been possible to translate my tiny writings on scraps of prison paper into a manuscript

Cherie A. Gaines, attorney-at-law (retired)

Linda Joy Kattwinkel, attorney-at-law, Owen, Wickersham, & Erickson, P.C., San Francisco

California Lawyers for the Arts

Katie Keene, University Press of Mississippi

Carol Cox, copy editor for the University Press of Mississippi

Barbara Bowersock, my sister, for her loving support now and fifty years ago

My mother and father, Mildred and Nathan Silver

Celia Tisdale, audiovisual curator, Archives and Records Services, Mississippi Department of Archives and History (MDAH), Jackson, Mississippi

Mississippi Department of Archives and History, for preserving not only a copy of the original manuscript but also my artifacts from jail: my clothing and my white bread chess set

Lindsey Mejia, digital artist at Samy's Camera, Los Angeles, who worked on the photos

Tracy Bennett, Digital Canvas, LLC, Los Angeles, who worked on and uploaded the photos

Adam Hurwitz, who worked on the captions and photos

David Lisker, without whom the 40th Anniversary Reunion of the Freedom Riders at Tougaloo College, Jackson, Mississippi, would not have happened

Craig Newmark, who created and was the original webmaster for the 40th Anniversary Reunion of the Freedom Riders, FreedomRidersFoundation.org

My New York roommate, Dana White

My aunts Fay Schneider and Rosalie Ehrenwald and my uncle Leo Silver, who responded to the pleas of my mother to help raise money for my bail

Terry Perlman Hickerson, Freedom Rider, my cell mate, who has remembered

Shirley Thompson, Freedom Rider, who died too early

Lee Dorfman and the iDictate Transcription Service

Professor Michelle Alexander, for the reality check of her book, *The New Jim Crow: Mass Incarceration in the Age of Colorblindness*

Honorable Michael Hennessey, sheriff of San Francisco

Aref Yaqubi, photographer

Lexie Gay, photographer

Dot Young, indexer

INTRODUCTION

—Raymond Arsenault—

In 1961, Carol Ruth Silver became a Freedom Rider. A twenty-two-year-old secretary working at the United Nations headquarters in New York, she was one of the 436 seemingly "ordinary" individuals who participated in an extraordinary civil rights campaign that transformed the character of American democracy. Breaking precedent and ignoring both conventional wisdom and the advice of their elders, Carol and her fellow Freedom Riders employed a confrontational strategy of nonviolent direct action that took the civil rights struggle out of the courtroom and into the streets of the Jim Crow South.

Through a remarkable display of courage and audacity, they achieved one of the modern Civil Rights Movement's greatest triumphs, bringing about the desegregation of interstate travel on buses and trains and in the public accommodations related to that travel. Overcoming the intense, sometimes violent opposition of militant white supremacists, the Freedom Riders—in less than a year's time—toppled a discriminatory and demeaning system of Jim Crow travel that had existed for nearly a century.

To understand the magnitude of their achievement, we need to recall what the South and the nation were like in 1961.

Rampant racial inequality and overt and systematic racial discrimination prevailed in virtually every aspect of American life, from employment, housing, and education to public accommodations, the legal justice system, and politics. In the South, this troubling reality manifested itself in a codified system of racial separation known as Jim Crow. Cradle-to-grave segregation in the region was sanctified and enforced by a network of state and local laws–especially in the Deep South states of Mississippi, Alabama, Louisiana, Georgia, and South Carolina. In the North, where a more haphazard de facto system of segregation based on custom and economic inequality held sway, the racial situation showed more promise. But even there the democratic goals of civic and social equality and "liberty and justice for all" were unrealized ideals.

Black Americans had experienced some progress since the "racial nadir" years of the early twentieth century, especially in the 1940s and 1950s. Large-scale migration to the North, accelerating the trend of the "Great Migration" that began during World War I, brought a measure of economic and social improvement to many black Americans. In the immediate aftermath of World War II, the nation witnessed the desegregation of the armed forces as well as the breaking of the color line in collegiate and major league sports—highlighted by Jackie Robinson's ascendance to the Brooklyn Dodgers in 1947.

The postwar era also brought a noticeable increase in black voting in several border states and across the upper South, due in large part to the landmark 1944 U.S. Supreme Court decision *Smith v. Allright*, which eliminated a white primary system that had effectively barred black suffrage for generations.

Other pro–civil rights Supreme Court rulings followed, most notably the 1954 *Brown v. Board of Education* school desegregation decision which struck down the 1896 *Plessy v. Ferguson* decision's "separate but equal" doctrine. The full implementation of the *Brown* decision would require decades of additional advocacy and litigation, but there were important portents of change in the pro–civil rights rulings of an increasingly liberal Supreme Court. While the trajectory of the other two branches of the federal government on racial matters was less promising, Congress did manage to pass a pair of civil rights acts in 1957 and 1960—the first federal civil rights acts approved since 1875. Though largely symbolic, this legislation provided a modest foundation for future progress by establishing a U.S. Civil Rights Commission.

Despite the constraints of a Cold War that often curtailed dissent and social protest, the decade of the 1950s also witnessed a renewal of grassroots activism and the emergence of a full-fledged national Civil Rights Movement. Civil rights advocates were encouraged not only by the maturation of the NAACP as a force fighting for legal change, but also by the successful use of nonviolent direct action during the Montgomery bus boycott of 1955–56, the rising stature of the Reverend Martin Luther King, Jr., as a potential American Gandhi, and finally by the emergence of a restless black student movement initiated by the Greensboro, North Carolina, sit-ins in February 1960.

While these signs of progress were clearly significant, discrimination and segregation continued to dominate and restrict the lives of most African Americans. Indeed, there was little or no indication that fundamental change would come anytime soon. In the white South, most obviously in the Deep South, the dominant spirit was massive resistance to desegregation—a determination to defend the "southern way of life" at all costs. By 1960 the white moderates and liberals who had advocated evolutionary change in southern race relations had essentially disappeared, silenced by political demagogues and conservative reactionaries who pandered to popular prejudices and bigotry.

In the North, there was a scattering of liberal voices calling for change, but for the most part there was apathy and complacency on matters of race and civil rights. The one issue that dominated public debate at the beginning of the 1960s was the Cold War struggle between the United States and the Soviet Union. This solitary focus extended to the federal government, including the newly elected Kennedy administration and its New Frontier philosophy. President John F. Kennedy talked about fighting for freedom around the globe, but other than a few rhetorical flourishes, there was no evidence that he intended to create a New Frontier on the domestic front, or to play an active role in propelling the more-or-less stalled freedom struggle in the South.

The early months of the Kennedy era represented a difficult and discouraging time for civil rights leaders. How could they cut through the complacency of politicians and the public? How could they restore the momentum that the movement had enjoyed in the mid-1950s, following the *Brown* decision and the Montgomery bus boycott? The sit-in movement had provided a model of student activism, but not one that held out much hope of seizing public attention at the national or international level.

What the movement needed—and fortunately what the Congress of Racial Equality (CORE) came up with—was a strategy that forced the nation to redress the broken promises of American democracy—to meet the demands of freedom now, not freedom later. A small predominantly northern and interracial civil rights organization founded in Chicago in 1942, CORE followed the lead of its new national director, forty-one-year-old James Farmer, organizing a daring campaign with the audacious title of "Freedom Ride."

The Freedom Ride was designed to turn the Cold War to the Civil Rights Movement's advantage, to convince the Kennedy administration and the American public that it was dangerous and counterproductive, and essentially immoral, for the United States to call for democracy and freedom abroad when that same democracy and freedom was denied to millions of black Americans at home. If the United States wanted to win the hearts and minds of the rapidly decolonizing Third World, it would have to practice what it preached.

Specifically, the Freedom Riders would test compliance with two Supreme Court decisions mandating the desegregation of interstate travel (*Morgan v. Virginia*, 1946, and *Boynton v. Virginia*, 1960). The idea was to force the federal government to protect the Freedom Riders' constitutional rights—that is, to implement and enforce federal law, regardless of the political consequences or temporary civil disorder that resulted from the Freedom Riders' determination to exercise their rights as American citizens.

CORE's basic philosophy was grounded in the Gandhian tradition of nonviolence. The Freedom Riders would act as a nonviolent and disciplined vanguard, a small band of activists dedicated to moral suasion and the power of unmerited suffering. Though eclectic in their social makeup (the Freedom Rides brought together young students and movement veterans, blacks and whites, men and women, northerners and southerners, and religious and secular activists), they were united in their commitment to nonviolent direct action and the ideals of freedom, justice, and equality. They were also unrelenting and impatient in their call for change. If the government or members of the public regarded the demand for "freedom now" as unreasonable, so be it. And if the Freedom Riders had to risk injury or even die to prove their point, they were willing to do so.

The original Freedom Ride—which turned out to be only the first of more than sixty Freedom Rides undertaken during the spring and summer of 1961—ended in disappointment and partial failure when a planned two-week journey from Washington to New Orleans was truncated by acts of violence in Anniston and Birmingham, Alabama. The original thirteen Freedom Riders made it to New Orleans, but they traveled the last link of the journey by plane, not by bus. After one bus was firebombed by a white supremacist mob in Anniston on May 14, and a second group of Riders was assaulted by an even larger mob at a Birmingham bus station later the same day, CORE leaders directed the battered Riders to retreat to New Orleans by air. To the relief of the Kennedy administration, the dangerous Freedom Ride experiment appeared to be over. But, of course, it was not.

In the weeks and months that followed, more than four hundred new recruits marshaled the courage and resolve to pay their fare and board regular commercial buses—repurposed as freedom buses—bound for the dark heart of the Deep South. Representing a cross section of America, they literally and figuratively put their bodies on the line. Roughly half of the Freedom Riders were black, slightly more than half were from the North, one quarter were under the age of twenty, and another quarter were women.

Among the one hundred ten women who participated in the Freedom Rides was Carol Ruth Silver, a Massachusetts native who had graduated from the University of Chicago in 1960. After a day of orientation in Nashville, Tennessee, she and five other Riders boarded a bus to destiny on June 7, 1961. During the previous two weeks, more than seventy Freedom Riders had been arrested in Jackson, Mississippi, and on May 29, Attorney General Robert Kennedy, responding to the pressure exerted by the surge of Freedom Rides into Mississippi, had formally requested a sweeping desegregation order from the Interstate Commerce Commission (ICC).

On September 22, the ICC issued such an order, effective November 1, and by the end of the year the shadow of Jim Crow was all but gone from the buses, trains, and terminals of the South. Other dark and malevolent shadows persisted—in the schools, hospitals, courthouses, parks, hotels, and workplaces of the region—all to be dealt with and largely dispatched later in the decade. But the mystique of Jim Crow was broken in 1961—the year of the Freedom Rides.

By the end of that pivotal year, Carol Ruth Silver and more than three hundred other Freedom Riders had spent a month or more as inmates of the infamous Parchman prison farm (Mississippi State Penitentiary). For them the price of victory was a temporary loss of freedom—an unexpected, sometimes frightening, strangely satisfying experience that changed not only their lives but also the pace and course of the ongoing struggle for civil rights and racial justice. The lessons they learned in Parchman, the added moral and intellectual strength that they derived from their prison experiences, and the bonds of friendship and common purpose forged during those trying but ultimately triumphant days served the movement and the nation well in the years to come.

Virtually all of the incarcerated Freedom Riders retained strong and lasting memories of Parchman, but only one, Carol Ruth Silver, managed against all odds to record and preserve a comprehensive diary/contemporary memoir of her experiences. The publication of this revelatory document more than half a century after its creation is both a supreme act of citizenship and a unique contribution to the canon of civil rights scholarship. Putting her life at risk for the sake of freedom so long ago, Carol Ruth Silver has once again risen to the occasion, this time as a chronicler of youthful wisdom, righteous struggle, and uncommon fortitude.

All Americans who seek to understand the complexities of the civil rights story, as well as those who cherish the dream of democratic promise, owe her a debt of gratitude.

RAYMOND ARSENAULT is the John Hope Franklin Professor of Southern History and Chairman of the Department of History and Politics at the University of South Florida, St. Petersburg. He has also taught at Brandeis University, the University of Minnesota, the University of Chicago, the Université d'Angers in France, and the Florida State University Study Center in London. One of the nation's best-known civil rights historians, he was educated at Princeton University and Brandeis University, where he received his Ph.D. in 1981. He is the author of several prize-winning books, including *Freedom Riders: 1961 and the Struggle for Racial Justice* (2006, abridged edition 2011) and *The Sound of Freedom: Marian Anderson, the Lincoln Memorial, and the Concert That Awakened America* (2009). The 2011 PBS American Experience documentary, *Freedom Riders*, based on his book and directed by Stanley Nelson, won three Emmys and a George Peabody Award. A long-time activist, he is the recipient of several social justice and human rights awards, including the 2003 Nelson Poynter Civil Liberties Award.

To the tune of Harry Belafonte's "Day-O":

Took a trip on a Greyhound bus—hey!
Freedom's coming and it won't be long;
To fight segregation, this we must!
Freedom's coming and it won't be long.

Chorus: Freedom, Freedom—Freedom's coming
And it won't be long;
Freedom, Freedom—Freedom's coming
And it won't be long.

Took a trip down Alabama way—hey!
Freedom's coming and it won't be long;
Met much violence on Mother's Day!
Freedom's coming and it won't be long.

Come, Mr. Kennedy, take me out of misery!
Freedom's coming and it won't be long;
And segregation, look what it has done to me!
Freedom's coming and it won't be long.

If you travel wherever you go—hey!
Freedom's coming and it won't be long;
Be sure that you travel non–Jim Crow—hey!
Freedom's coming and it won't be long.

Mississippi has spared our cause—hey!
Freedom's coming and it won't be long;
Because Alabama has no laws!
Freedom's coming and it won't be long.

Freedom, Freedom—Freedom's coming
And it won't be long;
Freedom, Freedom—Freedom's coming
And it won't be long.

FREEDOM RIDER DIARY

Chapter 1

NEW YORK

Sunday, May 28, 1961

And why not me? I have no excuse for not going—I am not in school, my job is not permanent, financially I can afford to spend two months or so not working. I can even afford a bus ticket to Jackson, Mississippi, since all year I have been planning to take a bus trip this summer.

The idea of my going first occurred to me a couple of nights ago. I think that even then it was already in the form of "why not?" Even at that point I knew that I would really have to go.

But it is such a big step; there are so many angles.

Next year is my first year of law school. Will something like being sent to jail in Mississippi for flaunting segregation laws keep me from taking my bar exam three years hence? Or would the University of Chicago refuse me a scholarship or even kick me out of law school if it found out that I had a jail record? Would I be denied a security clearance? I had a clearance when I was working as a secretary at the United Nations, so evidently none of my activities in college are considered "un-American." What if the next time I need a security clearance the bureaucrat who is supposed to put on the final stamp is a Klansman from Jackson, Mississippi?

But the students who have already gone on the Freedom Rides have just as much to lose as I do. Once someone at Chicago refused to sign a petition I was circulating for the South Africa Legal Defense Fund, on the grounds that anyone who signs anything is open to possible future trouble. Is that the kind of liberal and the kind of person I am? Or want to be? My interest in law has always been as an instrument for social justice—if I sacrifice my conscience to my career what have I left? If what I know is right is inconsistent with either going to law school or becoming a lawyer, then I guess I shall have to choose a different profession.

My mother gave me a lecture once, in the completely different context of being a Jew, about the necessity of standing up and being counted. There comes a point where it is no longer sufficient to stand up and say "I believe" in such and so; eventually one must prove it by actions. And I guess my time has come.

Monday, May 29, 1961

I tried calling CORE (Congress of Racial Equality) today, but the person I was supposed to talk to was not around. The office there sounded like a madhouse—I can only imagine. The (*New York*) *Times* said today that a new organizational setup has been created between CORE and a number of southern religious organizations to coordinate the Freedom Riders, and the Rides *are* going to continue.

About the only thing I accomplished all day was finally to complete and mail off the last of my scholarship applications. Of all the private foundations I have approached, about the only one which looks at all likely is the Educational Foundation for Jewish Girls, so I am really banking on getting something from the University of Chicago itself. I figure that it is my best bet because, in the first place, the scholarship committee knows both my work and how poor I am, as documented by four years of undergraduate scholarships, and, in the second place, the law school offered me a scholarship of two thousand dollars last year. I expect that the one thing against me there is that I did not take it, but I did tell the dean why I wanted to take off a year from school to work, and he seemed, if not sympathetic, at least understanding.

And I really think that I was right. This year away from school has given me the time to digest at least some part of the mass of information and misinformation I picked up in college. And also to find out how little it means to be a member of the "Society of Educated Men" (especially if you happen to be a woman).

Leslie has finished the portrait he was doing of me, and tomorrow I must send it to my parents. I am sure that Mother will consider it too realistic and "academic" (although what with the state of today's academy that is a distinctly wrong term), but I must admit that I like it. He flattered me greatly, of course, but I think not too terribly much. At least he did not make my nose shorter, although he did make my chin less sharp and he did not put in the circles I usually have under my eyes from insufficient sleep. It is a profile, and the most interesting thing is that he made my pale complexion ("anemic," my mother will say, "you should come out here to California and get some sun") contrast very sharply with gobs of very dark hair, and then put a light blue background behind the hair for further contrast. He insisted though that my eyes are gray, not green, and I could not get him to change it. Anyway, it is very elegant, which my mother should like.

I am becoming more and more convinced of my own personal responsibility to go down to Jackson, Mississippi. The Negro is being discriminated against in the name of white supremacy, and I am white. It is now up to the white race to prove to the Negro that the Black Muslims do not have the answer, that what we need is brotherhood and cooperation, not race hatred. Besides that, I am a member of a minority group which has suffered its own persecutions and repressions. In the United States today there is still anti-Semitism, but in most cases I do not feel it directly because I am sufficiently assimilated to "pass." The Negro, though, no matter how assimilated, cannot pass.

I think of my Negro friends in the North—and of Dr. Abram Harris, my tutorial professor especially; I could sit in his office, across a desk littered with term papers and erudite books, trying to catch and hold the ideas and criticisms he was throwing at me ten miles a second. But he could not eat in the same restaurant with me in Mississippi. How can I not go? It is disgraceful that a supposedly free country tolerates such discrimination.

I have been very lucky. Even though my family has no money, I managed to get myself an education on scholarships and work. Education is the magic key to the better way of life that the Negro and everyone else in this society is seeking, and yet in the vast majority of cases the system of segregation denies educational opportunity to all but a very few Negroes in the South. And then people come along and talk about "gradualism" and how there must be an "educative process" before the white community will be ready to accept the Negro as an equal. The beneficiaries of the status quo are never ready to accept change: Pullman was not "ready" to deal with the unions. The situation is really quite analogous. Today with Africa achieving new status and new independence, with the "white man's burden" a rancid joke, the Negro in the South is no longer "ready" to accept segregation.

Tuesday, May 30, 1961

Sometimes I think that this place is not large enough for the three of us, even if it is the biggest bargain on the Lower East Side. When I got home from work today, after pounding a typewriter for eight hours, the telephone screaming in my ear the whole time, all I wanted to do was eat something that would not give me ulcers and curl up quietly with *The Magic Mountain.*

But first there was the troop of little neighborhood kids who followed Dana home and all the way up our four flights of stairs "just to get a drink of water," and to poke around at her guitar and my books, and to ask when they could come back and paint some more pictures. These are the same kids who used to come up when Dana was out of work for a couple of months, and when she had the time to run a double class in arts and crafts and in how-to-act-like-ladies-and-gentlemen. She has little enough time for herself, though, now that she is teaching.

As much as they sometimes make nuisances of themselves, I cannot help but really love these kids. They are all terribly, terribly poor, all either Negro or Puerto Rican (a representative sample of our neighbors). Dana's favorite is still Mike—about two feet high, coal black, and five or six years old—because he is the shyest and was the most conscientious of her "pupils." But the one I really like is Eugene—tall and lanky for his nine years, lighter-skinned than Mike and aware of the distinction—already a juvenile delinquent. Go on, ask him, he'll tell you, got a record two miles long, see—he's tough, he is. Eugene was especially impressed with my collection of high-heeled shoes (I have about seven hand-me-down pairs from a rich aunt who wears the same large shoe size).

"Hey," says Eugene, "do ya wear them all?"

"Oh, once in a while, one at a time."

"That's a good one!" And his laughter echoes back up the stairs as he throws himself down at breakneck speed.

By the time we finally got rid of all of the kids, Les was on the phone asking if I wanted to go to the opera. They are doing *Tannhäuser*, and I really wanted to go, but I told him that I just could not face the prospect of standing up four solid hours (or more), straining to see over the heads of the men six-foot-two who invariably get to the best standing-room positions before anyone else arrives. Joan got home just at this point, and discouraged me further by gleefully telling us that it was raining very hard, also that the temperature felt like almost-January instead of almost-June. That cinched it, and I told Les that unless he had come into an unexpected inheritance and wanted to call for me in a taxi as well as pay for at least mediocre seats, he should pick up some rolls and come over for dinner. We can see *Tannhäuser* next season.

About eight o'clock, after having tried all day to no avail, I finally reached Gordon Carey, at the CORE office.

"Yes, may I help you?"

"Well, I hope so. I take it that you are running the Freedom Rides?"

He laughed. "Not quite. But I *am* the area coordinator for New York. If there is any information you want perhaps I could give it to you."

"First, my name is Carol Ruth Silver . . . What I want to say, I mean . . . I want to be a Freedom Rider!"

"That's very fine." (A pause.) "Are you a student?"

"No. I graduated from college at the University of Chicago in June of 1960."

"What do you do?"

I told him that I would be working at a temporary office job until this Friday, then blurted out some words about how strongly antisegregationist I feel, and how important I think the Freedom Rides are.

"How long are you willing to stay in jail?"

"Well, . . . how long will I be sentenced to stay in jail for?"

"The original group got a suspended jail sentence and a two-hundred-dollar fine. They are now all in jail serving out the fine at the rate of three dollars per day. That means they will be in for sixty-seven days. However, the judge has threatened to increase the sentence if the Rides continue. Freedom Riders are being asked by CORE to stay in jail for a minimum of two months."

For a second I stopped short—I had figured on about thirty days. But I heard myself saying, "OK, I can stay for two months."

"Fine."

"But wait a minute—what if our sentences are longer than that? I'm entering law school this fall, and have to be back in Chicago on the 15th of September."

"Each person who gets out on bail costs CORE five hundred dollars, because we have to put up cash bonds. That's why we want you to stay at least two months, or as long as you can, although we promise to bail you out after that."

"That sounds very fair. I can commit myself to two months."

"Now just a moment, hold on. Have you had any experience before this with nonviolence or passive resistance?"

"Well, I was not in the local CORE chapter in Chicago, but I did participate in picketing at Woolworth's, in sympathy with the sit-ins in the South. That was sponsored by the student branch of the NAACP (National Association for the Advancement of Colored People) and the University of Chicago's National Student Association delegation."

"But did you ever get any actual training in nonviolence techniques?"

"I suppose not. I am familiar with them though, both from reading about the demonstrations in the South and about the way they were used in India. And on our picket line we did have some trouble—no actual violence, but pushing, shoving, red-baiting, you know, that sort of thing."

"If you go on a Freedom Ride, you should really be given some workshop training in exactly how passive resistance works, and what to do 'in case . . .'"

"What are the chances that there will be mob violence?"

"Do you want the official estimate?"

"Yes—and also your personal one."

"CORE feels that the State of Mississippi is determined not to have the same kind of violence that occurred in Anniston, Alabama—the bus burning, you know—and Birmingham and Montgomery, Alabama. The State of Mississippi is doing everything in its power to prevent mobs and is trying to conduct Freedom Riders safely from the border of the state right into the jail at Jackson. The official line is that there is only about a 10 or 20 percent chance that groups going down now will be met by mobs or violence. No one can really know for sure, of course."

"And what's your own opinion?"

"I just plain don't know. I think that the situation is still extremely unsettled—I don't think that anyone can tell at this point."

"I'm still ready to go, if you want me to. But I really should leave this Friday. After that I'll be sitting around eating up my savings. I won't have a job, and someone else is probably going to move into my apartment."

"I'll send you a statement to sign. I guess that you'll be OK, even though we usually want more training in nonviolence techniques. I'll also send you some literature on CORE and so forth."

"Wonderful."

"Now, here is what you have to do. When you get to Atlanta, call SCLC, the Southern Christian Leadership Conference. They are at 197½ Auburn Avenue Northeast. They will have been notified that you are coming down, and will know when there will be a group leaving for Jackson. Are you going to get to Atlanta by bus?"

"Yes. And I intend to buy a ticket all the way through from here to Mexico City, since I was planning to go there and I might as well continue on to there whenever I get out of jail."

"That makes you an international passenger, as well as an interstate passenger."

"Yes, and someone was telling me that I should have some special rights under the Geneva Convention on International Travel . . . but I would have to look it up."

"Well, since Mississippi does not seem to recognize the government of the United States, I doubt that you can do anything about it. It might be interesting to try, though."

"Maybe so. Thank you very much, Mr. Carey."

"Thank you. And I hope some day to have the pleasure of meeting you—perhaps when you get out of jail. Good luck."

Wednesday, May 31, 1961

In the afternoon mail today I received the material from CORE, some descriptive little pamphlets and a mimeographed form to be signed and returned to them. For the first time I began to learn just who and what CORE is. Actually I never heard of the organization until the beginning of the sit-in demonstrations last year, and I got the impression then that it had been formed not more than a year or so ago, with participation in the sit-ins its primary activity.

On the contrary, CORE has been around for something like twenty years. In the beginning it was a small organization dedicated to bettering race relations by applying Gandhian techniques (although I could not get quite clear about what exactly this entailed). Its current ascendancy began with the beginning of the sit-in demonstrations. These broke out like a highly contagious rash over the face of the South after having been started (more or less) by a small group in Greensboro, North Carolina. The students had gone up to a lunch counter together, sat down, and waited for service. The lunch counter closed up.

CORE came in as the sit-ins began spreading, offering financial assistance to those in jail or otherwise in need of help. And some of its local chapters began challenging segregation by organizing their own lunch counter sit-ins, or wade-ins at beaches and public pools, stand-ins at movie ticket lines, read-ins at libraries and the like. The method used in all cases was nonviolent resistance, with Martin Luther King, Jr.'s bus boycott in Montgomery, Alabama, as the prime example.

I was especially impressed by one of their leaflets, in which was set out very clearly the how and why of CORE's actions. It said:

> In carrying out the action program, CORE first *investigates* to learn all the facts; second, *discusses* the grievance with those responsible for the practice in an effort to bring about a change of policy; third, *appeals* to the wider public for support in the action; fourth, *publicizes* the unjust racial practice through picketing, leaflets and press releases; fifth, if all the foregoing fail to end discrimination, uses *direct challenge*, such as Sit-Ins, Standing Lines, and boycotts.

And the Freedom Rides. The Rides seem to be about the most direct "direct action" that has yet been attempted on the civil rights front, primarily because they hit at the heart of the segregationist South. Last year's sit-ins were primarily in the border states, but Mississippi is the deep, deep South. I think that it was the governor of Mississippi who said, as one of the three-by-four planks in his platform for election, "Integration will never come to Mississippi!"

But not even the governor can stop this movement now. Even if it is only students, kids, who are willing to take jail and beatings for the sake of exercising their civil rights, they are giving the lie, once and for all, to the southerners who keep screaming that the Negro likes segregation and to the northerners who say he doesn't care. Negroes everywhere are becoming more militant in demanding their rights. I think it is lucky for the whites in this country that so many Negroes are taking the CORE sort of action rather than going into the Black Muslim–type of movements. They are both, in essence, an expression of the same frustrations and the same resentment of second-class citizenship.

The mimeographed form which came with the literature was a guarantee that I would adhere to the principles of nonviolence at least for the duration of the Freedom Ride, and also that I waived my rights (or that of my heirs) to sue CORE for damages incurred on the Ride. Just as I finished reading it, Dana came home.

"I'm pooped!"

"Oh, Dana—here, let me make you some coffee."

"We're out—and out of milk too, and bread, and cat food. Are you busy? I don't have any money . . ."

"Of course—I'll just run down to the corner. This has to be mailed anyway." And I signed CORE's form, put on a stamp as I went down the stairs, and dropped it in the mailbox.

It was only after I got back to the apartment—after I had climbed back up the four flights of stairs, after I had made coffee, after I had heard about Dana's troublesome first-grade class, after she had made toast and the second pot of coffee, after she had finally collected her pencils and gone off to a sketch class—as I sat in the kitchen with a well-fed cat on my lap and a half-finished letter to my mother on the table—that I really began thinking about the commitment I had made in signing the statement—and also in general by going on this Freedom Ride.

I wonder if I can really be nonviolent. My training in the New York subway system has made it almost automatic that if someone shoves me, I shove back. If some young punk came up to me and started beating me over the head, would I really be able to so discipline myself that I could just stand there and take it? The spirit is willing—I sincerely do believe that the nonviolent method is the only way to conduct civil rights protests—but when it comes to overcoming such a basic human trait as self-defense, I can only hope that I will be strong enough.

And if I can be nonviolent, and if we are attacked, what if I should get badly hurt? Blinded perhaps? Even killed? For the first time I am beginning to think of this commitment as one involving physical danger. If I should be crippled for life, would it have been worth it?

That is a question I cannot answer.

Except that if I am willing to risk my life crossing 42nd Street every day just to get to the other side, I should be willing to risk my life in a more noble cause.

I wonder what jail will be like. I have never even toured the inside of one. When I talked to Mr. Carey's secretary, she warned me that we would possibly be put in with real criminals—white, southern criminals. She also said that people are not being allowed to have books in the jail. Can I spend two months cooped up in one small area with nothing to do but contemplate the Ultimate Nature of Being? And not go stir crazy? That term, stir crazy, suddenly has a meaning separate from picaresque novels and bad movies. How much is this experience going to impact the rest of my life?

I had a long argument at work with a salesman from Portland, Maine, who kept saying that all these Freedom Riders were doing was stirring up racial hatred in an area which used to be peaceful. I wanted to cite to him the number of lynchings which have occurred in the state of Alabama, but unfortunately I did not have this statistic at my fingertips. The whites of the South cannot help being affected by these attempts to change their "peculiar institution," but their troubles are minor compared to what the Negro has undergone and is still suffering. The time has come when progress must occur not next year or even next week but later this afternoon. The South has had its chance for the past ninety-six years to develop Negro civil rights through "education" and "understanding." And these Freedom Rides only make it vividly clear. Change has not come. Do laws and rights of free citizens mean nothing in this country!

Thursday, June 1, 1961

Today I bought my Greyhound bus ticket—Mexico City by way of Atlanta, Georgia, Montgomery, Alabama, and Jackson, Mississippi. I asked the ticket clerk, just to check, and he assured me that on my ticket I could stop off for as long as I like (up to a year) at any of the cities on the way.

It looks as if Dana will be all alone in the apartment this summer. Joan announced tonight that she is going to be away for a month or, more probably, two, in Guatemala, on some sort of research project. I never have quite gotten straight what kind of research she does, except that it is biology. It always sounded rather unexciting—except for the time she swallowed some virus because of faulty equipment and got herself violently and contagiously ill.

"Do you expect to run into any trouble down there?" I asked her.

"Not the kind you're going to find," she laughed. "Anyway, all of Latin America is supposed to be much more integrated than any part of the states."

"Yes, so they say. You've never been there before, have you?"

"No—and you've never been down south before, right?"

"No. Unfortunately. That's one reason why I'm still quite scared of this Freedom Ride. Even if I were not going down as a Freedom Rider they would probably throw me in jail for doing something wrong that I didn't even know was included in their little perverted scale of right and wrong."

"Well, I expect that Guatemala will present fewer problems."

"I should hope so."

"And anyway, I'll be with my own team of biologists, all from the Rockefeller Institute. There should be at least two other Negroes in the group besides me." And Joan flounced away from our conversation as if she had won the point.

Most of my packing is now done. It amazes me that, having arrived in New York only ten months ago with a small overnight case, and preparing to exit with the same, I shall leave behind me two trunks, eleven cartons, a suitcase, and a role of prints.

Dana and I spent a couple of hours working out what to do with my mail. I finally typed three pages of "Instructions for Dana Covering Possibility that I Shall Spend Two Months in Jail," with this item:

"The University of Chicago: I am expecting them to send me some forms for scholarship application. If so, please write to them saying that I am traveling and therefore unavailable, but that the letter has been forwarded. You, however, being my close friend, know that Miss Silver's financial situation in re her family is the same as last year (for which they should have an application on file). The only difference is that she has saved approximately $600 toward her school expenses. This is what she asked me to tell you if you should request another application. Do *not* forward to me the copy of your letter, but rather, send me a postcard telling me what you have done. That way, if that mail gets stopped or lost, you will still have the copy to send to me when I get out of jail."

I have spoken on the phone to all of my relatives here and to the friends whom I shall not see. Especially to my relatives, I have not bothered to mention that I shall be traveling in an integrated group of Negroes and whites through Jackson, Mississippi, with an anticipated stopover of two months in jail.

"So now where are you going, darling?" said my aunt Rosalie in Winthrop, Massachusetts.

"You, know, Aunty, I always wanted to go to Mexico, and I have friends in Washington. I'll stop off in Charlotte, North Carolina, to see some other friends, and in New Orleans to see some of our other relatives on my dad's side."

"And you're going all the way to Mexico City by bus?"

"Oh, yes."

"Well, you're young. But you be careful, now. In the South, there's all that rioting on the buses. Are you sure it's safe? Why can't you take the train?"

"I'm sure it's perfectly safe, dear."

"There's all those riots—in the paper I read about a mob that burned up a bus altogether. Think of it! They burned up the whole bus. Now don't you get on a bus like that—are you sure you don't want the train?"

"Don't worry, Aunty—I've traveled buses all over the country, and nothing ever happened to me. I got to New York by bus, didn't I?"

"You'll write to us, yes?"

"Of course, dear. And you take care and don't work too hard. And maybe I'll see you next year when I have my school vacation."

"What, from Mexico you're not coming back here?"

"No, I thought I told you—from there I'm going to go to Los Angeles to see my mother, and Dad, and then back to Chicago. I'm going to go to law school there."

"Oh. Oh, yes, you did tell me. But I thought you were going to go here in the East, to Harvard or Columbia."

"Yes, I was thinking about it, but I'm probably going to go back to Chicago."

"Anyway, take care. And write to us."

Even to my closest friends, though, I did not have the courage to say that I was going to be a Freedom Rider. I said that I would "probably" join a group of Freedom Riders in Atlanta, that I would "probably" be arrested in Jackson, and would "probably" be in jail for about two months. At least this way if I get frightened and chicken out, I will not have quite so much embarrassment explaining my change of plans.

What does one take for a vacation in jail? The only practical thing I could think to pack was some athlete's foot preventative. I don't know, nor did Gordon Carey, whether we will be issued prison uniforms, although I am assuming so. I also put a thin pad of paper and four cheap ballpoint pens into my bag so that I can write letters. I can amuse myself as easily by writing as by reading. I am not taking anything of value except my watch, and am going to carry a minimum of money. I have planned with Dana that when I get out of jail I will call her and she will send me my passport and other such papers, and eighty dollars in traveler's checks, so that I will have enough to get to Mexico and then on to Los Angeles.

I have not been able to get out of my mind the gravity of the physical danger to which I am potentially exposing myself. The major question is "Is it worth it?" Will these Freedom Rides really do enough good to warrant the ugly possibilities? The only answer I come up with is an emphatic "Yes!" So I suppose that I will just have to go through with it.

I read a long letter to the editor today from some liberal southern group which said that even though they had supported the sit-ins last year they were dubious this year about the Freedom Riders. The sit-ins had been primarily native southern Negroes fighting their own battles in their own hometowns. But the Freedom Rides have not only involved southern Negroes, but also northern Negroes and northern whites, and they feel that these last two groups can not validly participate in a southern struggle.

I say, this is nonsense. In the first place, this is not just a southern battle. It is a fight of great importance to Negroes all over the country, because even if there is only one spot in which the Negro is degraded because of his color it must be the concern of every Negro, and of every white who has any sense of decency. What was happening to the Jews in Germany during Hitler's rise to power was the concern of Jews the world over (and should have been the concern of the world's non-Jews too). The responsibility for thwarting discrimination against a minority group certainly cannot be left solely to the minority group—if it could, they would not be in a position open to discrimination.

Friday, June 2, 1961

And, I'm off!

I got no feeling of impending adventure as I boarded the Greyhound bus. It was the same kind of bus in which I had traveled thousands of miles before, the double-decker kind (although that is merely an optical illusion created by the rear portion's being made two steps higher than the front to provide more space for baggage; the first time I boarded one of these buses I actually looked for the entrance to the "lower" section). There are relatively comfortable reclining seats covered in the usual strange kind of woven plastic with silver specks. It has a three-by-three-foot bathroom tucked beside the stairs, and the kind of green-tinted windows I especially dislike. The trend on buses seems to be to make the windows bigger and bigger and greener and greener, and to make the air conditioning more conducive to pneumonia the hotter it gets outside. But my complaints are not really to be taken seriously. Actually I enjoy traveling by bus more than by train—on the train I always have the feeling that I am hermetically sealed away from the land and the people and even the air through which we pass. On the buses, at least I get a chance every few hours or so to get off, stretch, and take a walk around whatever great metropolis we have reached.

Another reason that I like buses is that people always seem more friendly and open to talk than on trains. Today's ride to Washington was with a young man from Virginia, whom I am afraid I antagonized almost as much as he did me. (I had resolved when I first decided to go on this Freedom Ride that Principle of Action Number One was not to get into any arguments with segregationists whom I might meet casually on buses. But I felt that this ride from New York to Washington was still my own territory, and since I would be stopping in Washington, I would lose whomever

I argued with at that point.) We discussed the equality of the races, a point which is to me unquestioned and, in a sense, unquestionable.

This college boy from Virginia was not at all stupid or uneducated: "Take a random sample of Negroes, now, and a random sample of whites. Give them all the same I.Q. test, and the average score of the Negroes will be lower than that of the whites, always."

"OK, I believe you, but that does not necessarily prove that Negroes are inferior to whites."

"Of course it does. It proves that they are basically, fundamentally, less intelligent, as a race, than whites. It doesn't prove that any given individual Negro is necessarily stupider than any given white, because of course there are all grades of intelligence among Negroes and among whites. Except that among whites the number of high-intelligence people is always going to be greater than among the same number of Negroes."

"But you're basing all of these conclusions on the I.Q. tests."

"Sure."

"But these tests are not valid for most Negroes. What the I.Q. tests measure is nothing more than cultural sophistication. They measure how many books you read and how often you read newspapers and what are the interests of not only the individual taking the test but of the people who constitute his or her environment."

"So?"

"So, the things measured on the tests—vocabulary, association of concepts, geometry questions—are all things with which the average lower-socioeconomic-class individual, be he Negro or white or Puerto Rican, could not be expected to be familiar."

"Well, you may be right about that, although I do not concede the point. But the I.Q. tests, even if they don't indicate a basically lower intelligence, do indicate that Negroes have a lower operative intelligence. I mean that they just do not function in our society—that's why they are poorer and less well educated."

"How would a man from Mars function in our society?"

"What?"

"I said, how would a man from Mars function in our society? Would that mean that he was necessarily less intelligent than we are? That's just the extreme case of the individual who doesn't function in our society because he is not sufficiently familiar with and conversant in our culture."

To me, the equality of the races is just as much a given point as is the equality of men in "all men are created equal." In point of fact, all men (and women) are not equal, in strength, in intelligence, in morals, in appearance, and I suppose one could say that the fact that they are unequally pigmented makes races also unequal. But in a democracy one must assume that one individual is as good and valuable as the next, and afford to every single person the equal protection of law and equal opportunity for social and economic gain. The fact that people are so unequal in strength, in intelligence, and in chicanery, is just what makes law and government necessary, so that the weak and the naive can be protected. Give equal opportunity and equal protection to all and you will still find that some are "more equal" than others. But the idiocy of castigating a whole group of people on the simple basis of their membership in a darker rather than a lighter race is clear, in my opinion, from the difficulty in really defining what is meant by "race."

Saturday, June 3, 1961

I spent the day in Washington visiting with two old friends from Chicago. With one of them, a Negro, I went into a rather fancy restaurant to have a leisurely dinner. It was only when I realized that I was the object of a good deal of attention that I noticed my being the only white person in the place. The stares were not especially hostile, but after a while I began to feel a little uncomfortable. I began to think of how lonesome and cut off it must feel to be the lone token Negro integrating a white school in the South or eating in a "white" restaurant. I wonder if they resented me as an intruder. I hope not.

It has always been difficult for me to deal with Negroes except in the academic community. There and there only, I feel as if I do not have to bend over backward to prove that I am not prejudiced. I know a man, a very successful architect, who confided in me that he had shared office space for twenty years with a Negro lawyer whom he detested, a man with whom, if he were white, the architect would have had absolutely nothing to say. My feeling has been something like that, although I think not so extreme. I think that this man felt very guilty about his realization that the Negro is being discriminated against and his inability or unwillingness to do anything against this discrimination. When the Negroes in question are my friends, of my own age group, with similar interests and backgrounds, there just is no race problem. But every time I have anything to do with poor, uneducated Negroes, I am acutely aware of race. The Negroes with whom I come in contact in this way are usually maids or janitors in the houses of wealthy parents of school friends. I feel very resentful of the fact that a middle-aged woman should be expected to work six full days a week for just about a dollar an hour—and be grateful to get it. I know that I would never work that hard for so little. And still remember to say, "Thank you, ma'am" and "Please, Miss Debbie, come drink your milk."

And if I am resentful of their exploitation, I always have the feeling that they must be doubly resentful of me, as a representative of the white race. I want to start off every conversation by apologizing to the particular Negro involved because he or she has not had an education, cannot get a well-paying job, cannot find a decent place to live. And then I get annoyed with myself for taking the guilt of the world on my shoulders in such an unrealistic and silly way. Because of these ambivalent feelings, I cannot recall having been able to have a real discussion about anything important—religion, politics, or whatever—with any Negro whom I have met casually on a bus or train, although I have talked my way from one end of this country to the other and back again, many times.

The main reason I wanted to stop in Washington was to view the exhibition of Chinese art treasures from the Republic of China, on display at the National Gallery of Art. When I was taking lessons in Chinese at the United Nations, our instructor had told us that this was the first time these works were to be shown anywhere since the Nationalists fled from the mainland of China to Taiwan. He had hoped to arrange for our whole class of six to take a trip to Washington to see it, but I left my clerical job at the U.N. before the exhibit began. I was very glad that I took the time out to walk through it twice. Some of the individual works were breathtakingly beautiful. I enjoyed it especially too because it will probably be the last museum exhibit I will see for some time.

Late in the evening I took the bus for Atlanta.

Chapter 2

TRAVELING SOUTH

Sunday, June 4, 1961

To the northerner, to me, the honeysuckle was the first thing apparent in Virginia, an odor amazingly sweet and clear and fresh, and all-pervasive. The second thing I noticed was segregation, equally common and clear, but certainly not sweet.

The nominally integrated bus depot at Richmond, Virginia, still has two restrooms for women. The identifying signs "WHITE" and "COLORED" have been effaced, leaving an ugly scar on each door. In the restaurant there is a large cafeteria and a small, separate lunch counter. Most of the Negroes on our bus went to the counter, except for one slight, collegiate young man, a New Yorker, who chose the cafeteria. Richmond was my first stop in the South, my first real contact with any kind of open racial segregation, and I was more than a little shocked.

Our next stop was a few miles outside of Winston-Salem, North Carolina, where a motherly looking, middle-aged white woman boarded our almost-full bus. I thought nothing of it, until I realized that she was standing in the aisle, even though several seats were empty. Then I heard her remark, "They each have to have a seat for themselves—disgraceful." I looked and discovered that the empty seats were all beside Negro men. I was tempted to offer her my seat and make a big point of my lack of prejudice by sitting next to a Negro, but I did not. She stood all the way into town, almost an hour's travel.

At Statesville, North Carolina, a little town about an hour outside of Charlotte, I first actually saw "COLORED" and "WHITE" over the doorways of separate waiting-room entrances. I did not get off the bus, but watched the other passengers divide into separate docile streams and pass under the two signs. I wondered how the Negroes on our bus from New York felt at that moment.

Monday, June 5, 1961

In Greer, South Carolina, we stopped in a very dirty little restaurant at 9:30 a.m. for breakfast. I followed the arrow "LADIES" to the single dingy, dirty restroom. On the door were pressed-metal signs, reading "WHITE," "LADIES," "TOILET," and "PLEASE KEEP OUR RESTAURANT CLEAN."

There was no restroom marked "COLORED."

I arrived at the Greyhound terminal in Atlanta, Georgia, at noon, telephoned the number I had been given in New York, and said, "I've come to join a Freedom Ride."

"How long can you stay in jail?" the voice at the other end of the line asked.

"Two months."

"Take a cab to 197½ Auburn Avenue."

"Be right there."

The Auburn Avenue address is in one of the Negro slum districts which surround Atlanta's downtown business section like grime on the collar of a shirt. Most of it is old, rundown, and ramshackle. The office building to which I was directed, however, was new and looked quite out of place. On the second floor was the one-room office of the Southern Christian Leadership Conference (SCLC), one of the organizations associated with CORE. There I met Ed King, a Negro college student from New Rochelle, New York, who has become the regional organizer for the Freedom Riders going into Mississippi. Ed has scars from numerous beatings received at sit-ins last year.

Since the time in New York when I had decided to become a Freedom Rider, a ten-day restraining order had been issued, on June 2, 1961, by the Alabama federal district court (Judge Frank Johnson, Jr.) to enjoin CORE and the Movement from sending any more organized groups through Alabama. CORE was therefore bypassing Alabama altogether, and had moved the rendezvous point for Freedom Riders going into Jackson from Montgomery, Alabama, to Nashville, Tennessee. So at 5:45 p.m. I left Atlanta on a train headed northwest, along with two white divinity students from Yale, Ed Kale and John Gager, who were also taking this roundabout route to Jackson, Mississippi.

We were met at the Nashville train station by a red Volkswagen convertible and a young white man from New York who now teaches at Fisk, a Negro college in Nashville. He took us to a house in a respectable suburb (white), where the two white divinity students, our driver, some other guests, and I were to spend the night. Our hostess, Mrs. Genevieve Wilbur (whom everyone calls "Pinky"), is a charming middle-aged fashion designer, a native white southerner with two grown daughters. Sue Wilbur, the younger daughter, had been on the original Montgomery Freedom Ride, which had met with mob violence and bloodshed.

Tuesday, June 6, 1961, Nashville

Since the Negro students with whom we were to travel were due to arrive about midnight from Richmond, Virginia, we spent the day hanging around the Nashville "office" of the Student Nonviolent Coordinating Committee (SNCC, pronounced "Snick")—an unfinished house under construction near Fisk College.

All day long students from Fisk kept dropping in. I was immensely impressed by the religious feeling which most of them exhibited and by their complete acceptance of the Gandhian principles of nonviolence. Most of them had been in many civil rights demonstrations. One of them, I think it was William Barbee, related his experiences in Alabama, where he had been beaten badly and then, lying on the ground at the feet of his assailant, held out his hand and said, "Brother, I love you." It sounded unbelievable but I am sure it is quite true. During this time, we received a little formal training in the tactics and practice of nonviolence, and lots of informal advice and counseling from the students who had experienced it.

While we were in the office, a Negro minister came in with a letter from a young man who had just arrived in Detroit and an amazing, a fantastic story. The writer of the letter claimed that he had been working at the Birmingham bus station and that just before the Freedom Riders arrived there, he had seen the police changing into civilian clothes in the bus station restroom, and that later he had seen them leading the mob which beat the students and ministers. He said that he had run away but had been caught by a policeman who administered a severe beating and broke his arm. In the hospital the police visited him and threatened to kill him if he told anyone about what he had seen. Two days later he escaped from the hospital and hitchhiked to Nashville, then to Detroit, where, he said, he had relatives and hoped to move his family, to free himself to testify against the police. The letter reported his arrival in Detroit, and thanked the minister for his help while he had been in Nashville.

We met the three Negro divinity students, Reggie Green, Raymond Randolph, and Obadiah Simms, all from Virginia Union University Divinity School in Richmond, Virginia, at the Trailways bus station at 9:30 p.m. We decided with them that we would all take the bus for Jackson at 1:15 a.m. The hours between their arrival and our departure were spent in the station, getting acquainted, drinking coffee, and talking to Rick Smith, a lone reporter, from UPI (United Press International), who turned up. The only other people in the station besides us were two station masters and a few policemen.

We left on schedule with a minimum of wisecracks from the driver—and only the UPI reporter to see us off.

Chapter 3

THE CRIME

Wednesday, June 7, 1961

The ride through Tennessee and Mississippi was relatively uneventful. Two police cars fell in behind the bus at the Mississippi border and, sometimes joined by more, followed us all the way to Jackson.

At a whistle stop in Tennessee one of the Yale divinity students, Ed Kale, got out and began "discussing" the desirability of desegregation. The people there were getting rather ugly, with a grinning cop standing by observing, when the driver told him curtly to reboard the bus.

We stopped in Memphis for breakfast, and ate together in the integrated terminal restaurant—almost. I sat at a different table from the three Negroes. We did not want any incidents before Jackson and were afraid that if there was anything liable to make one, it was a white girl sitting with Negro men. Southerners are so chivalrous!

Before we ate, Ed had noticed a sign in the station barbershop which said "SHOWERS." He asked the barber how much and had a pleasant chat with him. After breakfast, however, when he went back with the intention of using the shower, the barber had found out who we were. He called Ed a "white nigger" and various other even less polite things. Ed did not take a shower.

When we again boarded the bus, two white boys, fourteen and fifteen, came to the very back of the bus where Ed and I were sitting, to look out the rear window at the police cars and to talk to us. They expressed great admiration for our courage, but not for our ideals. One of them exchanged addresses with me and promised to write to us in jail.

We were due in Jackson at 12:45 p.m. but did not arrive until 1:10 p.m. As we drove through the city, all traffic was cleared ahead of our bus by police stationed in the intersections. We did not get to see much of Jackson. The bus pulled into the station. We six Freedom Riders waited until everyone else got out of the bus before we held hands, said a prayer, then debarked from the air-conditioned bus into the hot, bright sunshine. For a few moments we were alone on the platform with the bus driver unloading luggage—three Negro divinity students from Virginia Union University, two white men of God from Yale, and a nice Jewish girl from New York.

In the shadow of the terminal I could see many uniformed police, a few men with cameras and notebooks, and some bus drivers. We shook hands with each other and moved forward to our destinations—the Negroes to the waiting room marked "WHITE WAITING ROOM INTRASTATE PASSENGERS" and the whites to the door marked "COLORED WAITING ROOM INTRASTATE PASSENGERS."

As we started walking in, a grinning reporter came up and asked if we were the Freedom Riders, and whether our names were correct on his prepared list. Then he said to me, "We were told there was a white woman in the group, but that she would probably not go through with it."

"Well, that certainly did not come from me," I replied and passed by him into the waiting room designated for Negroes.

Inside, our reception committee consisted of more police, all of them white, all armed, all looking terribly serious. I saw no Negroes or regular passengers in this waiting room. The whole thing, the elaborate preparations, the guns, the deadly serious police, contrasted sharply with the almost holiday-like, victorious mood in which we had been riding on our bus, traveling through the South, based simply on the fact that we had not been met by a white mob with clubs, at least not yet. Rather, there was an orderly process run by guys in law enforcement uniforms, taxed by their big beer bellies and the sweat dripping off their faces in the Mississippi summer heat. It became so ludicrous that I began to grin widely, and with this most indecorous expression I faced the still and movie cameras hedging the police who surrounded us.

We indeed *were* still moving when a police office stepped forward with great determination. "Move on!" he said. John Gager, our unofficial spokesman, replied, "We just want to get some coffee," and I at the same time piped up: "I just want to use the restroom, please."

"Do y'all refuse to move on?"

John: "Yes, sir."

"Then y'all are under arrest."

The police too, like the UPI reporter, had merely to verify our names on a typed list, rather than write them down, and we were quickly conducted out through the street entrance of the terminal to the waiting paddy wagon. The Negro students, who had obviously been subjected to the same treatment on the "WHITE INTRASTATE" side, joined us in the paddy wagon, and we rode to jail together. Someone said gleefully, "I bet this is the only integrated public transportation in the state of Mississippi."

Besides being integrated, the black paddy wagon was unbelievably hot—it had been standing in the sun for some unknown number of hours. Luckily, the police jail was only two blocks from the bus station.

At the modern-looking jail, we were herded onto an elevator and led from there into an air-conditioned office. We gave our names and our personal information, and then our pictures were taken, full face and profile, with numbers on little wooden signs hung around our necks. Our fingerprints were made and our possessions and eyeglasses taken away from us.

The whites had been taken first while the Negroes were ordered to "stand back." One of the interviewers asked our captor how many of us there were, and the latter answered, "Wal, they's three black niggers and three white niggers."

The formalities over, I quickly shook hands with all of my five companions, Negro and white, said goodbye, and was conducted out of the air-conditioning to a cell door labeled "ADULT WHITE FEMALES." Over other doors I could see other labels—"JUVENILE NEGRO MALES," "ADULT WHITE MALES," and, mysteriously, "OTHER ADULT MALES." The "ADULT WHITE FEMALES" door opened and then closed behind me with a deafening metallic clang.

Chapter 4

JUSTICE

Wednesday, June 7, 1961, continued

The Jackson city jail cell in which I found myself was the size of a large living room, divided down the middle by a set of bars in which there was an open sliding door. In the back section were four iron cots with thin, clean-looking mattresses. The front section contained a shower partially hidden by a transparent glass brick dividing wall, a toilet and a sink, along the wall in which the door was located. This wall also had a small window (four by four inches) and a slot (three by twelve inches), which was for food pans as I afterward discovered. Beyond the bars was a narrow corridor with four good-sized windows (all closed tightly) through which was provided a view of the county courthouse, the green space before it, and the city hall of Jackson with two clocks. The clocks were a welcome sight since my watch had been taken from me.

When I came in, the only other occupant of the cell was a woman lounging on one of the cots in a bra and black toreador pants. She did not look like another Freedom Rider, but I cautiously asked anyway. The negative answer was couched in a heavy southern accent, and I was just a little frightened.

But more than anything else, I had eyes for the cots—it had been Thursday night, almost a week earlier, that I had last had a full night's sleep, and that not very full. I took off my shoes, lay down, and immediately fell fast asleep, the hard bed notwithstanding, nor the lack of a pillow, nor my new cell mate's warning that "y'all better watch out for rats, they'll crawl right over while y'all're sleeping."

My sense of time was completely gone, but it was somewhat before dinner when I was awakened to come out of the cell and meet our lawyer, Mr. Jack Young.

Mr. Young appeared to be a rather well-to-do, well-educated member of the very small southern Negro middle class. I have the feeling that he is greatly jeopardizing his status in the community by taking on the CORE cases. He informed us that all of us would be tried the following day at 3:00 p.m., that the trial would take about five minutes, and that we were being charged with "breach of peace." In the interview room, once again our little integrated group of six was reunited. We each signed a paper asking Mr. Young to be our representative in court. He explained the procedure for us to get out on bail, if it became suddenly necessary, and told us we were to expect a stiffer sentence than the previous groups of Freedom Riders, probably four months in jail with two suspended, and a two-hundred-dollar fine. (Previous groups had been getting two months, suspended, and gone to jail upon refusing to pay the fine, working it out at the rate of three dollars a day.) The limit for filing an appeal and being released on bail is forty days, so on the thirty-ninth day, July 17 for our group, I shall have to be bailed out. The full penalty of two months, plus nine weeks to work out the fine, would take me beyond the date on which I have to begin law school.

After the interview, I was told I could make the one telephone call allowed each of us. I had been collecting change for days so that I would have it for this phone call, but, of course, they had taken all of my money away from me. I called Mother, collect, in Los Angeles. Up to this point she had been with me all the way, but when this call came through, her anxiety temporarily got the better of her. I talked, and she cried, about ten dollars' worth. And then I was conducted back to my cell.

It was now dinnertime and I had my first experience with jail food. Surprisingly, it was hot, and the three biscuits were excellent. The other sections of the tin pan were filled with turnip greens and a large mess of beans with a lump of some kind of animal fat in it. The latter two items were completely impossible to my not-yet-adjusted palate, even though I had not eaten all day. There was nothing to drink but lukewarm water from the tap. The response from the jailer to a question of mine was "There ain't no cold water in Mississippi." The big tin spoon that was served instead of a fork was only insulting, rather than inconvenient, considering the nature of the food.

After dinner I went right back to sleep again, not even the hard cot, an empty stomach, noisy neighbors, and further warning about rodent animal life being enough to keep me up.

Thursday, June 8, 1961

My second prison meal, breakfast—at about 6:00 a.m.—was three more biscuits, some thin molasses syrup, grits, and coffee. Aside from the grits, which I ignored studiously, I was almost embarrassed to pronounce it much to my liking. The coffee was black and sweet and not too strong, the biscuits were light and hot, and the syrup in which they were to be dipped was quite palatable.

At about 10:00, four girls were clanged into the "ADULT WHITE FEMALES" cell. Freedom Riders? Yes! Hello! Hi! Hello! Welcome to Jackson! They had come by train from New Orleans and had been arrested in the same manner as I. They were Helene Wilson (age twenty-six) from Washington, D.C.; Terry Perlman (nineteen), New York City College; Joan Trumpauer (nineteen), Virginia, and Jane Rosett (eighteen) Durham, North Carolina.

During the day we were each called out to be "interrogated" by a couple of detectives. To me they were almost paternal, and our discussion was carried on in the subdued manner of a cocktail lounge. They asked me if I had ever dated Negro boys (yes), and if I would be willing to marry a Negro (that, I said, is a matter of personalities, not generalities). I said that I had been engaged to a Negro boy once (which was not exactly true), but that it had broken up because we had arguments about our divergent tastes in music, among other things. The younger and quieter of my two interrogators practically jumped out of his seat at this: "You see! You see! They are different from us!" I told him that I did not exactly follow his logic since my white friends had as diverse tastes in music as my Negro friends, etc. (The "etc." gets overworked in my description of southern prejudice, but I am afraid that I just could not stand to write down all the nonsense of "red birds and blue birds" and "if God intended us to be the same . . .") They brought up discrimination in the North and said that "we love our southern niggers." I neglected to object to that appellation, which I should have. The interview took about half an hour, much too long for my taste. I spent about ten minutes distinguishing between private places, in which one may make any kind of personal discriminations, and public places (even if privately owned) such as a restaurant. We spent another ten minutes discussing my religious beliefs, and especially the word "agnostic."

The young detective said, "Wal, I've been all around the world and back again, and I ain't never heard of that one." (Evidently they liked the term, because they asked one of the girls whose turn came after me if she was an agnostic. She said no, but they made her spell the word for them.)

Back in the jail cell, I discovered that I could talk to the white boys who had been arrested with me, through the little food slot. Their cell was directly across the hall from ours, and stooping uncomfortably made it possible to communicate with them. They told me that someone else had joined them, a Canadian boy from the University of British Columbia named Michael Audain. He had been in San Francisco and, independently of CORE or any organization, had decided to participate in the Freedom Rides. He had walked into the Greyhound "COLORED INTRASTATE" waiting room in Jackson and, to the surprise of the police, refused to "move on." They were upset at the appearance of an unannounced "odd" Freedom Rider. Actually, it was a very dangerous thing to do, because if the police and FBI are not notified, Freedom Riders run the risk of facing segregationist mob violence. We had been quite glad to see the police when we came in, for just that reason. The Canadian was trying to get in touch with his government, but he, too, was to be tried with us.

At a few minutes before 3:00 p.m., we were ushered out to experience our share of "southern justice." The whites—the four girls and I, my two Yale divinity students, the Canadian, and New York State Assemblyman Mark Lane (who had arrived and been arrested early that morning at the airport)—were instructed to sit in the front row of the courtroom. Then the Negroes, among them Percy Sutton, the Manhattan Borough president, City of New York, were conducted to the two rows of benches behind us. Sutton and Lane had been arrested as they used the men's room together at the Jackson airport. Lane, an attorney, was sitting beside me, and he took careful notes of the proceedings on the back of a New York Museum of Modern Art brochure. I asked him if the New York City jails were as modern and clean as the Jackson city jail, and he said, "Definitely not."

As Mr. Young had explained to us, this was not a court of record, and therefore no attempt at a defense was being made on our behalf. Mr. Young was asked how the defendants pleaded and he said, "Not guilty." Captain Ray then testified that we had each been arrested by him (or by one of his men) for refusing to "move on" after having been so ordered, and that the reason for the order was that the officer was exercising his right to prevent an assembly which, in his opinion, might possibly create a situation that could lead to an incipient "breach of peace," which was the specific charge against us.

When the prosecutor was through reading from his prepared list of questions, Mr. Young asked the witness (Captain Ray was the only person who took the stand during this whole farce) if he would, upon questioning, give the same answers this time as he had in the previous trials of similar groups.

"I would."

"Defense rests."

With great pomp, the prosecutor paced back and forth in front of the judge and said, "Your honor, I ask you to sentence these prisoners, if you find them guilty, of course, to four months in jail and a two-hundred-dollar fine, with two months of the sentence suspended."

The judge, after a thirty-second show of deliberation, said, "Guilty. Now I told y'all that if these rides continued, I was going to increase the penalty. Y'all'll get four months and a two-hundred-dollar fine, with two months suspended. Court is adjourned." The whole proceeding had taken about four and a half minutes, belying Mr. Young's estimate by thirty seconds.

Convicted criminals, we were then taken back to the jail office where we were given back our glasses, our valuables and suitcases, and checked out in preparation for being transferred to the county jail to serve out our sentences. The space problem had already become acute in the city jail, so all Freedom Riders except white males were being taken to the county jail.

In the office I ran into Percy Sutton, whom I did not know personally, but to whom I introduced myself. Since he was posting bond immediately and returning to New York, I hurriedly gave him three dollars and a request for a one-month subscription to the *Washington Post*, c/o the Jackson County Jail (a mistaken address as I afterwards found out; I also found out that we are not allowed newspapers and that I would probably never get a single copy of the *Post*).

While we were waiting to be checked out, I pulled out my notebook, a little pencil, and a paperback book from my suitcase and carried them under my arm to the county jail, my new "home," on the theory that the jailers would be more likely to let them through in that case than if I had to open my suitcase. We went down the elevator again to the basement (the five white girls, all of us just a little bit scared) and then, not handcuffed but under the charge of two heavily armed male policemen, walked across the street and up another elevator to the county jail. The outside of the jail building of Hinds County (not Jackson County, as I had thought) is pseudocolonial. The inside looks much more like a movie set of an ancient prison than did the city jail. There was a locked, barred door at the turning of every passage. We were forced to leave our suitcases in the office upstairs, but with some verbal pleasantry convinced the jailer to allow us our purses, and I did manage to take in my papers and book. After we had left our stuff, two of us took our courage in our hands and ran back to grab something else from our suitcases, I my tube of athlete's foot preventative and she her toothbrush. We got back just in time to join the group, which was waiting for the jailer to open the cell door. When one of the other girls asked if she too might go and get something, he said, in a surly way, "No!"

Finally, the cell door was clanged open, a trusty threw some mats on the floor, we were shooed in, and we had arrived. I got a distinct feeling of "for *this* I traveled two thousand miles?!!?"—and then we settled down to settling down.

Chapter 5

HINDS COUNTY JAIL

Thursday, June 8, 1961, continued

The county jail cell was about half the size of the city jail cell and much less modern. Instead of cream-colored tile, the walls were painted, cream-color cement, with the cement floor painted battleship gray and worn bare in spots. Two barred windows looked out on the upper edge of a cement wall which filled three-fourths of the view; a lowering sky completed it. Four steel shelf beds were ranged along the walls, two side by side under the windows and one each on the side walls. A shower and a toilet and sink combination (sort of like a Pullman train bathroom) completed the appointments. The room was approximately thirteen feet by seventeen feet. The entire fourth wall was bars, like a cage in a zoo, so the jailer walking in the corridor could see into every corner of the cell.

The occupants, when we arrived, were three: Betty Jo, my acquaintance from the city jail who had been tried earlier in the day and had been given five days because she could not pay a fifteen-dollar fine; Betsy Wyckoff, a dignified, gray-haired woman who, up to my arrival, had been the only white female Freedom Rider arrested in Jackson; and Emmy, a local alcoholic, asleep on one of the bunks. Betsy had been there for about a week, and was in one of the earlier groups of Freedom Riders who had gotten the lighter sentences, two months suspended and a two-hundred-dollar fine, which she was now serving out at the rate of three dollars per day.

The five of us made eight in the cell, built for four, and the old, dirty, lumpy extra mattresses spread on the floor for our beds did not look at all inviting. But there was a certain pleasure in introducing ourselves to Betsy, in being made acquainted with the jail routine—and in discovering that the two cells beyond ours contained more Freedom Riders! They were Negro females whom none of us in our cell had previously met. Nonetheless, there was much shouting back and forth, welcomes and greetings, and a few songs—"We Shall Overcome," "Oh Freedom,"—to make us feel again the importance and value of our victory in defeat. Supper—so called—brought us back to the bitter realities of being prisoners. It was navy beans with a lump of fat, grits, and cornbread, all ice cold.

Since we were quite tired and hot and dirty, all the new prisoners took showers, more than a little embarrassed to be in full view of anyone (including the male jailer) passing in the hall. None of us had any clothes to change into, so we had to run around in our slips or else get back into the sweaty clothes in which we had been traveling. Some of the girls asked the jailer if they could make the one phone call which they should have been allowed (usually a privilege to be exercised before trial!) when he came to collect the supper pans, but were denied their right, being told that he was "too busy now, maybe tomorrow."

As we were quite tired, even the mats on the floor looked good to us and we were ready to go to sleep right after dinner. But Betsy informed us that there was one more event to the day—the "store." A little while later that phenomenon actually turned up—the jailer, yelling "sto' taime." A couple of his trusties walked by our bars with two cardboard boxes of cigarettes, candy, writing paper, and pencils. We pulled cash from our purses and rushed to buy cigarettes and to supplement the sweet, salty, and nourishment-free prison diet with chocolate and peanuts. A half hour later all the lights went out—and I, for one, fell immediately asleep.

Friday, June 9, 1961

Our first full day as prisoners of Hinds County, Mississippi: we were awakened for breakfast at 6:30 a.m. by the clanking of metal pans. My watch, which had been in my purse, is definitely contraband but somehow a comforting reminder of the outside world, where minutes do count and the time makes a difference.

After breakfast—cold grits, hard biscuits, three stewed prunes, and black, unsweetened, bitter, half-chicory coffee—we rolled up the mattresses and cleared the floor for sweeping and some exercises. The fear of inactivity has hit us all and we did some bending and pulling and a few modern dance exercises.

When the jailer came by, we all clamored to get our clothes from our suitcases and for some of the girls to be allowed their phone calls. (The same clamor was coming from our Negro friends next door, but somehow our white, fat, lecherous jailer did not seem to hear them.) We were allowed finally to go upstairs one at a time and get access to our suitcases. Books, glass containers, metal of any kind, and newspapers were the major items forbidden us, so rather than pull my suitcase out into the light, I opened it in the dark closet where all of our cases were being stored. I grabbed all of my books and wrapped them in a dress, took a plastic bag of cosmetic bottles (all plastic—I had been warned in Nashville), a pair of clean underpants, and my nightdress. Luckily, the jailer was concerned enough inspecting my bottles not to ask me to unroll my clothing! This was one of life's minor triumphs.

Back in the cell we had "lunch"—but it is time to stop wasting paper complaining about the prison food. Grits and beans seem to be the staple combination, and anything else is a major deviation.

New excitement in the afternoon—two more Freedom Riders! Del Greenblatt from New York (Cornell student in medieval history) and Winonah Beamer, Dayton, Ohio. They had come from Nashville by train with a fairly large group. The trusties threw two more mattresses on the floor, these two in really bad condition with the stuffing dripping out and the covers filthy.

All of the white girls had by this time been allowed to make their calls and get their clothes (except Del and Winny) but none of the Negro girls. There seemed to be nothing we could do about that injustice except complain and be annoyed. We passed over to the next cell whatever books any of us were not reading and offered to share toothpaste and shampoo.

We have finally realized that we have two jailers, not one. The fact that they are both of about the same rotundity had caused some confusion. The night man's name is Kelly, and he is even more sour than jolly Mr. Hutto.

After dinner we started singing—all the girls, and occasionally we could hear the boys singing upstairs, answering us. The Negro girls seem to have a much more musical group—some of us are pretty off key, but enthusiastic.

Saturday, June 10, 1961

New aspects of the prison routine display themselves. Today we exercise more strenuously, as we feel more the effects of our inactive life. Del, one of yesterday's newcomers, offered to teach a beginners' class in ballet, and six of us hung on the bars and to the wall while she called out the traditional command to bend up and down with back straight, and demonstrated for us: "Plié (a French word pronounced plee-AY) and up, plié and up, grand plié, two, three, four, relevé (re-li-VAY), and two—heads up now—and four . . ." As I listened to Del, I closed my eyes for a moment and thought, "This is jail!" About halfway through the session every muscle in my legs, including some I never knew I had, became agonizingly painful. But when I complained about it, Del said, "That's good—it means you're doing it right. Now—heads up, knees straight . . ."

We can pass things back and forth with the Negro Freedom Rider girls in the cell next door to the right quite easily. On the other side of us is a cell of local Negro girls-in-trouble, and although we cannot reach them, we can toss them cigarettes and they can toss us a contraband newspaper (given by one of the Negro trusties to a girlfriend there). We also have a very ragged contraband broom which passes back and forth among the cells. There seems to be another cell of Freedom Riders beyond the one next to us, whose inmates have been here longer than our immediate neighbors or we have been.

Mr. Hutto, our day jailer, likes to park himself at the bars to our cell while his trusties (all of whom seem to be skinny Negro boys about eighteen) pass out Epsom salts or food pans or collect the mail we write. He delights in telling us that he'll be glad to do anything he can for us because we are his kind, but not for *them*, indicating the cell of the Negro girls. We try not to make any comments but he provokes some responses. After one such "discussion" we received a note from the Negro girls in the next cell saying, "Don't say anything to him—that's how distorted statements get into the papers about what the Freedom Riders said." And we also learned that he was leaning on their bars and telling them that he would do what he could for *them*, but not for that white trash (indicating our cell), because they at least were southerners and he understands how they feel.

Every time he comes by, we ask Mr. Hutto about our mail and the censorship of it. And every time he comes by, he complains of the volume of mail which he must censor. "What will happen to anything you don't pass?" I ask him.

"I won't stop nothing that says the truth," says Mr. Hutto, and we must be satisfied with his view of The Truth. He says that any letters which are censored will be torn up and tossed away. We are not allowed stamps (which might facilitate smuggling letters out) but are to put the money for stamps in the open envelopes. One of the girls next door noticed, when she was finally allowed to make her phone call, that a stack of letters she had written to the Interstate Commerce Commission (ICC) and to the

U.S. attorney general and such had been deposited neatly in the wastebasket. Later on she asked if she might have her postage money back. Mr. Hutto with a smirk: "Why, I threw that out with the letters."

But we have a find in Betty Jo, my old friend from city jail. She, out of the goodness of her little heart, has offered to smuggle out some of our letters (in her draws) and she leaves on Monday. Everyone has given her postage money and a letter or more—I have sort of abused the privilege by giving her ten letters. These included letters to President John F. Kennedy and various senators and congressmen, all urging support of the ICC regulations and other such things. The letters all had "Hinds County Jail, Jackson, Mississippi," as a return address and began, "Out of my deep commitment to the cause of Negro equality . . ."

As we were sitting around in the Mississippi heat of the afternoon, trying to be cooler in various states of dress and undress, we had visitors. A group of about thirty white boys in tee shirts printed "American Legion—Boys' State" were ushered into the corridor by Mr. Hutto. They are high school students from all over the state who got to come to Mississippi's capital and try their hand at "running" the state government as an exercise in civics. Betsy told us that they had been coming around all during the week she was alone in the cell. Needless to say, we rather resented being put on exhibition like monkeys in a zoo.

Sunday, June 11, 1961

Today some people got telegrams of congratulations. Betsy got one in Greek, from her twenty-five-year college reunion, which was a sort of football cheer. (Betsy—I think I forgot to mention this—taught ancient Greek at two prestigious liberal arts colleges, Mt. Holyoke in Massachusetts and Bryn Mawr in Pennsylvania, for about twenty years.) She was surprised that the jailer did not censor the telegram as possibly being some sort of code. She also got one from Gordon Carey, the New York CORE representative, saying, "Congratulations! Wish I was there!" Someone who had seen Terry's name in the newspaper, a casual acquaintance, sent her a longish quotation by telegram, the gist of which was that she would rise with renewed strength from her vale of troubles. This was the first incoming mail that anyone had received, and I was most intrigued to see it stamped on the back in big block letters "CENSORED" and a date and initials scrawled underneath.

We have a new chore to occupy us: so many showers are being taken by the ten of us that our contraband broom is put to good use in sweeping the puddles of water out into the passageway. Mr. Hutto came by and wanted to know where the water came from—I told him that the floor slanted that way and it had flowed out.

Betty Jo, our "regular" prisoner, is on very good terms with Mr. Hutto. He told her that seventeen more Freedom Riders were in the city jail and that some of them would be coming here to the county jail. That is good news! He also told her, and us, that the Reverend C. T. Vivian, a Nashville Negro minister (who is, I believe, the prisoner who was beaten up by a guard on the Mississippi County Farm for refusing to say "sir") had been giving them some "trouble" and had been put into the "hotbox." Mr. Hutto would not elaborate on the specific nature of this punishment.

Evidently the jailers were rather upset over the singing last night. One girl is not allowed to make the phone call to which she is entitled and was promised, "Because," Mr. Hutto says, "them boys was singing all night!" I was asleep, but evidently there had been a late concert, accompanied by applause and shouts from the girls' quarters. We do not know what punishments will be inflicted on the boys—they are already prohibited books—but we fear that the "shakedown" with which we have been threatened might come through and then we too will lose our books. Or that the "store" will stop coming.

Joan Trumpauer, who is a really devout Christian, insisted on dressing up this Sunday morning—she polished her white shoes (shoe polish was the furthest thing from my mind when I packed to come to jail) and put on her last vestige of clean clothing. Joan has been sleeping the better part of every day, but this morning she managed to stay awake until 10 a.m., when the Salvation Army preacher came by to tell us to have faith and we too might get to heaven.

Joan has a three-inch round mirror (although mirrors are strictly forbidden), and today we made the discovery that by holding the mirror through the bars out into the hall, we can actually *see* the Negro girls in the next cell with whom we have been singing and conversing. With our mirror we can also tell that ours is not a dead-end hall—a passageway to somewhere bends off the end of our corridor, and the cell on the other side is about ten feet away. Mr. Hutto says that we are on the fourth floor of the building—that the county courthouse and offices are below us and the men's jail quarters are above us. We had thought we were on about the first or even basement floor. It is a strange feeling to be so disorientated.

The lack of privacy (with now ten girls in this cell built for four) is beginning to bother some of us. Jane Rosett and I had sharp words this morning over I forget what. Betsy is angelic—her forty-six years and decades of teaching seem to have given her infinite patience which those of us less than half her age seem to lack.

Monday, June 12, 1961

I woke up before anyone else this morning, before the lights were on. In the predawn light I brushed my teeth—and suddenly noticed The Bug. It was two inches long, shiny and fast moving on multitudinous legs. I chased it into the corner by the bars and it disappeared down the hall. When I turned around, there was another one on the other side of the cell. Maybe I'm going stir crazy.

Betty Jo has failed us. On her way out she got "shaken down" and this morning Mr. Hutto brought back our letters which she was to mail for us, with righteous indignation at our abortive attempt to smuggle out mail uncensored. The only letters opened were those to President Kennedy and to our lawyer, Mr. Young, but Mr. Hutto made no comments about them. The jailer said that if we tried it again we would be denied all incoming or outgoing mail. This fiasco so depressed me that I could not face the noon meal of navy beans and cornbread. I lunched instead on a hoarded candy bar and a biscuit left over from breakfast. Now I shall have to rewrite as censored mail my letters to my friends and to my mother! And my letter-writing exercise in good citizenship, petitioning my government representative for redress of grievance, is completely wasted.

After lunch we had a meeting of our whole group, a real "cell meeting." We decided that our attitude toward the jailer had been too free and easy. Rather than joke with him as we had been doing, we should be respectful and reserved, and at any possible opportunity we should say "sir" to the Negro trusties.

More Freedom Riders! Three girls for us, making a total of eleven in our cell (with locals Betty Jo and Emmy having been released and gone). They are from Chicago and Minnesota: Lee Berman (age eighteen), Claire O'Connor (age twenty-two), and Kathy Pleune (age twenty-one). Claire is a nurse, which should be useful.

Emmy left on Sunday (I forgot to mention it here). She was directly out of a Faulkner novel. At fifty-three years old, she had just been divorced by her fourth husband for being an alcoholic, but she has been an alcoholic since she was twenty. Her brother committed suicide and a sister is in the Mississippi state mental institution at Whitfield. Her father collects and spends Emmy's alimony checks every month, and she thinks he has also arranged for his nonresident mother to get an old age pension from the State of Mississippi, which he also collects and spends. While she was intoxicated, her family had called the police to take her to jail and off their hands until she could be committed to the psychiatric ward at Whitfield where she has spent a good many months in times past. She is a frail-looking woman and the police had managed to pretty well work her over—when we came in she had two black eyes and numerous bruises.

Late in the evening we have still one more arrival, but not a Freedom Rider—a middle-aged woman named Polly, with whom the last three Freedom Riders had had some experience in the city jail. She came into their cell drunk, and immediately began beating up on them. She socked Kit and beat her over the head with a shoe, all the while insisting that the girls sign a statement that the Freedom Riders were Communists, atheists, and professional agitators. Being committed to principles of nonviolence, all they could do was try to protect themselves as best they could without retaliating. When she sobered up she was relatively pleasant to them. (Polly is of a racial type which, to me at least, seems distinctly Negroid, but she evidently passes as Caucasian.)

When "sto' taime" came around, the night jailer, Mr. Kelly, called Polly out of the cell to talk to her—about what we could not manage to hear. This incident capped the suspicions already fermenting in our too-little-occupied minds, and we became convinced that she had been placed in our cell in order to spy on us. In addition, we were afraid that she might get into a fight with someone (thirteen people in a relatively small, completely confined area might have a certain amount of trouble getting along even if all of them know exactly why they are there and believe in their cause) or that she might try to steal from us either our few valuables or the multitudinous papers which we had assiduously hidden from the jailers. We decided to keep a watch all night. Helene took lights-out to about 2:00 a.m., Jane and Kit the middle section, and I was to be awakened as soon as dawn began to creep up.

Other news: although we did not notice it at first, the female Negro Freedom Riders had been divided into two cells down the hall from us, presumably because of their greater numbers.

Tuesday, June 13, 1961

The "watch" was uneventful; Polly did not so much as snore in her sleep. But after she left this morning the local girls in the other cell told us that the last time she had been in the jail she had stolen eight dollars from a fellow prisoner.

Helene Wilson is writing to her husband in invisible ink. She is using deodorant, after we tried every liquid we had. We burned the paper a couple of times, trying to make something appear, using cologne, contact-lens antiseptic, and a few other oddments, but the deodorant was the only one which showed up. To get him to heat the papers, she is going to put "please iron my things" in each of her letters and hope that he'll get the point.

Bad news: the jailer came by in great glee to tell us that we were all to be transferred to the state penitentiary, Parchman Farm. This rumor has been abroad for days, but his information is to be taken as semiofficial. He said also that "the papers are all ready" but claimed not to know if this means all prisoners or only the boys or only the Negro boys or what. Or maybe it is all just to frighten us.

Further news later about the state pen: only the boys (both the Negro boys from here and the white boys from the city jail) will go, the girls will not. We have decided, though, that if they are sent we are going to go on a hunger strike until either the boys come back or we are sent there. The newspaper this evening (smuggled in by our "local" neighbors) said that the Negro Freedom Riders transferred to the state prison would be put to picking cotton and kept in the maximum security section of the penitentiary. We had been told that cotton does not ripen until September, but I expect that they could manufacture it especially for us, if need be.

The implications of a hunger strike have been very thoroughly discussed. Terry Perlman, the CCNY student, has decided not to participate, and also Helene Wilson, of D.C., both of them because of health conditions among family at home (a father and a husband) who are already under a great deal of strain.

Jack Young finally came to visit us. Martin Luther King, Jr., could not have gotten a warmer reception. He took our clothing sizes and orders for bras, panties, and the like which some of the local (Negro) churches want to buy for us. We tried to slip him a note saying that we intend to go on a hunger strike if the boys are moved, but cannot be absolutely certain that he did get it.

Today, finally overcoming my disappointment at Betty Jo's failure to smuggle out our letters, I wrote twelve letters to various people. I wrote to Ed Kale, one of the Yale divinity students with whom I had arrived in Jackson, adding a phrase in Greek (courtesy of Betsy) saying that we would go on a hunger strike if they went to the penitentiary; literally translated, it read, "If the boys go to the big prison, the girls will stop eating."

Chapter 6

THE BOYS GO TO PARCHMAN

Wednesday, June 14, 1961

Big excitement all day (and night)—the boys to the penitentiary? or not?! They did not go this morning, and Helene offered to make book that they would not go at all.

Things were quiet all day, except for a variation on our visitors from Boys' State. This time it was Girls' State, a dozen or so girls in starched and ironed summer dresses, with hair stylishly neat and careful makeup. I cannot tell why, but these I resented even more than I had the boys. It took all of the nonviolence I could muster to keep me from disliking them intensely.

In the late afternoon there was much shouting to the boys upstairs concerning, especially, a note being passed by string and wire from their floor to ours. The note was not significant, but it precipitated Mr. Kelly's closing all of the windows in the corridor at dinnertime (as he had warned us he would do if the shouting continued). After he had come again at "sto' taime," and after much discussion back and forth between the cells, we managed to open the windows by some fancy manipulation with the broom. The danger in this was that, if he should notice the open windows, he would know that we had a contraband something-or-other with which to have opened them, and that this might bring on the shakedown of which we are all so afraid. We decided to open them, however, on the reasoning that (1) the day jailer would probably not notice in the morning, (2) it would be insufferably hot and stuffy with the windows closed, and (3) since the threat of removal to the penitentiary still hung over the boys, this might be our last chance to yell or sing to them.

About half an hour after we opened the windows, to our horror we heard the "jingle bells" of the jailer's keys. We all dived onto our mattresses and pretended to be asleep. He ushered a young girl into our cell, slammed the door, turned the key, and left, apparently without noticing the windows. We all breathed a sigh of relief, and turned to examine our new arrival. She was not a Freedom Rider, but a local girl, who told us that she was being held because someone had forged her signature on a note and then defaulted—she expected to be out of jail the next morning or possibly even the same evening.

During our shouting with the boys, we had been told that Dan—one of the boys who had been mysteriously called out of his cell the previous day, and about whom we had begun to worry—had turned out to be an informer, and that he had held a press conference the previous day at which he discussed, among other things, a controversial trip to Cuba by one Freedom Rider girl. We were therefore most suspicious of our new addition, who looked like one of the Girls' State visitors. Helene Wilson swore that she actually recognized her, and before five minutes had passed, we had all decided, each independently, that she was possibly, if not probably, sent to spy on us. What they wanted to know, we thought, was what protest we were going to make over the boys' transfer. We decided that we would have to set a watch, be careful of our talk, and warn the girls next door. (This simultaneous unanimity among us, which occurs often, never ceases to amaze me, although under the circumstances our solidarity is probably quite logical.)

After the lights went out, we were struck that the boys did not sing, as they had done every night after lights out for the whole time we have been here.

The Negro girls in the cell next door refused to sing when we wanted them to do so in hopes of a response, and so we pretty much settled down. I took the early morning watch, and had already gone to sleep when, at about midnight, male voices singing our theme song, "We Shall Overcome," were heard from upstairs. I woke up with a start on the second verse, even though I have slept through many such concerts which included shouts and clapping and much more noise. The first thing I said as I sat up was, "That's *not* our boys." The rhythm was ragged and much of it was off-key, and someone was shouting out each line before it was sung.

We finally decided that this was the "regular" Negro prisoners from upstairs, who had been singing along with our Freedom Rider boys on previous nights. With much shouting, however, we discovered that at least some of our boys were still up there. They sang a few songs, much diminished in volume, and we sang a few back. Then there was much shouting of "Hey, Gwen!" "Yeah?" "Good-bye!" "Good-bye!" "I love you!" "I love you, too!" "It's Dion—good-bye, Terry," "Hey, Pat, this is Lowell," "Hi, Lowell," "Take care of yourself, Pat," "You too. . . ." And so on, into the night.

At one point, during a period of comparative silence, a man's voice was heard close by saying, "Tell the girls the boys are leaving right now." It was one of the trusties calling through the door to his girlfriend in the cell down the hall. We heard him give the message and started shouting to the boys, but stopped immediately when the trusty shouted, "Hey, wait a minute, give me time; don't let me lose *my* head." We waited a few minutes, and then, again, shouted, but in vain. His message had meant they were already downstairs in the van, actually taking off for the state penitentiary, too far away to hear us.

Now was the time to make effective the hunger strike which we had been discussing for a couple of days. In breathy conversations and brief match-lit notes we decided to start with breakfast the next day. All of this was done in whispers and writing, while two people occupied and "covered" our little visitor. She caught herself in so many lies, and we saw her watching us so attentively and asking such pertinent questions, that we became fully convinced that our suspicions were justified. But I doubt that she learned anything of significance.

Thursday, June 15, 1961

First day of the hunger strike. The jailer woke us up at the proper time with breakfast and Betsy asked for "just two pans, please" (for Terry and Helene), informing him that the rest did not want any. He got the point very fast and took the remainder of the pans away. A day not even broken up by the diversion of meals can drag on interminably. And this one did.

In the evening, Christmas in Jackson: the Negro ministers who had come to see the girls on Sunday had told Mr. Young that they wanted to do something for us, and tonight they came through with a load of shampoo, soap, rubber sandals, tee shirts, and shorts. Also, wonder of wonders, paper shopping bags. No longer will our few odd possessions have to be piled untidily on half-sheets of newspaper and placed under the beds. We were also overjoyed to have the plastic bags in which the clothes and shoes arrived.

One strange thing—Kit got a shout from Lowell, upstairs. Evidently he is alone up there, and it is most curious. It is quite certain, though, that the rest of the boys have been sent to Parchman.

I finally finished a letter to Mother which has been in the writing for some days and it pleases me very much:

Hinds County Jail
Jackson, Mississippi
15 June, 1961
Letter #5

Mother dear, thinking about it, I have been getting more and more pleased about the support for my action you expressed in your last letter. The only thing that has really bothered me about all of this is that (after I talked to you on the phone) I felt that I might really be hurting you. I have done so in the past, I know, sometimes unthinkingly and out of a youthful carelessness. But this situation is a different one, where I feel that I am distinctly right in my actions and that if you are suffering on my behalf, I could do nothing but feel terribly sorry. What I must do, I must do.

Very relevant to this is part of the book I just finished, Martin Luther King, Jr.'s *Stride Toward Freedom*, about the Montgomery bus boycott. He writes there of having to leave his parents' home, with his mother already made sick by worrying over him, and return to a Montgomery torn by mob violence and house bombings. How can a parent fail to envision every possible danger? How can a child not feel guilty at worrying his parent? But how can an individual shirk his responsibilities and continue to look his parents straight in the eye?

If I have a social conscience I inherited it from you and Dad, and if I must speak out for the causes of justice, freedom, and truth, I learned to do so from you. You must not fear for me when I am in physical danger. It is better that I live a shorter or longer life and live it well and fully than that I live to senility a vain and meaningless existence.

But forgive me for being so serious.

I love you.

Carol

Friday, June 16, 1961

Second day of the hunger strike—almost. In the morning we did mild exercises rather than the full ballet routine. Then showers and "peace and quiet" for a couple of hours. As I had suggested for some time, we began a class in Spanish with Claire O'Connor teaching. She has had two years of college Spanish and two of the others in the original class have had almost as much. What I really want is someone to give me correct pronunciation, and I figured I could manage to keep up by studying the text in advance.

This Spanish class, rather desultory and not too helpful, led, however, to the most exciting thing which we have tried since being here. Someone asked Betsy to teach us Greek, and she agreed! We had assembled and were about to begin with the six of us who were awake when Del, our medieval historian, woke with a start, crying, "Wait for me!" and joined us. She said that she had been dying to ask Betsy to do this but had considered it too much of an imposition; since someone else had initiated it, however, she was horrified at the thought of being left out.

At about 2:00 p.m. Mr. Young came by, as always to an enthusiastic reception from all of us. He pulled Betsy out of our cell and two Negro girls each from the other two cells. He told Betsy that the newest attempt on the legal front is going to be for the lawyers to try to get a habeas corpus release for Betsy in the federal district court—on the grounds that she is being held illegally on a false charge. If this strategy succeeds, she will be released immediately and we would be released soon after. And the most immediately exciting thing about it is that Betsy gets to take a trip to Biloxi, Mississippi, since in a case of habeas corpus the sheriff must actually produce the corpus (the body of the prisoner) before the judge.

Mr. Young also reiterated to us his advice that hunger strikes do no good. And evidently he convinced one of the Negro girls, our elected spokesman on the hunger strike, Pauline Knight, that it should be called off. Her cell announced to us that they were going off—period. The other two cells, Ruby's and ours, were then sort of left in the lurch, without a spokesman (Pauline) and yet without a decision of the whole group that the hunger strike should be ended. Ruby's cell decided almost immediately to quit also, but a rather long and upsetting meeting was held by our cell on whether or not we should go off.

All eleven of us in our cell, all the white female Freedom Riders, had considered very carefully the value, implications, etc., of this strike, its objectives and purpose and how it should be run. We felt a great deal of resentment toward Pauline for not having consulted with us, in the first place, about her refusal to announce by a written or oral statement to the jailers the reasons for the hunger strike—that by being sent to Parchman penitentiary the boys had been subjected to "cruel and unusual" punishment for a minor offense and were being given different treatment than the girls—and our conditions for calling it off—that the boys be moved back to Jackson or we be moved to Parchman, and secondly, about the decision to quit the strike. We had all felt very strongly that the spokesman for the strike and the leadership of it should come from one of the Negro girls rather than from one of us in this white cell, but we also felt that, as individuals involved equally with them in a democratic movement, we had the right to be treated equally. There was much talk of sending a note to Pauline explaining our grievances and suggesting everything from a continuance of the hunger strike to better communications in the future. In the end, we decided that we could not continue the strike independently of the other two cells. Betsy sent a note to Pauline and Ruby, in the other cells, saying that we too were going off the strike, and we decided to have a meeting tomorrow to discuss the whole affair and also to decide on whether we needed another note to be sent.

Just as we finally finished this business, the cell door clanged open and three more Freedom Riders—Jo Adler, from the University of Wisconsin, Slade (Elizabeth) Hirshfeld from Cornell, and Kay Kytle from Oklahoma—were added to our cozy little group, making fourteen in all. A might tight, indeed!

And almost before they had been introduced around, we had our first real emergency. Winnie had been complaining of headaches and dizziness, even this morning, after not eating all day yesterday, and suddenly she sort of keeled over in what Claire (the nurse) described as a "mild coma." Her head began rolling from side to side and we could not rouse her. The only thing to do was to call the jailer to get a doctor, so we started shouting for Mr. Kelly. He did not answer, but about twenty minutes later came in with supper. His response to our demand that he get a doctor was, "Now listen here, y'all better just shut up that noise. *I* run this jail, not you." But evidently the sight of Winnie, propped up in the middle of the floor on multitudinous mats, her pale appearance and the movements of her head convinced him that we were not kidding. With a few more angry words, he stormed out.

We tried feeding Winnie some mashed-up food, and managed to get a few teaspoons of potatoes down her, but it did not seem to do any good. Claire reported that her pupils were still dilated, and we could see that she still looked very sick. When we heard nothing from Mr. Kelly after half an hour, we began screaming again and banging on the bars. This time he came, again with the angry demand that we shut up. But he told us that he had called the doctor, and a little while later that phenomenon, a doctor, actually turned up—a short fat man in a rumpled suit. He looked at Winnie (and all of us) disdainfully, listened to her heart, refused to look at her eyes on Claire's suggestion, and finally said, "Wal, there's nothing much wrong with her." Then he pulled out a vial of something, gave her a shot, and left. Claire's professional opinion of him was that he probably got his sheepskin (his medical degree) out of a Sears Roebuck catalog. But the shot he had given Winnie (which Claire said was probably a respiratory stimulant) did begin to revive her. We fed her some more food and after a while she was OK, still weak but able to sit up and make self-deprecating comments about zaftig girls who faint when they don't eat for a day.

Saturday, June 17, 1961

Last night, for the first time, the "sto" failed to appear. We could not decide if we were being punished for having been bad girls and not eaten for almost two days or if Mr. Kelly was too busy or what—but "sto" did not come.

Last night also we got the benefit of the ingenuity and genius of one of our new girls, Jo Adler. She had concealed a transistor radio in her girdle under a full skirt, and our contact with the outside world has now been reestablished. On the 10:00 p.m. news we heard for the first time that President Kennedy is on crutches, that the Mariners are striking, and the tractors-for-prisoners deal with Cuba's Castro had fallen through. We also got the latest dope on the Freedom Riders, and on the legal maneuvers being attempted to free us. After almost two weeks of complete isolation from the outside world (aside from an occasional Jackson newspaper smuggled our way), that almost made worthwhile the additional crowding from adding the three more girls with their three more sleeping mats.

The big event of the day was the meeting held after lunch, as planned yesterday, to discuss the abortive hunger strike.

It started out with a general discussion of household matters, the organization of periods of "peace and quiet" and "noise and chaos" and various kinds of time between, like classes and meetings. This was felt necessary predicated on the new fact that we are now fourteen girls in a cell built for four. This led us to what we would do if a fifteenth person was shoved in here, either another Freedom Rider or a local white drunk. There was hot argument by Jane Rosett and myself that our procedure should be to ascertain if the addition was a Freedom Rider or a drunk and if the latter, to throw ourselves before the door (more or less literally) and physically prevent her from coming in. A Freedom Rider we would accept without murmur. But the majority vote was different: on the reasoning that we had come here expecting to be treated as regular prisoners and that we should not try for special handling, the decision was that we should just accept anything and anyone they threw our way.

We then began discussing the hunger strike and our disappointment at the way it had ended. After much general discussion, Joan Trumpauer, from Virginia, launched into a disquisition on the nature of the Civil Rights Movement in the South. She pointed out, among other things, that to southern students in the Movement the word of the lawyer always carried tremendous weight; therefore when our lawyer had said that there was no point to the strike and that he did not approve of it, the strike was, of course, off. We also discussed our chief grievance about the conduct of the strike, that Pauline had refused absolutely to do what we considered so necessary, that is, to state the terms and conditions of our strike. Here again Joan pointed out that Pauline had felt it too obvious for discussion that (as she finally wrote us in a note) any statement would have gotten no further than the jailer except in the form of garbled and perverted releases to the local press. In the South, Joan continued, the Civil Rights Movement has a firmly religious nature, with Gandhi's principles of nonviolence and passive resistance grafted onto Christian morality and brotherly love. Pauline, firmly rooted in and faithful to these principles of the Movement, felt that no other decision was possible, that this fact should be obvious to everyone, and that discussion was not only unnecessary but ridiculous.

The liberal objection to Joan and Pauline was voiced by Winnie (Winonah Beamer)—that she was not interested in a mystic faith in "the Movement" which precluded democratic processes and consultation among the individual members of the group, that this was not her understanding of the activities to which she had committed herself in Dayton, Ohio, nor was it the kind of an objective, either ultimate or immediate, to which she would have dedicated her summer.

My own small contribution to the discussion was to point out the difference between these two attitudes as one of philosophical significance—that in the North the Civil Rights Movement is the concern of the ACLU (American Civil Liberties Union) and in the South of the SCLC (Southern Christian Leadership Conference)—on the one hand a distinctly individualistic and libertarian fight for civil rights, and on the other hand a religious movement based on love and brotherhood, with nonviolence as a technique adopted by both. Both elements are extremely important; both are necessary to the eventual success of the Civil Rights Movement as a whole. But the problem of communication which these differences set up between the northern and the southern members of the Movement is very great and cannot be either sloughed off or explained away. The northern whites, representing the liberal democratic segments of the Civil Rights Movement, are welcomed by and to the Negro movement in the South, but they must recognize that it is essentially both Negro and southern, that they may join it but must not attempt to lead it. The southern Civil Rights Movement is essentially revolutionary in its objectives, and only its early infusion with Gandhian principles of nonviolence has saved it from being a more bloody revolution than it has been.

Anyway, the upshot of our very long discussion was that any resentment against Pauline was dispelled and we resolved to try to improve communications between the three cells in general, especially by whatever personal contact is possible with Ruby's cell, the one next to us. This experience is a perfect example of one of the greatest evils of segregation. By precluding meaningful communication it fosters misunderstanding on both sides.

Sunday, June 18, 1961

All day today, Kit and Joan, Helene and Jane (and occasionally others) kept getting into political discussions, even though these had been outlawed by general agreement. The possibility of a Gleason-type innocent turning up among us and being shocked at the polemics of a hot political argument was the reason for this, although all of us chafed under this restriction on our favorite indoor sport. ("Gleason" refers to the Rev. Richard Gleason of Chicago, one of the early white male Freedom Riders, who was convinced by the Jackson authorities that his fellow Riders were all Communists and atheists. He signed a statement to that effect on June 5, 1961, which made every newspaper in the country.)

Sunday is Bible and Salvation Army day. At 10:00 a.m. a pretty blond nineteen-year-old in a starched pink dress read us the Bible in a thick southern drawl and reached out with faith and redemption for all us sinners. We were polite.

At 3:00 p.m. a small group of singers came around, this time accompanied by a man with a trumpet, and it, too, was aptly described as "rhythm ragged and one note flat." We asked for and were lent a copy of the little songbook they were using, so that at least we could sing along. The girls in Ruby's cell sang beautifully, as usual, and we asked the group to lend Ruby a songbook too. They only hesitated a little, then lent her one. As they left, I asked if we could keep one of the songbooks and one of the women started to say "yes" when the trumpeter, somewhat flustered, began insisting that there were not enough, and that they could not get any more. As they hurried out, with their trumpet and all their songbooks, we were handed a stack of Salvation Army tracts and a Gideon Bible, all of which we gave to the Negro girls in the cell next door.

Later on, two Negro men, ministers from Jackson, came to visit the Negro girls. The ministers were not allowed near the white girls. I suppose that in Mississippi, heaven, too, is segregated. As they were leaving, they had to pass by our cell, however. We asked them to try to get us a rabbi for the Jewish girls (more than half of our number). They said they would try.

Monday, June 19, 1961

Nothing of note. No rabbi, no mail, no new Freedom Riders, no visitors, not even any rumors or arguments.

Tuesday, June 20, 1961

A relatively uneventful day again, but still not dull: somehow, what with ballet in the morning, Greek classes, and a very interesting crowd of people, no day is ever really too dull.

Today I got a package from my father, a carton of Spring cigarettes. Having vowed to give up smoking when I ran out of my favorite brand, and faced anyway with the disappearance of our main source of supply, the "sto," I was steeling myself for the thought of giving up smoking completely. All day I had been saving the last cigarette from my last pack to give myself an after-supper treat. I was somewhat surprised that the package was allowed to come through. Maybe no one in the jailer's office likes my brand, even for free.

Our small store of reading matter has been increased courtesy of the Prison Mission Association, Inc. Mr. Hutto today brought us their newsletter, a single sheet printed on both sides with inspirational material, like: "WHAT IS A COMMUNIST? A world wide organization advocating . . . absolute social and racial equality, promotion of class hatred." And, especially for prisoners, "Dear Friends: Have you wondered what will come to pass if communism takes over this great land of LIBERTY? . . . you will lose your freedom . . . the people are not allowed to travel or visit friends. They cannot choose their kind of work or place of residence . . ."

Winnie spent most of today fooling with the statistic that the cell is thirteen by fifteen feet with a chunk out for the shower and toilet (about six by four) and that there are fourteen of us. She figures that we each have an allotted space smaller than the size of the shower.

Wednesday, June 21, 1961

Four more Freedom Riders were added to our cell today, from the University of California at Berkeley and from Oakland City College—Jorgia Siegel, Joan Pleune (Kit's sister), Peggy Kerr, and Lestra Peterson. This brings to eighteen our number, and the girls who were busy figuring out how many square inches we each are allocated have just given up.

Bursting with California sunshine, Jorgia with her robust and buxom tan has made the rest of us sad and woeful about our prison pallor.

There is not enough room on the floor to put down all the mats, so two mats were put on each bed and we will try sleeping across, three people to two mats and five to four. And today the Negro girls also got a taste of overcrowding. A white woman, drunk and in very bad shape, was literally dragged in. In order to put her in a cell by herself, the jailers doubled up the two Negro cells of six and seven each into one of thirteen. The poor woman banged and screamed for a while, but then shut up and went to sleep. It is fantastic to think that a few hours earlier she had been driving a car.

One of the girls is to leave tonight, and after long discussions of the morality, practicality, and possible consequences of the move, we decided to smuggle out on her (in a Kotex pad) two letters. One was more or less the same as the one we had tried to get out by Betty Jo to the *New York Times* and the other some notes to be the material for a news story, sent to an Associated Press reporter that Helene knows in Washington. When the letters which Betty Jo was carrying had been returned to us, on our prior try, we were warned that if we ever tried it again, the jailers would cut off all of our mail both in and out. But we figured that the chances of their catching the letters were rather dim, and that, anyway, it was worth the risk to break the silence of our "silent witness."

The good citizens of Jackson have come through again with a load of clothes and toiletries. This time, surprisingly enough, we are told that the gift was from some sympathetic whites in the community—unknown benefactors, since they had gotten in touch with Mr. Young through a dozen intermediaries. I was especially grateful for the shampoo, even though I cut my hair (with a contraband razor blade) a day or two ago. I did it as an act of impulsive desperation when I found that I could not get my hair anywhere near clean here, but I still have enough to be concerned about. (When I was a kid, my mother cut our hair, mine and my sisters', into long page-boy style, and for the past years, at college and working in the Big Apple, New York City, I asserted my independence by letting it grow to almost waist length; times change.)

Still no "sto' time." We have decided that it has been permanently removed either as a punishment for our hunger strike or on a general policy of trying to make us less comfortable, that is, encouraging us to bail out.

Thursday, June 22, 1961

Today was Betsy's day in court—and out of Hinds County Jail. The hearing on her application for a writ of habeas corpus was held in Biloxi, Mississippi, about a hundred and fifty miles away, and so they took her out early in the morning for the trip. When she came back, late in the afternoon, she gave a full report on the hearing and the issues involved: CORE and its attorneys are arguing that she is being wrongly held in jail because the law under which she was convicted is unconstitutional, that is, a disguised segregation law. This is the major argument which they will use when and if the writ is issued and a hearing is held. Today's affair was just a preliminary application to ask the judge to issue the writ, and actually Betsy did not have to be present at all. But the Jackson authorities are sufficiently scared that they wanted her there just in case.

Today's arguments centered around why the issue should be heard in the federal courts, Mississippi saying that Betsy must first exhaust all of the remedies offered by the state courts, and her CORE lawyers arguing that since her sentence is only sixty-seven days (her two-hundred-dollar fine at three dollars per day) she does not have time to go all the way to the state supreme court before seeking relief in the federal court. The CORE lawyers also focused on the fact that by issuing this writ, the judge has a chance to make a momentous decision and write his name large in history. He is to give his decision some time around the beginning of next month, but it does not look hopeful.

When Betsy came back, we were in the middle of a big meeting on what to do about our dwindling supply of cigarettes, to ration them or not, and if so, how. After adding to our supply the two packs she had managed to buy, Betsy regaled us with the tales of her excursion. They had chartered a seven-passenger plane and had accompanied her with a special matron, the sheriff, the state prosecutor, and some other big shots. She also got dinner out, and the menu made our usual supper of beans and cornbread taste all the worse.

About the cigarettes, we decided on self-discipline rather than actual rationing, and to keep all cigarettes and matches in the far corner of the cell, hoping that our natural laziness will perhaps help cut down on our smoking.

Again, more Freedom Riders! This brings our number to twenty. And we complained when we were eleven! After the new girls came in, we asked Mr. Hutto what the authorities considered the maximum capacity of our cell to be. "As long as we can still close the door," he said. And I believe him.

One of the new girls got a call today from some radio station in her hometown, and, to our great amazement, they let her talk to them. Of course, it was under the watchful eye and ear of Mr. Hutto, but she did answer fairly frankly to questions about our conditions. She figured that the only thing the jailer could do would be to cut off the call in the middle, which might embarrass Jackson as much as anything she could say. She said that she had heard on the phone the little bell ringing periodically, which meant that the call had been recorded.

When the two new girls were allowed to get their clothes, they made a real haul. Carefully coached by all of us veterans, they not only managed to get about thirty books (by slipping them into various parts of their underwear when the jailer was not looking) but also dipped into the shopping bag full of cigarettes which had been confiscated from the packages sent to us and which we knew was being kept in the same closet with our suitcases. They got two and a half cartons' worth. How they managed to get that much by Mr. Hutto I shall never know.

Friday, June 23, 1961

No one got much sleep last night, because the floor was so very crowded—even with the three largest girls on the cots and two smallest ones sharing the fourth cot. But I expect we will get used to this in time, as we have gotten used to everything else.

Today we started something I had wanted for a long time, a class in conversational French. Judy Frieze, one of yesterday's arrivals, Jo Adler, Helene Wilson and I were the main conversants, even though only Judy knew the language very well (she hopes to teach French some day). With Judy correcting our grammar we chattered happily for almost an hour.

Sometime during the afternoon we heard the boys calling for the jailer, and then for the doctor. These were the Freedom Rider Negro males who had just come in and were waiting to be transferred to Parchman. We called up and asked what the matter was, and they yelled back that one of them was having an asthma attack, and that they could not get the jailer to respond. So we started calling too, on the theory that we were closer to the jail office. We yelled and screamed and banged on the cement floor with our contraband food pan–ashtrays. Finally Mr. Hutto came to see what the racket was about. We told him that one of our boys was sick and needed attention. He said "Your boys? Your boys is all over in the city jail. They ain't nothing but niggers upstairs." Ignoring this bit of pleasantry, Claire, our nurse, threatened him that the boy could die if he did not get immediate medical attention. She insisted that Hutto take up to him Judy's atomizer of respiratory stimulant, a standard emergency remedy for asthmatics. With a great deal of bad grace, he did take the medicine, and went out. We shouted to the boys about what we had done, but it was almost a half hour later before they stopped shouting, "Jailer! Doctor!"

At about six in the evening, our jailer and some strange man came by and asked us how many there were in our cell. We told him twenty and he, the stranger, said, "Get your stuff together, y'all are being moved."

A tremendous uproar and clamor of "Where? Where?"

"To Parchman!"

Chapter 7

MAXIMUM SECURITY UNIT

Friday, June 23, 1961, continued

The night ride in the paddy wagon between Jackson and Parchman took about four hours, and was more frightening than any previous part of this whole jail experience. Twenty-three girls, about half and half white and Negro together, were crowded into one old army-transport-type truck. It was completely lacking in springs, and bounced us along toward an unknown future. Many of us had black-and-blue marks when we arrived, because the drivers delighted in stopping and starting suddenly, which threw us against each other and the sharp corners of the seats. We sang, of course, to keep our courage up.

The most terrifying part of the ride was the three occasions when the driver suddenly jolted off to the side of the highway—and stopped. We imagined every possible horror from a waiting ambush of the Ku Klux Klan to mined roads. I suppose that they may have been waiting for some kind of escort, of state police or FBI, to catch up with us, or something equally innocent, but until we were moving again, none of us breathed an easy breath.

When we finally arrived, we could not see anything through the tiny grilled windows of the truck but a huge, modern-looking barred gate. We had been singing steadily (to the great annoyance of our driver-guards) and continued while we waited for something to happen. Then, to our unspeakable joy, we suddenly heard an answer—men's voices, singing "We Shall Overcome," the song that has become more or less the theme song for the whole civil rights movement. After that, nothing and no one could frighten us.

Our induction to the state penitentiary was quick and thorough. Our paper shopping bags full of clothes and the other items which we had been allowed in our cell in the Hinds County Jail were taken from us "for safekeeping" by the men in charge. Then three women in striped skirts (two white and one Negro) took us into another room and searched us—with particular attention to our brassieres and underwear—and gave us prison skirts of black and white striped denim to replace the shorts which most of us had worn. We kept our own blouses, mine being a flimsy sleeveless thing printed with blue and green circles, the perfect thing to go with stripes. The women did not take away our eyeglasses, as we had most feared, but they did take away all of our bobby pins, hairpins, rubber bands, and barrettes. When they were done with us, we were as sorry looking a bunch of females as ever one did see.

We were ushered down a long row of cells by one of the men and stopped before one of the cells. Since we were being inducted in threes and fours just as we came in, the choice of cell mate was random except that they would not allow Negroes and whites in the same cell. Terry and I walked close together in hopes of being put in the same cell. The jailer shouted "Open three!" Metal clanged, a motor whirred, the electric door to one of the cells slid back, and Terry Perlman and I were locked into our new home.

The cell had new-looking mattresses (much thicker than the ones we had at Hinds County Jail) on both tiers of the steel bunk beds, a toilet (looking very bare without a toilet seat or cover), and a tiny sink. It was, we estimated, nine feet by six feet by ten feet high. Beyond our bars we could see the wall opposite with a row of small windows just under the ceiling. Our stock-taking disclosed the fact that, aside from prison-issue furnishings, that is, a skirt, towel, and an unbleached muslin sheet and pillowcase each, our total assets consisted of one safety pin, which had been pinned on my blouse and somehow been missed by the women who searched us. We were barefooted, too, and looking at each other we realized, even without a mirror, how dreadful we looked. I felt suddenly very lonely and homesick.

Saturday, June 24, 1961

Despite all the yet-to-appear but possible disadvantages of Parchman Prison Farm, I must admit that I prefer the sleeping arrangements here to those at Hinds County Jail.

Terry has claustrophobia and I am a little afraid of heights, so it worked very well that she took the top bunk and I the lower. With one exception, I slept very well last night. The exception was when I suddenly was awakened by some sort of large bug crawling across the back of my neck. I screamed and tried to jump out of bed, but, getting tangled in the sheet, fell out instead onto the concrete floor. The bug, unconcerned by my traumatic experience, crawled slowly away—I had nothing with which to smash it, and was not about to step on it with my bare foot.

Breakfast, our first meal here, was unexceptional, the usual grits, coffee, and biscuits. But lunch was, to our Hinds County Jail–trained palates, truly magnificent: in the first place, the tin trays were easily twice the size of those at the Hinds County Jail, with six rather than three compartments. And for this memorable first lunch at Parchman, each of the sections had something in it! There was cornbread, potatoes, a very peppery but still edible spaghetti, cooked cabbage, and, truly the pièce de résistance, a half of a fresh, raw peach. None of us had seen anything that was not overcooked in the southern manner, let alone fruit, since we had arrived in Mississippi.

During the afternoon we were taken out cell by cell and fingerprinted, again. Then we were given a bar of soap with which to wash off the ink. And a little while later a man came around passing out toothbrushes and tooth powder in little packets made from prison stationary envelopes. From the same carton he passed out Gideon Bibles, the New Testament with Psalms and Proverbs.

We are beginning to settle down and adjust to our new situation. Claire O'Connor, in the cell next to ours, discovered that she could pull threads out of her towel, and pulled enough to braid into a passable piece of string, which she immediately, of course, used to tie back her hair. This great discovery was relayed to Terry and me, and we spent a few happy hours pulling and twisting and braiding, and then, finally, admiring each other's ponytail.

The fact that we are in an integrated cell block, even though no individual cell is integrated, pleased us quite a bit. On the other side of Terry and me is a cell with Ruby Doris Smith and Shirley Thompson, two Negro girls respectively from Nashville and New Orleans. When we were at the Hinds County Jail, individual contact with girls in the Negro cells whom we had not known on the outside was almost impossible, but now not only had we shared the horrible ride to Parchman but we had a chance to really get acquainted on a one-to-one (or rather two-by-two) basis. It is impossible to see into the next cell, but verbal contact is almost as good.

After dinner we played Botticelli (a famous-person guessing game), up and down the cell block, making a great deal of racket. And it was after this that Shirley and Ruby discovered that they could talk to the prisoners in cells on the other side of the wall from us: our cells are back to back with Death Row. The man with whom they talked said that he had been convicted, along with two other Negro men, of raping a white woman, but that the NAACP has appealed his case. He has been in Parchman, waiting for action on his appeal, for over a year. The conversation was carried on through a hole in the wall which seems to lead to some sort of blower system. When Shirley told this man who we were, he said that he knew all about us because he had a radio and got newspapers and magazines. He would not believe, at first, that we were without shoes, cigarettes, and our personal belongings. After Shirley had more or less finished talking to this man, we decided that it would probably not be a wise idea to talk to him again, because it might get him in a lot of trouble. He would be dealing with the prison authorities long after we had left.

Sunday, June 25, 1961

In spite of the fact that the Salvation Army did not represent the religious views of very many of us, we were all somewhat disappointed not to have even that contact with the outside world: no chapel, no services, no Sunday variation in the established routine of the Maximum Security Unit of the Mississippi state prison.

We are only beginning to catch the full implications of this business of our being in the Maximum Security Unit. Just before dawn every morning, at about 4:30 a.m., one of the jailers comes by and rattles the door of each cell. The first day it woke everybody up, but we are getting accustomed to the tremendous amount of noise which accompanies every action on the other side of our bars, although Terry and I still jump every time the last and loudest of the metal corridor doors clangs shut.

After breakfast we tried having our regular ballet practice. Del called the steps from her cell (near the other end of the block from ours) and even added in things like "Heads up!—two, three, four; grande plié, two, three, four; keep those arms up, backs straight, two, three, four and again—one, two, knees straight, four . . ." But somehow it was not the same as when we were all together in the same cell.

About the middle of the afternoon, one of the jailers came clomping down to about the middle of our cell block and stopped. He was one of our two more frequent visitors, and we have decided that he is someone especially in charge of us. Although I do not like stereotypes, he was a perfect stereotype of a tough prison guard: tall, heavyset, with a mean face and big heavy boots (which showed because somehow he always managed to have one leg of his pants caught on the edge of one of the boots). He was usually smoking a cigar, and that, to those of us still having nicotine withdrawal symptoms, was the ultimate insult. They smelled like bad cigars, too.

Standing there, in the middle of the block, he began addressing all of us in a booming voice. "Y'all are going to cut out all of this noise and singing. Y'all are going to quit talking to them niggers back of y'all. If I hear any more noise from y'all, y'all ain't going to get to write no letters. If y'all don't quit singing I'm going to take away your mattresses and y'all'r going to be sleeping on that cold, hard steel." And he chomped on his cigar and stomped out. Clang—the first door. Crash!—the outer door. As the echoes began dying away, we were already involved in heated debate about his threats, an activity reminiscent of the "good old days" in the Hinds County Jail.

We decided, of course, that we were not going to be intimidated. The question then became one of tactics. In other words, did "not being intimidated" mean that we were going to sing louder in defiance, or try to keep the volume down so that we could point to our at least partial cooperation, or sing less often, or what? Many of us felt that there was a good deal too much noise anyway, for our own sakes rather than for that of the authorities, since even a polite conversation in one cell reverberates up and down the cell block. I was rather vociferous on this point for I found it impossible to even read our little Bible with so much general noise always going on.

But the ones who won the day were not the peace-and-quiet advocates but the love-thine-enemy-and-walk-the-extra-mile southerners. Under the principles of brotherhood, with which the southern girls are so imbued, we should try to do as our jailers asked within the framework of our own desires and needs, that is, the need to sing both as an expression of our feelings and pent-up energy, and as a major morale booster. If, as many of us insisted, their asking us not to sing was primarily a harassment designed to dampen our demonstrably high-spirited excellent morale, we should show them that nothing they can say or do can break it. At the same time we want to be able to say that we cooperated to the fullest possible extent with them by being somewhat quieter. As far as their specific threats are concerned, they have not yet given us mail privileges and there is no assurance that they will do so; they have not yet given us showers and there is no assurance that they will do so; they have taken away everything that can make us feel like civilized human beings instead of animals—shoes, combs, bobby pins, reading matter, communication with the outside world—so they might as well take away our mattresses, too.

The upshot of the whole very noisy discussion about quiet is that we decided to elect a spokesman, whose job is to answer comments addressed to the whole group, and to set up periods during which relative quiet will be observed, principally right after breakfast and for a shorter period after lunch. Pauline was again elected spokesman, with Joan Trumpauer and me elected as sort of vice-spokesmen in case an attempt should be made to split us up or to remove Pauline as a troublemaker.

Sometime during the late afternoon Del got a bad attack of what seemed to be asthma. She has great difficulty in breathing and felt dizzy and weak. We hollered for the jailer, who came with not too great a delay, although grudgingly. He looked at Del, and walked out without a word. A half hour later he brought down a pill which he said the nurse had sent. About an hour after that, Del's cell mate reported that she remained as bad as before, so we called again. This time a male voice shouted down to ask what was the matter, and we told him. A short time later he brought in the nurse herself, who gave Del another pill.

When Del still had gotten no relief after dinner, we hollered again. This time they took a long time to answer, and when two of our jailers finally did come in, our we'll-take-your-mattresses intimidator of the afternoon remarked angrily as he passed our cell, "If y'all keep up this yellin' and screamin', we're gonna take away yer damn mattresses and then see how y'all like sleepin' . . . ," and the rest was lost as he continued on down the cell block.

All of us were very worried about Del. So far as she knew, she did not have asthma, but had occasionally gotten mild attacks of hay fever. It probably could be some especially high pollen count in the middle of the Mississippi farmlands, or it could have been anything, but whatever it was we believed she needed to be seen by a doctor—not just to be seen by Tyson (which we had discovered to be his name) standing with arms crossed, chomping on his infernal cigar, in front of her cell. Finally he said,

"C'mere, you" to Del, who had been resting on the lower bunk. She was helped up and came to the bars where, again, he stood looking at her. Del told him politely, "I need to see a doctor." No answer. She then asked him if it would be possible for the prison to call Mr. Young and ask him to post bond and have her released. He turned and stomped out. Del's cell mate reported that he had said something to the effect of "Now you're talking!" And as they were going out past our cell, Tyson remarked to the other man, "These girls won't last long."

Monday, June 26, 1961

Last night was a really bad night for bugs. Ruby Doris Smith, in the next cell, told us that she woke up with five painful bites on her legs and a number of bugs crawling on her. She had torn a strip off the sheet and bound her legs with it, but still woke up a couple of times, screaming, with bugs on her. Our plague seems to us to be of the beetle kind rather than cockroaches, which is what I would have expected. These monsters range from a half inch to an inch and a quarter in length, and can fly, but not too well—they keep hitting the wall, whereupon they sort of slide down to the floor, crawl around for a bit and then take off again. What most infuriates us, of course, is that we have nothing with which to kill them. I could not conceive of stepping on them, even with my bare foot wrapped in toilet paper. The one hard object in the cell is our only reading material, the three-inch by two-inch Gideon Bible. Far be it from me to make such a use of the Holy Word, but I think it was Jesus who said, somewhere, something to the effect that "the Sabbath is made for man, not man for the Sabbath."

At breakfast we complained about the bugs, and Sergeant Storey (the other jailer, an older, sort of fatherly looking man—we had learned another name) said to us, "Why, they ain't nothing to do with bugs—just step on them," and he demonstrated for us, with his heavy black cordovan size twelves.

Our after-breakfast nap was interrupted, to our great delight, by Storey and Tyson, with short little pencils and prison stationery on which we were, finally, to get to write our weekly allotment of two letters. The "stationery" was mimeographed sheets with about three-quarters of the page taken up with lines, the other part of it being taken with the prison heading, like this (my mother saved all my letters):

MAXIMUM SECURITY UNIT
MISSISSIPPI STATE PENITENTIARY
PARCHMAN, MISSISSIPPI

RULES FOR RECEIVING MAIL AND VISITORS:

(1) MAIL:
(a) All letters addressed to inmates must be limited to two pages; family and business matters only.
(b) Each inmate shall not receive more than one letter per week from any one person or a total of more than TWO letters per week. NO PACKAGES WILL BE RECEIVED AT THIS UNIT.

NB—one letter

N.B.

(2) VISITORS:
(a) NO VISITORS WILL BE RECEIVED AT THIS UNIT.

TO:
Name Mrs. N. Silver
Street 1020 N. Hoover
City Los Angeles, 29,
State Calif.

From:
Name C.R. Silver
Number cell #3—Freedom Riders
Camp No. MAXIMUM SECURITY UNIT

Parchman, Miss. 26 June, 1961

Mother love, I am alive and well, which is something anyway. the main reason for our being transferred here was that the jail in Jackson was very overcrowded—here we are 2 to a cell, 9X6', with bunks, a commode + sink. the food here is much better than in the little Hinds County jail—one of the 'guards' said proudly that the biscuits were the best in the state. We will get showers twice a week, on Tues + Fri, + if we are good + don't sing or talk loud, maybe they will give us combs. I have finally come to an adjustment with my entomological ambitions—when I get out I expect to be able to do very well with my extensive knowledge. We conduct classes among ourselves—anthro + Chinese are at our end of the block, + our ballet classes continue—even though one of the girls who taught it, Del Greenblatt, is ill + returning to N.Y.C. next week. I suggest that you not worry about me, + resign yourself—as I have—to the fact that I am cut off from the outside world until the 2nd or 3rd week in July, when my 40 days are up. Don't expect to hear from me again, although I shall try to write. If an emergency arises—ie you have another heart attack or daddy or grandma is ill—do not hesitate to call Mr. Young, who can post bond for me at any time. But don't be foolish about bothering him (I love you, remember)—you must not worry about me. Give all my love to dad + the kids (I got a letter from Barbara but had no time to answer it) + to Leo + Grandma. Love, Carol

P.S. I have lost weight, given up cigarettes and am reading the bible every day. Also, I'm getting lots of sleep. P.P.S. SAVE my LETTERS!!

Both Terry and I spent agonized hours deciding whether saying this or that or the other thing might make our letters subject to censorship, and choosing every word with deliberate care. I wrote to my mother in Los Angeles. To my roommate in New York, in order to come within the "family only" restriction, I began the letter "Dear Sis" and addressed it to my middle and last name, since I had instructed her to open all of my mail while I am in jail.

After we wrote our letters, I took the pencil and chewed (literally) the wood away from about two inches of pencil lead. This I carefully broke off and carefully placed on one of the bars, being carefully inconspicuous, close to the wall. The wood shards I flushed down the toilet. I also managed to make my letter to my mother, which in essence said, "I am happy and healthy and don't worry about me," cover only one of the two sheets which we had been given for each letter, so that, with my pencil lead and the extra sheet of paper, I was back in the diary business! The diary I kept in Hinds County had been one of the most comforting and time-consuming of my activities, and one of the things I most missed when we were transferred to Parchman.

While we were still supposed to be writing our letters, Sgt. Storey came through distributing our first delivery of mail since we had been in Parchman. I got one letter, from my father, which was very gratefully received, although I was unhappy to see that because of his very poor eyesight he had scrawled over every inch of both sides of the paper. But there's always the inside of the envelope.

I asked the good sergeant at this point just what he would consider proper for us to write in our letters. He said, "Just write the truth."

"What is the truth, Sgt. Storey?" I said with my most innocent smile.

He bit: "You know, nothing about this here cause y'all are here for, or nothing like that."

The chaplain came by to see us this afternoon. He started with our end of the cell block, asking each girl her name, her religion, and where she was from. For each cell he seemed to have some small bit of pleasantry, starting with Claire O'Connor and Jo Adler in cell number two: "Y'all girls must feel that the whole world is against you."

"No, sir, just the state of Mississippi."

Then to Terry and me in cell number three: "And where are you from, little girl?" (to Terry).

"New York."

"What denomination are you?"

"I'm Jewish, sir."

"And how about you, young lady?" (to me).

"I'm from New York, too, and I am Jewish."

"Oh, then of course you two must have known each other."

Cell number four, two Negro girls, Ruby Doris Smith and Shirley Thompson: "Where are y'all girls from?"

"I'm from Atlanta, Georgia."

"Well, that's just about as Deep South as y'all could be."

"Yes, sir, but at least it's still in the United States."

And so forth. When they got to Joy Reagon's cell, she was asleep with her head near the bars, and so the guard pulled her hair to wake her up.

The cell block was very quiet after lunch. Suddenly there was a sound as of the rattling of a cell door. Lee Berman was heard saying, in a nasal Chicago twang and a very disgusted tone, "Damn door's stuck!" Our laughter echoed through the cell block, and when we finally could control it, we all agreed that it was a joke which no one on the outside could possibly appreciate. You had to have been confined to a six-foot by nine-foot space for a considerable time to even understand it properly.

Tuesday, June 27, 1961

Today makes the fourth day that we have been without combs or showers. The fact that we are all so concerned about how terrible we must look to our rather restricted group of beholders just proves that the feminine concern with personal appearance is really basic to her psyche or, at any rate, more deeply ingrained than I had believed. We have been filling up many hours in washing our blouses, underwear, and selves from the tiny sink with our bar of pink, prison-issue, Ardmore Super-Fatted Lanolated Soap. When more than an inch of water is run in the bowl, the color of it turns a distinct rust brown, and at first, I was squeamish about washing in it, let alone drinking it. But one adjusts.

Perhaps Tuesday is washday in back country Mississippi instead of Monday, for right after breakfast the female trusty came down, announcing that "today is shower day," and that we were to bring up our sheet, pillowcase, towel, and prison skirt to be exchanged when we took our shower.

When it was our turn, the electric bar door slid back with a whir and a crash, and Terry and I went gaily up to the end of the cell block. We had not been out of our cell since we had arrived at Parchman, and of course we stopped to peer in at the girls whose cells were next to ours. This was accompanied by the shouts of both the jailers and trusties to "hurry up."

The shower itself is an area about the size of two cells, with two sprays. These are each operated by a button. Push the button and the water comes for about thirty seconds; then it stops and you have to push it again. The soap was not bad smelling, but I found it very difficult to wash off the lather, and even after we were done, I felt sort of slimy. Because of that I did not wash my hair, even though that was what I most wanted to do. We dressed in the hall and were halfway through when Terry suddenly pointed through the barred gate to a little window beyond, which led to the offices of the prison, and shouted, "There's a MAN in the window!" I looked too, and saw Sgt. Storey, with a big lascivious grin on his fatherly old face. By the time we finished dressing the female trusty had put a piece of cardboard over the window.

In the next cell down the block from ours, Ruby had said that she was not going to take a shower unless she was given shower clogs, to prevent her from getting athlete's foot. She was in jail at Rock Hill, South Carolina, last year for the sit-ins, and had gotten a very bad and painful case of it, so was legitimately frightened. She was quite willing to make do with hand baths from the sink in her cell, rather than risk getting it in the shower. When the door to her cell opened, only Shirley went up, with Ruby's skirt and linen, and told the trusty that Ruby was not taking a shower and why. The trusties tried to convince her to come out, then passed over her and went on to the rest of the cell block.

After everyone else had had a shower, the hall bars opened and down the hall came Sgt. Storey with three hefty female trusties. One of them was holding a floor brush, and the other two had a kind of pressure handcuff with a gadget which twisted in. The following drama I shall never forget: Sgt. Storey: "Is this the girl who wouldn't take a shower?" A nod from the trusty. "Open four!" The cell door opened.

Ruby: "Well, if that's the way you feel about it, I guess I will have to take a shower."

Sgt. Storey: "Go in there and get her."

Ruby at this point walked out herself into the hall of the cell block. The trusties put the handcuffs on her. She was wearing only her blouse and a pair of underpants, since they had not given Shirley a fresh skirt or returned her old skirt. The three women walked Ruby past our cell to the shower, one on each side and one in front.

When they brought her back, she was stumbling a little. They pushed her into the cell, the door closed, and, when they had all left, we asked Ruby's cell mate to tell us what had happened to her.

Shirley told us that they had taken her into the shower, turned the water on a couple of times, and scrubbed her down with the floor brush, concentrating especially on the sensitive areas of the skin and between her legs. They had also knocked her down a couple of times, while they continued to hold on to the pressure cuffs. (Ruby was having her period at the time and was also suffering from a bad case of ulcers—she had vomited after every meal we had since we had been in jail). They did not bother to use soap, nor to undress her.

We were all, especially Terry and I who had seen the dark welts on Ruby's wrists as she passed by our cell, burning with anger and frustration. Our subdued comments to each other and up and down the cell block were distinctly unprintable as well as unforgiving, uncharitable, and unnonviolent.

But then from Ruby, lying on the top bunk in her cell, in her soft drawl began a lecture on Christian brotherhood, and love, and how we must not hate because that is a victory for the evil forces which we are fighting. She talked of mental nonviolence, which is just as important as physical nonviolence—of returning love for hate, sympathy for oppression. These women were not evil, only their actions were evil, and what we must do is to hate the sin and love the sinner.

I had never been so close before to this kind of religious feeling, and in a sense I felt I could not really understand it. But for the rest of the day I lay on my stomach thinking about Ruby's lecture, and very late, after everyone else seemed to be asleep, I began to feel finally that I did not hate the women who had done it, and, maybe, I did not hate Sgt. Storey.

Wednesday, June 28, 1961

This morning Sgt. Storey and some strange men came around to spray the cell block for bugs. The experience was hideous, since they laid down a thick cloud of the insecticide while Terry and I commiserated on the top bunk. Nonetheless we were very glad of it. When they were done, the floor was littered with dead bugs, some varieties of which we had never even noticed before.

We had white bread for breakfast this morning, as we have had before, only this time with a difference. Under instructions from Jo next door, who has read lots of modern-day adventure novels, I collected extra bread from anyone who did not like it and used about six slices to mold a set of chess pieces. By wetting the bread with spit, we could mold it much like the plasticine clay I remember having as a child. The project occupied most of the morning very pleasantly, and just before lunch I set out all of the thirty-two pieces to dry.

Then came the problem of coloring them to make one set black, and of course, Jo suggested using blood. With my trusty safety pin I tried jabbing my fingers, but the pin was so dull and I was so gentle with myself that I never could get more than a tiny spot at a time, which was not even enough for a pawn. Finally, with sore fingers and fourteen pieces left to go, I decided to be the first in history to put the woman's curse to an immediate practical use. My cell mate was in squeamish horror, but the chess set looked great.

One of the girls was pulled out of her cell today to talk to what she describes as "Mississippi's own HUAC (House Un-American Activities Committee)." They had discovered that she had been in Cuba some time last year. They asked her if she was a Communist, implying that she was one even if she denied it, asked if she knew that all of the national leaders of CORE and the NAACP are dedicated Communists, and insisted that she had gotten training in how to organize and lead civil rights demonstrations from the Russian agricultural experts who were known to have been in Cuba at the same time as she was there. To her great credit, she remained mentally nonviolent throughout, even to the extent of respectfully adding "sir" to her answers of "I'm sorry, but I really don't think that I care to answer that question."

We have been expecting any day that Del would go out on bail, since she is still sick. She finally got a pill which gave her some relief, but still has some trouble breathing and still gets fits of dizziness. As they were serving lunch today, Sgt. Storey was standing in front of my cell and I asked him if he knew when Del would be leaving. He replied, with a malicious smile, "Y'all girls are just being used by them Communists in New York—she ain't going to get out till they're good and ready." He claimed that he had called Jackson and asked the lawyer to post bond for her, but that he had had no further word.

Wonder of wonders, today we finally were given combs! Two cheap plastic ones, to be passed up and down among us. By the time one of them got to our cell it already had a couple of teeth missing, but the luxury was still tremendous. Sgt. Storey gave them to us saying that he hoped we appreciated what he was doing for us, since he had had to go out and buy them himself at Woolworth's, and that if, as he has said just about every day since we have been in Parchman, if we would cooperate with him, he would cooperate with us: "If y'all'd cooperate with me, why I'll. . . ."

We combed our unwashed hair as if we were brushing it, and Terry and I inspected each other's head for bugs—nothing so far. Then we made neat pigtails and tied them with our braided string.

A new group of girls came in today, Betsy among them. We were delighted to see her, of course, but disappointed because her being transferred here means that the application for a writ of habeas corpus on her behalf has probably been denied. All of the cells in our block are already full, so putting in the extra girls gave some of the cells three girls instead of two, but not in ours. They threw in extra mattresses on the floor for the extra girls. Before they did that, though, they finally gave us brooms, and mops with a Lysol solution, so that we could clean our floors of the accumulated dust, dirt, and dead bugs.

Thursday, June 29, 1961

We had showers again today.

And our first shakedown. When she brought up her sheet to be changed, the trusty noticed this time that Ruby had torn strips off of the end, and this precipitated their searching us all. After Ruby, they searched each cell while the girls were out taking showers. We had already been up, so we were called out into the hall and frisked by one trusty, while another one searched our cell. My precious papers—my diary and chess board—I had put in the Bible, which I displayed prominently on the bars at the front of the cell, and they did not even look at it. The little chess set they evidently did not notice, sitting on one of the lower bars. My most prized possession, the remaining inch of pencil lead, I slipped into a narrow hem in my bra, and although they felt me over with great enthusiasm, they did not catch it.

In the afternoon we began a program of lectures to each other, in lieu of books, to help pass the time. Del, our medieval history Ph.D. candidate, gave us her version of the causes of the decline and fall of the Roman Empire, essentially Gibbon with her footnotes. Then someone else talked on mental health in Nigeria, a topic on which she had done some research. Jo recited as much of T. S. Eliot's "The Waste Land" as she could remember, and gave us an interpretation of the images and symbolism. We decided to make lectures a regular part of our routine, and to plan a real workshop on Gandhi and nonviolent techniques.

My own contribution to this program was to talk on Mann's *The Magic Mountain*. The concept of time in that book is very similar to what we are experiencing, and in many ways our situation is analogous to that of the character Hans Castorp. Of course, his imprisonment was by his own mind and ours is by steel bars, but the intellectual battles which have raged among us as a group were similar to those that he had been exposed to in his beautiful Swiss mountain retreat—and I enjoyed making the comparison.

Ruby is still vomiting, and Del is still having trouble breathing. We keep urging Ruby to ask to be taken out, or at least to ask to see the doctor, but she refuses stubbornly. Today the jailer volunteered the information to Del that he had "heard" that CORE did not have enough bail money to get us out, and that was why she had not yet gone. This suggestion got us very upset, since many of us planned on going back to school in the fall and most of us had sentences which would last well past October if we did not post bail. The worst part of it is that there is nothing any of us can do but wait, and stew, hope that Del will not suffer any permanent damage, and hope that the bail money will be found somewhere.

Late in the evening Judy Frieze, one of the group that had just come, had an asthmatic attack. She had had an attack in the Hinds County Jail, but since this is an old condition and well under control, she had just sniffed on the little atomizer which she always carries with her and been feeling fit in a few minutes. At Parchman they had not allowed her to take her medicine into her cell, however. Her two cell mates began getting panic-stricken when she started wheezing and gasping. We began calling, "Jailer! Doctor!" and called and rattled our cell doors for about half an hour before Sgt. Storey finally came. Judy eventually got a pill like the one Del had first been given, which did help her somewhat.

Chapter 8

PARCHMAN CONTINUED

Friday, June 30, 1961

Del was sick again today, this time feeling really bad. We yelled for the doctor and got the jailers, who repeated their comments of the first time. As one of them was walking out he remarked in a loud voice, "Y'all know, we've got a graveyard at this prison, too." We were infuriated, and when Del was feeling even worse after about a half hour, we began shouting and banging again. This time the trusty answered, from the outer hall, saying that the doctor was coming, and that we-all had better be quiet or the jailer would take away our mattresses, and then we would be sleeping on the cold, hard steel.

Finally, the doctor did come. He was very young and looked anemic and short as he walked in with our husky jailers. Del got a shot of some sort, and as he went up the block he talked to the other girls who called to him. Judy told him that the pills were not doing the job completely and that she really needed an atomizer. Jane Rosett asked for something for athlete's foot, and, at our insistence, Ruby mentioned that she had an ulcer condition and had been vomiting constantly, also that she had had blood in both her vomit and her stool. All of the girls told him that they had medicine for whatever ailed them in the luggage which had been taken from them on their arrival, but the jailers told the doctor that it was absolutely impossible for any of us to get anything from the luggage, period.

The jailer also told us again that there was no bail money for Del, and reiterated that we were all just being "used." Terry and I talked about this for hours: about our plans based on the many different possibilities, about what we would do if we had to stay in jail four months. She will be in her second year at City College next year, and there is a danger that if her family's financial situation deteriorates she might have to get a job before she gets her BA degree, and so any time that she has to take off from school is terribly frightening. Also, she had figured her stay in jail so that she would have enough time left at the end of the summer to go back and get a job for two months to earn enough money for her expenses in school, since the class schedule she has planned is too heavy to allow her to work part-time. As for me, if I get a scholarship for the University of Chicago Law School (and in all of my plans I have assumed that I will, since they approved me before and I cannot possibly go back to school without one) and then do not turn up for registration, I can only be pretty sure that the university will never give me another scholarship.

Saturday, July 1, 1961

I finally won a chess game with Jo today! She and I manage to play with each other, even though we are in separate cells, by calling out the moves. We can only do it when the cell block is reasonably quiet, since a mistake can be disastrous. Jo is just enough better than I am to make it challenging for me and interesting for her. It sounds very funny, I am sure, for other people to hear us calling out:

Me: "Pawn to queen four."

Jo: "Pawn to queen four."

Me: "Pawn to king four."

Jo: "Pawn to king three."

Me: "Pawn take pawn."

Jo: "Why must you stick to that silly opening? Pawn takes pawn."

Me: "Queen to king two, check."

Jo: "Queen to king two—I dare you."

Me: "I'm chicken—queen's knight to queen's bishop's three."

And so on. I did teach Terry to play chess, but since I can still beat her easily, I usually prefer playing Jo—to my dear cell mate's often annoyance.

Today we had our workshop on nonviolent techniques. Joan Trumpauer started it off with a lecture on Gandhi's techniques as understood by Martin Luther King, Jr., and when she got into some difficulties, Jo offered to give us a talk on Gandhi "straight." Then we had a long discussion of how these techniques actually were applied in violent and nonviolent situations. There were some girls with us who had been mobbed and beaten in Montgomery, Alabama, and in Rock Hill, South Carolina, and almost all the Negro girls had participated in more than one sit-in demonstration.

We finally got to what, at this moment, interests me more than anything else, the methods for applying nonviolence when not actually threatened physically—for example, now that we have been jailed, in our dealings with jailers and other such. I began to get a better feeling (I cannot yet call it understanding) for what Ruby had been talking about after she was beaten up by the trusties, the assumption basic to the Movement that "love will win out over hate in the long run." Without this, all of the suffering and hardship has been useless. And so, in our situation, we are supposed to make a concerted effort to treat our jailers with respect and consideration. Ruby was the one who said, "I may not like Sgt. Tyson, but I can love him."

After the theoretical discussion, we went up and down the cell block and had various girls tell about their own experiences either as Freedom Riders or in sit-ins. Curiously, the most bloody story did not come out of the South but was told of last year's Rainbow Beach wade-in in Chicago, where an integrated group of University of Chicago students, NAACP members, and high school students had attempted to use a part of the Lake Michigan shore traditionally reserved for whites. The girl told us that they had been mobbed by a crowd of about five hundred and beaten with chains and fists, while the cops, who had been much in evidence a moment before, were all suddenly called to the parking lot. One of the students had to be taken to the hospital with a concussion. All of them had some wounds or bruises, when the police finally came back and broke it up. Chicago, not Mississippi. Food for thought!

Sunday, July 2, 1961

Something very bad must have happened to someone last night, because all day today we heard groans and short screams as of pain from across on the other side of the prison wall. There was nothing we could do, and the noise was most disturbing and depressing, so we decided to sing to drown out the sounds. We sang most of the day, and it was very eerie to hear those moans every time we stopped even for a minute.

We got to write our letters again today. Both Terry and I wrote desperate letters to our parents about this suggestion of there not being enough bail money. I told my mother that, if there was a question of my being stuck because CORE did not have enough money for our bail, she should use five hundred dollars of my school expenses money (of the eight hundred which I had managed to save in my year off from school, working in

New York) and get me out. If worse comes to worst I can try to start borrowing money again, but at least I will be in law school.

Lunch today was really funny—two kinds of potatoes, macaroni, and biscuits.

My relations with Terry are deteriorating rapidly, but I do not know what to do about it. We are jumpy and I am sure that she is as annoyed with me as I am with her, even though we both know that it is a function of the situation and not anything either of us has done or said. I practically bawled her out for leaving a puddle of water on the floor, and she asked me rather shortly to quit playing chess with Jo because she wants quiet time to read and write. "Read the Bible?"

"Yes, that's all there is."

"OK."

Monday, July 3, 1961

Del left this morning, finally.

In the middle of a very dull afternoon, we suddenly saw through the little windows the top of the same old green truck out in the yard of the prison and heard the very hoarse voices of men singing "We Shall Overcome." More Freedom Riders! We began singing in response, then shouting to ask for news of the Freedom Rides, of the court cases, of the world. (The big story when I went into jail on June 7 was the degenerating Laos conference between U.S. President John F. Kennedy and Russian Premier Nikita Khrushchev over neutrality of Laos in the Vietnam War. The first question I have asked of any new group coming in has been "What's happening on Laos?" The boys said that they did not know.)

The boys told us that we could expect some Freedom Rider girls, and a few minutes later we realized that indeed there were some girls being inducted in the outer hall of our cell block. So we sang them the great (although not very original) new song which someone had written that morning to the tune of a football song: "We welcome you to M.S.U.; We're very glad you're here; We'll set the air reverberating, with a mighty cheer, Rah! Rah! Rah! We'll sing you in, we'll sing you out; For you we'll raise a mighty shout—Hail, hail, the gang's all here; And you're welcome to M.S.U."

Most cells now have three girls (each cell still carefully segregated, all Negro or all white). Our new addition is Marion Kendall, from Oakland, California. The new group is mostly from the West Coast, San Francisco and Los Angeles, and they filled us in as much as they could on the news. The Laos conference has broken up although it looks as if it will resume shortly. There are many more Freedom Riders expected, and the rumor is that there will be a major convergence on Jackson on the Fourth of July. Betsy's habeas corpus case is being appealed to a higher court.

About an hour after dark, the cell block was relatively quiet. We decided to have a bedtime story. Betsy volunteered to tell the ancient Greek story of Oedipus Rex. She was in the last cell, and we, in cell number three, could barely hear her, but rather than complain we strained our ears. In the middle of the story, however, Sgt. Tyson came tromping into the cell block and stopped in the middle of it. He was rather obviously angry, and began, "Y'all girls are going to cut out all of this here shouting and hymn singing and noise. Y'all are going to cut it out or I'm going to take away your mattresses and y'all are going to be sleeping on the cold, hard steel. Now are y'all going to cooperate with me or am I going to take away your mattresses and y'all'll be sleeping on the cold, hard steel?" There was a dead silence. "Y'all hear me?" He glared at us all. And started walking out. After the door crashed, thinking that he had already passed out of hearing, Pauline, our chosen spokesman, called down, "Betsy, will you please continue."

And Betsy started again. "When Tiresias, the blind seer, arrived at the palace of Oedipus in Thebes . . ."

"Didn't I tell you girls to shut up?" And Sgt. Tyson was again among us. "Are y'all going to keep quiet or am I going to take away your mattresses and y'all be sleeping on cold, hard steel?"

Betsy had stopped when he came back, so Pauline said, "Sgt. Tyson, we feel that we have been cooperating with you and Sgt. Storey. At the moment we were not making much noise at all."

A glowering look.

Our policy, decided upon long ago, was not to be intimidated by unreasonable threats. "And so, Betsy, would you please start again?"

Betsy: "He got to Thebes, and was led into the presence of Oedipus by a young boy. There were many people present, priests of Apollo and local citizens, all of whom had come to supplicate Oedipus to do something effective about the terrible plague. Jocasta, Oedipus' wife . . ." Sgt. Tyson walked down to Betsy's cell and stood in front of it with crossed arms. He must have stood there for a good five minutes, while she went on with the story. Then he turned on his heel and started walking toward our end of the block.

In his biggest voice: "Open up two, and send a trusty down here." The electric cell door to cell two clanged open. Tyson came into the cell and took the mattresses, and a Negro male trusty—the first we had seen—carried them out. "Close two." Clang. "Open three." Clang.

At first, between the clanging of the doors and the clomp of Tyson's boots we could still hear snatches of the story as Betsy continued on, but by the time they had taken the mattresses from Terry and Marion and me and moved on to the next cell, there was too much noise to hear Betsy at all. Evidently other people were having the same problem, because suddenly someone began singing "We Shall Overcome." We all picked it up, and sang two or three verses. Then we sang "Oh, Freedom," "Old Jim Crow," "I'm Going to Get My Civil Rights," and just about all of the other songs we know, including "He's Got the Whole World in His Hands," with special verses—"He's got Sgt. Tyson in His hands," "He's got the mattress-bearer in His hands," and of course, "He" always "has" Governor Barnett, Judge Spencer, and Captain Ray in His hands. While we were singing they finished taking all of the mattresses out. Then Tyson started at our end of the cell block again, taking from each of us our pillow, then our sheet and pillowcase, then our towel, and then, finally, our toothbrush. Our singing had gotten progressively louder until towards the end we were practically shouting. In a break at the end of a song Pauline shouted, "And now we will all sing 'The Star-Spangled Banner,'" which we did. Then a few people, out of the need to make noise and the frustration of being almost hoarse, began banging on the steel bunks, and soon others joined in until the noise was deafening. (I would have objected to this on the grounds that it was not nonviolent, but of course no one could hear anyone's objections.) As a final move, having taken away from us everything but the clothes on our backs, Tyson closed all of the windows. Then he turned, gave us one last, furious, black look, and clanged out.

When the noise finally stopped the three of us in cell number three looked at each other and at the cold, hard steel bunks, and the cold, hard dirty floor—and began laughing.

Tuesday, July 4, 1961, Independence Day

Last night Terry and I tried sleeping two on the lower bunk, and gave Marion, our "guest," the honor of a cold, hard steel bunk all her own. None of us got much sleep. Our dear jailers had turned on all the fans, and Mississippi can be pretty chilly in the middle of even a summer night on cold, hard steel. I was using a clean Kotex pad as a pillow and Terry was using the little Bible. Thankfully, the bugs were not especially bad—perhaps they were hibernating. During breakfast Lee and I started singing "Oh, What a Beautiful Morning," to bolster our flagging morale and also to drown out the complaints. Everyone picked it up, and those few rousing choruses really made us all feel better about the mattress situation.

Today, THE event was dinner. In celebration of the holiday, we were served one half of a tender, juicy, southern-fried chicken, coleslaw (I had not had any raw vegetables for almost a month), sweet potatoes, potato salad, corn, biscuits, and lemonade—and cake! We put our trays down on the cold, hard steel, and savored every morsel!

Since most of us had gotten little sleep, some of us were more than ever interested in having a quiet period after lunch to try to nap. But others insisted that they could not sleep even now, and that the strain of keeping quiet and awake for an indefinite period of time would be too much for them to take. After much noisy wrangling, we decided that we would have, from now on, quiet periods of finite extent, approximately one hour in the afternoon and two in the morning. Since we had no clocks, the question then became, who is going to call the beginning and the end of the quiet periods? Pauline was unwilling to take on the burden, and so with the remark "I know you will all get to hate me, but it is worth it to have quiet hours," some idiot volunteered to be timekeeper—me. The timekeeper has to be someone who does not usually sleep during these nap periods, which I do not, preferring to continue my first-ever reading tour through the fascinating contradictions of the Christian gospels in our little Bible. I gauged the time by the shadows falling from the windows on a wall that I could see standing at the top bunk, and this first day, at least, no one complained about my timekeeper decrees.

The female trusty (white, the first we met coming in) seems to be around all of the time now. Evidently they have moved a bed and some of her personal stuff into the outer hall, since she came by with the predawn door rattler dressed in a robe and slippers. She also seems to be dressing in street clothes instead of prison skirts these days.

Wednesday, July 5, 1961

I slept on the concrete last night, and it was not too bad. It was warmer than the steel, and I did not have to worry about kicking Terry when a bug lit on me and I started awake.

In the middle of the morning, Sgt. Storey, accompanied by Sgt. Tyson, came down and began talking to us. "Are y'all girls ready to cooperate now?" Sgt. Storey said. He was opposite our cell. Terry told him to "please speak to our spokesman, in cell seven." He marched down to Pauline's cell, and repeated his question.

"Well, Sgt. Storey," said Pauline, "we are always willing to cooperate, but we don't think that we were doing anything wrong."

"Now if y'all girls want your mattresses back y'all are going to have to cut out all of this singing."

"I'm sorry, Sgt. Storey, but we are going to continue to sing."

"We expect y'all girls to keep quiet, y'all hear me? And we're going to give your mattresses back, and I want y'all to be quiet, y'all hear me?"

"But Sgt. Storey, we can't promise to keep quiet, because we have decided that we are going to have to sing."

"Now you shut up, young lady, or you are not going to get your mattress back."

And so we got the mattresses back. And towels and toothbrushes and sheets and pillows and pillowcases. We even had our floor washed too. Why they were returned, and why Sgt. Tyson had allowed himself to fly into such a rage with us as to take them in the first place, we still none of us understood. Obviously they now wanted to give them back, and so we decided just to enjoy the luxury. Having lost so much weight, I have little natural padding left, and that concrete was pretty hard and uncomfortable last night. And the bugs were worse. There was no point to question the ways of the powers what be. We all brushed our teeth and went to sleep, even I, for our morning nap.

During the afternoon Lee Berman shared a little private joke—that she and her cell mate had been calling any of the civilized luxuries which they most missed "watermelons." And so we got a laugh out of sitting around talking about all the "watermelons" we were going to smoke when we got out, and how we would feast on charcoal-broiled "watermelon" with French-fried "watermelons" and tossed green "watermelon."

The only exercise we have been getting since Del, our ballet-master, left us, has been to run in place in the middle of the cell. We figure each pace as the equivalent of three feet, and so have been counting how far we have "run" by the number of steps. Today, for the first time, I was able to run a full mile—1,761 steps. Since I have been losing weight steadily since I have been in jail, exercising muscles I never used before, and improving my wind by giving up smoking, I expect that when I get out of here I shall be in better physical shape than I have been in years.

According to the schedule with the lawyer when we were first arrested, I should have my bail posted and be out in about a week or ten days. I feel as if I have been here forever, forever and ever and a day.

Thursday, July 6, 1961

In the middle of our morning nap, Sgt. Tyson came down, took nine of the Negro girls out of their cells, and spirited them away. They were not going home, we figured, because they did not stop for the registering-out process which Del had gone through, but our queries to the jailer about their destination met with no answer—not even a retort, just silence. The rest of us, who had been three and in one case four in a cell, were then distributed evenly, two to a cell, and the extra mattresses taken out. Then starting from our end of the cell block, we were all swept and mopped, and then we were taken to be showered. Next, wonder of wonders, we were given two hairbrushes and a comb with all its teeth to pass from cell to cell! We kept asking each other what the occasion could possibly be.

In the afternoon, we found out. A team of women had been sent by the governor of Minnesota to inspect the conditions at the Mississippi State Penitentiary, and this was the inspection. Claire O'Connor was from the Minnesota group, but the women were talking to the jailers as they came in, and they continued doing so as they paraded down the cell block and back out. One of them did try to stop and talk to Joan Trumpauer, who was standing at the front of her cell just waiting for a chance to say something to them, but when the Minnesota lady paused for a moment Sgt. Tyson put a protective arm around her waist (he really did), said something in southern, and conducted her out.

Today I reviewed my growing collection of manuscripts. Most of my writing is on toilet paper—the outline of a short story, some bad poetry about Michael, my long-lost love, and a complete play for radio. My diary I am keeping in a kind of shorthand mostly on the two sheets of prison stationery I managed to steal. My chess board, lists of our names and addresses, and the words to some songs have just about used up all of the letter backs and insides of envelopes.

Last night the bugs were really bad, worse than they were before we were first sprayed. Rita Carter, one of the last group to arrive, told us this morning that she had not been able to sleep all night because of the bugs, and even I, who am a heavy sleeper, was awakened by something crawling over my leg. And it has been abysmally hot for three days.

Friday, July 7, 1961

Today we got showers again, the second day in a row, so we were prepared for more visitors. They came about noon, a delegation from the grand jury of Hinds County, Mississippi. Officially and legally we are still the prisoners of Hinds County, since it is against Mississippi law for misdemeanor offenders to be sent to the state prison. By a special ruling of Governor Ross Barnett, however, Hinds County had been allowed to rent a section of the prison for us, since all of the cells in both the city and county jails in Jackson were full of Freedom Riders and more were coming in. This inspection team was allowed to stop and talk to some of us. They asked me how I liked the food. I said, "Well, it's much better than Hinds County Jail, but it's not the Four Seasons."

"Tell them about the Fourth of July," Sgt. Storey interjected. I smiled and told them, or rather started to tell them, but they impolitely wandered off down the cell block as I began talking.

About an hour later we got still another group of inspectors, which Mrs. Lee (we had finally found out the name of our matron-trusty) told us was from the office of Governor Barnett himself. This group not only got to talk to us, but they actually asked us if we had any complaints and stayed to listen to our answers. No one had the nerve, with Sgt. Storey very close in the background, to tell about the fixing-up we had been given in preparation for their arrival (not that we got the feeling that they would have cared), but someone did complain about not being given her mail. Then the inspectors started asking questions like "Why did y'all come down here? Just to cause trouble?" and "Why don't y'all go on back where y'all belong?"

In the afternoon, all of the Negro girls who had been removed yesterday came back. They told us that they had been held in a prison hospital ward, about a mile from the Maximum Security Unit. They had been treated well and fed very well. They told us that they had been fed actual meat, which we have gotten only once (a vile stew) since being in Parchman. We were green with envy. With their return, we were again three in most cells, although Marion did not come back and so Terry and I are still two. And when we sang a few songs to celebrate our reunion, Sgt. Tyson again came blustering down and said, "Now y'all keep quiet or I'm going to take away your mattresses and y'all be sleeping on that cold, hard steel." I guess we are done with the inspections for a while.

Four of the girls left for Jackson, just before dinner. The group included Pauline, who was quite mystified because she had been serving out her fine (she was in one of the earliest groups and got a two-hundred-dollar fine and two months suspended) and had expected to stay her full sixty-seven days.

Saturday, July 8, 1961

Maybe our complaints paid off. Sgt. Tyson came by and distributed a large stack of mail this morning. This seemed like the most uneventful day since we have been here. The only other incident of interest was that Sgt. Tyson asked which of us wanted to see Jack Young, the lawyer. Since we are all very worried about the bail money question, and since we had not seen anyone except Mississippi state prison officials and the two women from Minnesota for over two weeks, we all of us said we wanted to see him.

Sunday, July 9, 1961

And today we did get to see, not Mr. Young, but another Negro lawyer named Mr. Hall. He asked each of us when exactly we wanted to be released on bail, and assured us that there was plenty of money for our bail. Evidently the jailers had just been trying to scare us with their stories about there being no bail money for us. Well, they had certainly been successful.

Terry and I both asked that bond be posted tomorrow, Monday, the tenth, so that we could be released on Tuesday, the regular day for discharging prisoners from Parchman. That would be our thirty-fourth day, but we were afraid if we did not bail out then we would be held until after the forty-day limit on posting bail and appealing our convictions. Ruby told us after he left that because of her continuing stomach problems she had also asked to have bond posted immediately. As she was in one of the original sit-ins in Atlanta, Georgia, where the strictly observed principle was "jail, no bail," this had been the result of a great inner struggle, and she cried when she told us about it.

Rita Carter, another of the Negro girls, also asked to be bonded out, because she also is sick. Her mother had flown from Los Angeles because she knew that Rita was ill, and had driven over 110 miles, about three hours, up from Jackson with Mr. Hall. She was allowed to see Rita—for one minute, under the watchful eye of Sgt. Tyson. Mrs. Carter brought along Rita's sister, an adopted Korean War orphan, and Rita reported that Tyson kept looking from the child to Rita to her mother and back again.

I wrote to my mother saying that I hoped to be out before she got the letter, but then changed it because I was afraid that they might not bother to mail it. We are all in a jubilant mood, and I wrote my other letter to a former professor of mine who will probably say, "Now what will the postman think?" when he sees the return address on the envelope.

Monday, July 10, 1961

I woke up feeling wonderful, after dreaming all night about getting out tomorrow and thinking about all the "watermelons" I am going to eat. Ever since the first morning after the night we spent without mattresses we have been singing "Oh, What a Beautiful Morning" right after breakfast, and this morning we sang that with gusto and then broke into "I've Got a Bluebird on My Shoulder." The food was, for the first time, completely disgusting to me. I could not stomach any of it all day, but was not in the least hungry. I guess I am really now so ready to get out of here that I am beginning to think as if I already was, and on the outside I would not touch this slop with a ten-foot pole.

We were all very quiet today, in consideration for Mrs. Lee, who turned up about noon with a patch over her eye. She told us that she had had a growth removed from it at the prison hospital, and that it was still very painful.

Marion Kendall, who is going to stay in Parchman for six months, asked me to call her mother in San Leandro, California, when I get to Los Angeles, and also to write to her in jail. We set up a code which will allow us to pass in and out both news and information, and are both to memorize it. It is based on numbers and name equivalents:

1	=	they took away
2	=	mattresses
3	=	beds
4	=	towels
5	=	food
6	=	bread and water
7	=	soap
8	=	toothbrushes
9	=	showers
10	=	solitary
11	=	toilet paper
12	=	clothes
13	=	Bibles
14	=	mail

15	=	visit from Attorney Jack Young
16	=	call CORE
17	=	want out, in a hurry
18	=	they are giving us
19	=	physical abuse
20	=	dangerous
21	=	call Parchman
22	=	someone is sick
23	=	windows
24	=	blankets
Blue	=	small
Green	=	big
University of California	=	good
Los Angeles City College	=	bad
George	=	Interstate Commerce Commission
George has gone to Cal	=	the ICC has issued an injunction against arresting Freedom Riders
George returns to Washington	=	the injunction will become effective
Roberta	=	federal writ of habeas corpus
Has gone to NYC	=	writ was issued
Rosalie	=	Mississippi Governor Ross Barnett
Tom	=	Cuba's Fidel Castro
Paul	=	Russian Premier Nikita Khrushchev
Bill	=	Attorney General Robert Kennedy
Ken	=	U.S. President JFK
Richard	=	French President Charles de Gaulle
Judy	=	CORE
Norman	=	NAACP
Sam	=	SLATE (University of California at Berkeley Student political organization)
Andy	=	ACLU
Winston	=	West Berlin
Salem	=	East Berlin
The experiment	=	the Civil Rights Movement
No. of mice	=	no. of Freedom Riders
Dot under the last letter of a word	=	use the whole word in the code sentence
Dot under the first letter of a word	=	use a word that rhymes with

Tuesday, July 11, 1961

Well, evidently bond was posted for some of us yesterday, but Terry and I were not among them. Rita went, and we will no more enjoy her beautiful voice; also Ruby. As for the rest of us, no one knows.

I was in a fit of black depression all day, and Terry broke down and cried. Since we did not leave today, we cannot expect to leave until next Tuesday, and next Tuesday is two days after the forty-day limit within which we can appeal our convictions. We tried to convince ourselves that it would not be so terrible to stay the full sentence, but neither of us believed the other. I was even too miserable to play chess.

The only relief in our bleak mood came with the arrival of a new group of eight female Freedom Riders and an unknown number of males. They brought news, including the fact that they had been told that there was absolutely no problem of money for bail bonds for us. Since our number is now thirty-one in a cell block with beds for twenty-six, all but one cell has three people in it. (There are actually fourteen cells to the block, we have learned, but the first one is solitary, or "the hole," as Sgt. Tyson so charmingly called it when he offered to put us in it if we were not quiet—and that is empty.) Our third girl is Norma Matzkin, also from New York. She told us that she had contracted trench mouth while in the city jail and that she was worried about it but had some medicine in her suitcase which would clear it up in three days. We told her that she would not be allowed to get it, and told her to begin asking for the doctor immediately since it would probably take multiple requests for her to get any relief. Terry and I were scared to death of getting it from her, especially with the possibility that we will be spending more than just a few more days here.

Wednesday, July 12, 1961

Norma saw the doctor quickly, after all, because he came to see Janice Rogers, one of the girls from Los Angeles, who had requested to see the doctor a few days ago. Her husband, Johnnie Rogers (a professional boxer), is on the men's side. The doctor told her that the reason she has been vomiting and getting dizzy is that she is about two months pregnant.

Janice is a very light Negro, more Caucasian looking than many whites, and when she first came into the jail the authorities insisted that she was white. They had actually put her into a cell with some white girls before they checked her identification, which quite officially listed her as Negro. So Sgt. Storey came tearing down with a very red face and transferred her to a Negro cell. We were all amused.

Seeing the doctor did Norma very little good, because all he sent was some patent medicine, a mouthwash which, Norma said, a dentist had once told her was no good at all for trench mouth. She took the stuff, though, in lieu of anything better, even though it burned her gums most painfully.

Our group morale is rather low at this point. There have been many arguments in the last two days, primarily between the girls who just arrived from Los Angeles and some of the "old" girls. The subject matter of the arguments was nothing serious, but the bad thing is the way they were handled. We have had many disagreements among us, but today was the first time I ever heard an angry voice.

All afternoon Jo Adler and I played chess and, at the same time, played the game of "ins and outs." She said that the most "in" thing she could think of was peach ice cream with chocolate sprinkles, and I barely matched that with the "in" bit of wearing a large ring on the second finger of the right hand. We decided that striped skirts are definitely "out" and so is Mississippi, but that Oregon was "in," and especially any suburb of Portland. Grits are always "out," and lobster is still "in," unless it is from South Africa, in which case it is absolutely "out." Trips to Europe are "out," and so is *Playboy Magazine*, but *True Confessions* is so far "out" that it is "in." The most "out" thing we could think of was a yellow polka-dot bikini, but a close runner-up was the Coca-Cola Company because they contribute heavily to the white Citizens' Councils.

Thursday, July 13, 1961

A man came by today who was introduced to us (a strange enough occurrence in and of itself) as Mr. Lawrence, the assistant superintendent of the prison. He asked if we had any complaints. To every girl who said "yes," amazingly, he actually listened, but then replied, "Well, that's not my affair. Y'all'll have to speak to someone else." He neglected to tell us how to arrange to speak to whomever we are supposed to speak to.

Lee Berman and Claire Toombs put on a set of skits today that were really hilarious. The first was an imitation of Elaine May and Mike Nichols doing the psychiatrist scene, and in spite of the lack of polish, we enjoyed it immensely. Then we spent the whole afternoon telling "sick" jokes, one after the other. Lee is without compare as an amateur comedienne.

Some of the new girls have begun complaining to the jailer about the food. We have never really complained seriously about food because no matter how bad it has been here at Parchman, it has always been better than Hinds County Jail, and also because most of us felt that bad food was one of the relatively minor inconveniences attendant on being in jail, one which we had fully expected when we agreed to become Freedom Riders. Some of the girls even went so far as to propose that we should all go on a hunger strike until they improved the quality of the food. I offered the comment that we are not here in Parchman to concern ourselves with prison reform, but rather had committed ourselves to fight racial segregation by accepting our unjust and unjustifiable punishment in a nonviolent manner. I doubt that anyone convinced them, but, in any event, they decided not to go on a hunger strike.

This incident reminded me of something important. When Terry and I and a couple of others have left Parchman, all but one or two of the group which had been together at Hinds County Jail will be gone, and, especially, all of the southern Negro girls who had provided the moral leadership of our group will be gone. I really wonder if the girls who remain will be able to maintain their morale, as we have, and just how they might react in any emergency situation which might arise.

Friday, July 14, 1961

Maybe they were right to complain about the food, after all. This morning we got oatmeal for breakfast instead of grits, and those of us who like oatmeal ate it with great relish. And then Sgt. Storey came down and said that he wanted to hear our official complaints. We directed him to Joan Trumpauer, who had taken Pauline's place as spokesman for the group. She told him that we objected to the food's being cold, sometimes spoiled, overcooked, and having ten times too much pepper in everything; that we should be allowed to have more than one change of underwear; and that we needed to be allowed some exercise. Then, when he continued to stare at her after she had finished, she launched into our underlying and most major complaint, the fact that we are being kept under maximum security conditions when our offense was at most of a minor sort. He took no notes and finally deigned to reply, saying something to the effect that the rules were the rules and as long as we were in this unit we would be governed by the Maximum Security Unit rules. Then he turned and went out.

I talked and played chess with Terry most of the afternoon. A third cell mate has had a good effect on the two of us, somehow ameliorating the differences which had been cropping up between us. We have certainly not felt the need to unite against a third person, but somehow it has brought us closer together.

Chapter 9

OUT!

Saturday, July 15, 1961

"July 15, 1961—Saturday—want out, out, out!!! Washed floors."

That was the last entry in my prison diary notes, for at 2:30 p.m. that day we were in a truck bouncing toward Jackson. Terry and I, Shirley Thompson, Joan Trumpauer, Gwen Greene, and three boys, one white and two Negro, were all in the truck, integrated every which way—boys and girls, Negroes and whites—and bound for freedom!

None of us had expected to be sprung that day, and Terry and I had already resigned ourselves to spending not only until the following Tuesday, the regular release day from Parchman, but the whole two months remaining of our actual sentences, in that crummy prison. And suddenly! Hoorah!

On the way out they examined our letters and confiscated anything that had even the most innocent writing on it. I lost my poetry and story writings, my list of names and all the words to our songs, but, being forewarned by what Rita had called down the cell block when she was being processed out, I did not leave my precious diary in with my other papers. Instead I pinned it with my little safety pin to a loose place in my blouse which I was pretty sure would not be touched in a shakedown. And I also walked out with my chess set, just because the matron did not notice while she searched me that I was holding something in my hand, a lumpy, dirty, used envelope.

We asked about the mail which had been withheld from us during our stay at Parchman, and Tyson told us that we would get it in Jackson. When we got there they did give us the packages which had been received for us, but no letters.

We had to sign bail agreements which stated that we would show up to our new trial, and we also signed agreements with CORE that we had no claims to the five hundred dollars CORE had put up for our bail. When she was asked to sign the bail agreement, Joan refused, since she was not supposed to be bailed out. She had decided to serve her full sentence. The Hinds County deputy sheriff said, "Well, why didn't you tell us?"

And Joan replied, "Nobody asked me." She was not averse to taking a free outing to Jackson and back, and so, back she went.

And then we were free, almost.

We were turned over to the custody of Mr. Young, who had promised to get us out of the city without further incident. His custody was rather more pleasant than that of Sgt. Tyson.

We were driven to the house of a Negro minister, Reverend Mays, where some of the ladies from his church had prepared a dinner of fried chicken, coleslaw, potato salad, the works! And for dessert we had peach ice cream! It was Fourth of July ten times over, even without chocolate sprinkles.

Then these wonderful ladies of Jackson treated each girl to a beauty session in the beauty shop around the corner. Even I, who had not sat under a hair dryer for many years, had my hair done. It made me feel as if I belonged to the human race again. Then back to the reverend's house where we all took baths, and put on whatever clean clothes we had, and makeup—even though it was by now very late in the evening.

As we dispersed by twos and threes to various transportation terminals, there were hurried good-byes, promises to write, and plans for future meetings. Shirley and I, the last to leave, took a train for New Orleans at 2:00 a.m.

At the Jackson train station the Negro cab driver let us off at the Negro side, but, in observation of local custom and under strict instructions from Mr. Young, I walked around to the white side. I could see Shirley across the counter, asking for the New Orleans train. Then I did the same, walked up the "white" stairs, and we joined each other again on the platform. The idiocy of segregation had never seemed so marked. At the door of our coach, the white porter took both our bags and put them on the train. He mounted the steps and (even though we were obviously traveling together) put her bag in the right-hand car and mine in the left. Shirley wanted to make a fuss then, but I just followed the porter to my seat in the white car and left her to go to the Negro side. As soon as the train was under way, I picked myself up and quietly marched over to join her. I felt this to be very cowardly of me, but, by hook or by crook, I was determined to get out of Jackson that night.

A few minutes after I sat down, the Negro woman sitting in the seat directly in front of us turned around and whispered, "You girls wouldn't be some of those Freedom Riders, would you?" I guess that even leaving Jackson, Freedom Riders give off that peculiar scent which made them so easy to spot on the way in. The woman was from New York, which warmed the cockles of my heart, and we talked about discrimination in the North versus segregation in the South. I really must admit that I kept thinking that I would have preferred talking to some of the white Mississippi natives in the other car of the train, agreement never having made for very interesting conversation, but the lady was very pleasant. She wanted to give us some money, but we insisted that she send it to CORE instead.

Shirley and I did not get any sleep at all because, rather than being a two-and-a-half-hour Jackson-to-New Orleans express, the train we were on was the real milk run, which stopped at every mud hut on the way and took about six hours. Mostly we read the newspapers, a two-day-old Jackson paper and a three-week-old *New York Times* which my cousin Nancy Rubin had sent to me in one of the packages I was given on my release. The news was old, but that was just as well since I had forty days to catch up on.

Sunday, July 16, 1961

We arrived in New Orleans at 8:30 a.m., at the sparkling new railroad depot which, so far as I could see, was integrated. From the pay phone Shirley called her mother and I tried to get Dana in New York. Because she did not understand our prearranged signals for not answering a long-distance collect phone call if Dana was not there, I talked to my other roommate, Joan, but she did not have any information on my scholarship application. But it was great to hear a real, genuine damn Yankee accent.

Shirley's large family lives in a six-room house in a Negro suburb of New Orleans. Her mother works as an attendant in a hospital, one of her brothers works as a stevedore, and the other also works as a hospital attendant. Both brothers have had some college work and are army veterans of the Korean War. Her sister Grace is a schoolteacher, and the other two girls, Alice and Jean, are still students. Jean was one of the first Freedom Riders, and it was after she got slapped around at the county farm that Hinds County stopped sending Freedom Riders there. Her father is now in Denver, Colorado, looking for a job. He got fired after working fifteen years as a stevedore for the same company, because of the civil rights activities of his daughters Jean and Shirley.

When I realized how crowded the house already was, I felt a little strange about staying there, but the cordial welcome of every member of the family soon dissipated my discomfort.

The weather was abysmally hot and humid. We took a nap, then spent the day sitting around and talking, reading the New Orleans newspaper, generally relaxing, and washing clothes.

I managed finally to get hold of Dana, who told me that I had been granted a $1,050 scholarship by the University of Chicago, which will cover my tuition exactly.

I was overjoyed, because this was one of the things which had bothered me most while in prison—what I would do if I did not manage to get the scholarship? I charged all of my calls to my phone in New York, and in a few hours called about fifty dollars' worth: to my mother and family in Los Angeles, a friend in Chicago to try to get her apartment there for next year, to my friends in Mexico City to tell them I still was going to come even though my vacation would be a little later and shorter than originally planned, to a realty company in Chicago about housing, and again to my mother to let her know my plans. It was expensive, but I had not used a telephone in forty days, and I sort of felt that I had a right to make up for lost time.

Every once in a while during the morning Shirley and I would turn to each other and say, "Yesterday at this time I was playing chess with Terry," or "Yesterday I was betting my cell mate that we would all stay for four months."

In the evening we went over to the house of Oretha Castle, a Negro girl who was already a CORE leader and movement activist, and about whom I had heard so much from Terry, who had stayed at her house on the way into Jackson. We sat around and talked, swapping experiences in civil rights protests with six or seven members of New Orleans CORE, including Jerome Smith, the current president.

Among other things, Oretha told us about her experiences with Betty Jo, the local Jackson white woman whom we had met in the Jackson city jail and again in the Hinds County Jail in Jackson. She had called from somewhere outside of New Orleans to ask if Oretha could give her and her husband a place to stay and some money, claiming that she had smuggled out seventeen letters for the Freedom Riders. I told Oretha that in addition to not having gotten the letters out she had "borrowed" something over five dollars from us before she left. At the time Betty Jo called, Oretha had a house full of Freedom Riders and was terribly busy, but when Betty Jo arrived in New Orleans she did manage to get five dollars and a meal from someone in CORE, and then disappeared again.

Monday, July 17, 1961

We had planned to go shopping downtown this morning, but were called by Jerome Smith of CORE, and told that TV people were going to come over and interview Shirley and me, so we had to hang around the house looking proper and dressed, despite the heat. They finally showed up at about one o'clock, and the actual interview took about three minutes. We each got a chance to talk—Shirley was asked about medical treatment at Parchman, and I was asked, "What do you hope to accomplish on the Freedom Rides?" I said something I thought was relatively coherent: "We will demonstrate to the state of Mississippi that this intolerable situation of segregation cannot continue to exist," and so forth. Later in the afternoon we saw the interview on TV, about thirty seconds of it, and I must admit my satisfaction with my first press conference and my television debut. I was not at all nervous during the interview, and in the part of it that they aired I looked ascetic and pale (as befits someone who has suffered for the cause), my voice was well modulated, and my thoughts sounded well connected.

There was another interview and some still pictures were taken by a reporter from one of the local Negro weeklies. I related to him the outrageous story of Kit's having been asked by one Jackson police detective in her official induction interview: "Would you rather f— a nigger or a white man?" and about the unsanitary conditions under which vaginal exams were given to the last group of girls who entered Parchman. Those were the only sensational bits I could think of. He will also get a copy of the statement which Jerome asked me to prepare for a press release. This last I wrote in about an hour, but it pleased me very much—it is distinctly rhetorical, which is what I think is called for in this case. Here it is:

"I came to Jackson because I believe in American democracy and because I believe in the capacity of American democracy to meet its present and greatest internal challenge—the systematic persecution of one minority of the citizens of America by another minority.

"I came to Jackson because I believe that in the world struggle for power between fascism and democracy we cannot, we must not lose—as we shall lose unless we rid ourselves of the cancer which cripples our relations with the uncommitted nations of the world, which retards the growth of our own country with wasted lives and wasted minds.

"Segregation is evil and breeds evil, is racial hatred and breeds racial hatred, is a denial of human dignity and breeds human degradation.

"Every citizen has a moral responsibility to cry, 'Stop, thief!' when he sees the robber in the very act of committing his crime; so has every citizen the responsibility to protest the thief, segregation, which robs the nation of vital human resources, the Negro of his birthright and the segregationist of his ability to reason, and to love.

"My own personal obligation is very great, for not only am I fortunate enough not to be subjected to the kind of discrimination experienced by my Negro fellow citizens, but, in addition, I suffer the guilt of the crimes committed in my name and in the name of the whole white population. For me, on June 7, 1961, the Trailways bus terminal in Jackson, Mississippi, was merely my station on the not-so-new frontier at which the battle for the equality of all American citizens was—and is—being fought.

"I have experienced a great deal and learned a great deal from it. But more than any other single incident, I learned from the following, which happened early in our stay at the Maximum Security Unit of the Mississippi State Penitentiary at Parchman:

"One of the Negro girls in the cell next to mine, when she refused to take a shower because she was afraid of getting athlete's foot again, was scrubbed with a floor brush by three female prison trusties. When they brought her back to the cell, she showed us the bruises around her wrists from the pressure manacles with which they had held her and told us that they had knocked her down a couple of times and scrubbed on all of the more sensitive areas of her body.

"We were furious, we were outraged, we were seething with anger. But she, from the depths of her belief in nonviolence as a way of life as well as a policy of expedient action, from her deep commitment to the tenets of Christianity and to the brotherhood of all mankind—it was she who ministered to our pain, it was she who urged us not to feel so badly about her beating, it was she who turned this physical defeat into a victory of love over violence and oppression."

Tuesday, July 18, 1961

I called up a relative of ours who lives in New Orleans. To my knowledge I have never met him, but the family in Boston was insistent that I get in touch with him. He wanted me to come and see him while he was working at the drugstore he owns. Until, that is, he found out that I would be accompanied by a couple of Negro girls (I did not mention the Freedom Rides or Jackson at all). We left it that he would come over to Shirley's house and see me when he got through work, but of course he did not come.

This afternoon I finally got to see something of the city of New Orleans. I had offered to treat Shirley, Jean, and Alice either to a fancy lunch downtown or to a sightseeing bus tour of the city, but of course they just laughed at my northern naiveté: all those things were still segregated, even though the train terminal looked integrated. Instead, we went down to the old French Quarter, walked about and peered into antique shops and historical museums.

About the time our feet were beginning to complain, we saw a horse and buggy sightseeing taxi driven by an old Negro man in a strange top hat. I asked him how much he charged and whether he would take our integrated group. His price was an exorbitant six dollars for half an hour, but even at that it was worth it. And when I asked him about a set of mixed passengers, he grinned and said, "Folks is folks, I treats them all alike." So we rode up and down on the narrow streets, while he pointed out the famous houses—the old slave market, the Confederate headquarters, the house in which the only Negro governor ever elected (during Reconstruction) had lived, and so forth. At one point I impolitely asked him if he gave the same lecture for white passengers as for Negro, and in a very insulted tone he informed me that he did not believe in discrimination.

Extrovert that I am, I found very amusing the double takes and long looks we were given all along our route, and the great number of cameras that were directed at us. At one point someone screamed out, "Look at the Freedom Riders!" in a distinctly hostile manner, but aside from that there were no incidents. Our ride lasted much longer than half an hour, and when we were finally dropped back at our original starting point the driver told us that he had given us an extra ride because he wanted us to see more of his beautiful city. He shook our hands warmly, told us that if we wanted to take another ride some time he would take us for free, and that he was "all for" the Freedom Rides.

After dinner, we sat around all evening and I got a chance to talk to Shirley's brothers and various neighbors who dropped in. I was very glad of the opportunity, among other reasons because this few days in New Orleans was the first chance I had ever had to speak to southerners about the South in relaxed circumstances. Certainly these Negroes had

Door to one of the two waiting rooms at the Trailways bus station in Jackson, Mississippi, on June 7, 1961, this one labeled "WHITE WAITING ROOM INTRASTATE PASSENGERS." When Freedom Riders who were not white entered through this door, they were met by the Jackson police (all white, of course), and told to "move on." Then they were immediately arrested for "breach of peace." Courtesy of the Mississippi Department of Archives and History.

A sign outside the Jackson, Mississippi, train station waiting area on June 8, 1961, made the point: "WAITING ROOM FOR WHITE ONLY, BY ORDER POLICE DEPT," with an arrow. When Freedom Riders exercised their federally recognized right not to be segregated in interstate transportation, despite the dictates of local officials like the Jackson, Mississippi, police, they were arrested and jailed. Courtesy of the Mississippi Department of Archives and History.

Right to left: Ed Kale (age twenty-four), Carol Ruth Silver (age twenty-two), and John Gager (age twenty-three), on June 7, 1961, entering the Jackson, Mississippi, Trailways bus station, defying the sign on the door which said, "COLORED WAITING ROOM INTRASTATE PASSENGERS." Almost immediately after they passed through this doorway they were arrested for "breach of peace" by the Jackson police, who were lined up inside the waiting room. Courtesy of the Mississippi Department of Archives and History.

Carol Ruth Silver (age twenty-two), center, was arrested with John Gager (age twenty-three), to her left and, with back to camera, Ed Kale (age twenty-four), both Yale Divinity School students from New Haven, Connecticut. They are being processed by the Jackson police after having been arrested for "breach of peace" at the Trailways bus station for entering through the door marked "COLORED WAITING ROOM INTRASTATE PASSENGERS." Courtesy of the Mississippi Department of Archives and History.

This photo is of an oil painting of Carol Ruth Silver which was completed in New York City in May 1961, about a month before she was arrested as a Freedom Rider in Jackson, Mississippi. The artist was Leslie Rosen, a student of Raphael Soyer at the New School for Social Research in Manhattan. Painting is in the private collection of Carol Ruth Silver. Photo by Carol Ruth Silver. All rights reserved.

Carol Ruth Silver shown in Jackson Police Department official photograph, front and side, with jail number, taken shortly after she was arrested on June 7, 1961, at the Trailways bus station in Jackson, Mississippi. She was twenty-two years old. Courtesy of the Mississippi Department of Archives and History.

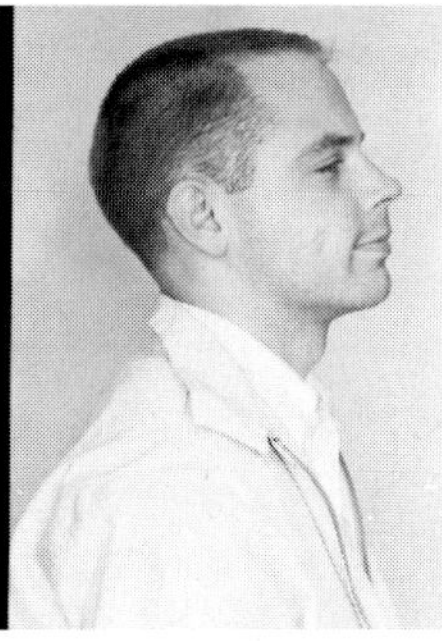

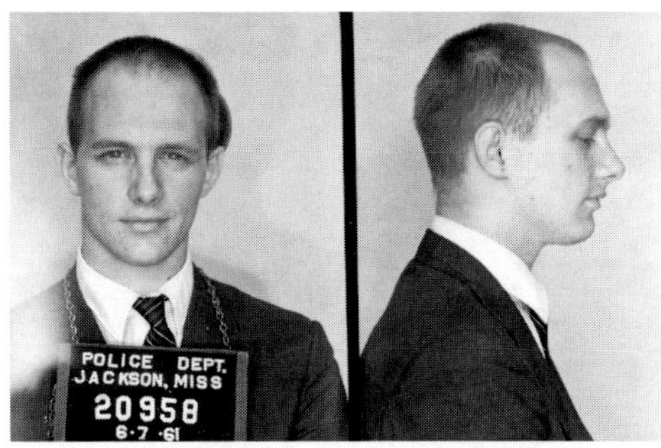

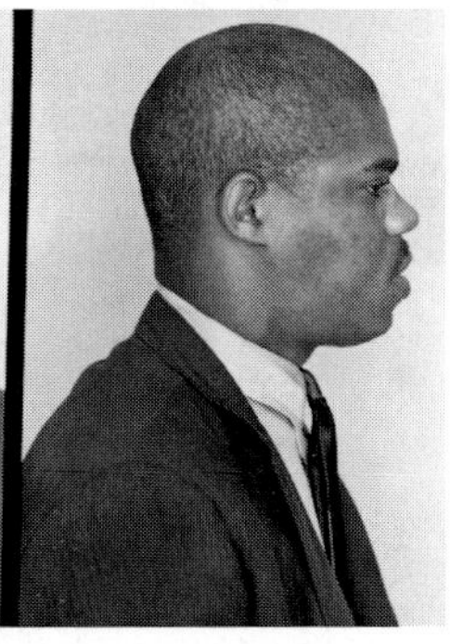

Arrested together with Carol Ruth Silver on June 7, 1961, at the Trailways bus station in Jackson, Mississippi, after having traveled together from Nashville, Tennessee, were the following, starting top left:

- Ed Kale
- John Gager
- Reginald Green
- Raymond Randolf, Jr.
- Obadiah Simms III

Courtesy of the Mississippi Department of Archives and History.

View of front of the Trailways bus station, Jackson, Mississippi, June 7, 1961, with traffic and pedestrians moving normally, no mob or police in evidence prior to arrival and arrest of Freedom Riders. Courtesy of the Mississippi Department of Archives and History.

Bus in the arrival area at the rear of the Trailways bus station, Jackson, Mississippi, June 2, 1961. Courtesy of the Mississippi Department of Archives and History.

The black Jackson, Mississippi, police wagon, sitting in the hot Mississippi sun in front of the Trailways bus station, waiting to transport arrested Freedom Riders to jail. Courtesy of the Mississippi Department of Archives and History.

Inside the Jackson, Mississippi, police wagon, June 2, 1961, after being arrested at the Trailways bus station for entering the waiting room designated "WHITE WAITING ROOM INTRASTATE PASSENGERS" are: (front to back) Joy Reagon (age nineteen), from Nashville, Tennessee, Charles Butler (age eighteen), Nashville, and Ruby Doris Smith (age nineteen), Atlanta, Georgia. Courtesy of the Mississippi Department of Archives and History.

Freedom Riders came to Jackson, Mississippi, by bus, train, and, as did Gwendolyn Jenkins (age twenty-one), dressed in her Sunday best including white gloves, by airplane. She is shown being arrested on Wednesday, June 7, 1961, with Freedom Riders (not shown) Robert Jenkins (age twenty-seven) and Ralph Washington (age twenty-four), all from St. Louis, Missouri, at Hawkins Field, the Jackson, Mississippi, airport. Courtesy of the Mississippi Department of Archives and History.

Left to right: Freedom Riders Jane Rosett (age eighteen), from Washington, D.C., Gwendolyn Greene (age nineteen) from Washington, D.C., Terry Perlman (age nineteen) from New York, and Helene Wilson (age twenty-six) from Washington, D.C., at the Illinois Central Railroad Station in Jackson, Mississippi, immediately before being arrested on June 8, 1961. They were charged with and convicted of "breach of peace" for integrating the train station waiting room because, or so the police later testified in court, the actions of these young ladies in traveling together in an integrated group, contrary to the laws of Mississippi, could have caused a white mob to breach the peace by attacking them. Courtesy of the Mississippi Department of Archives and History.

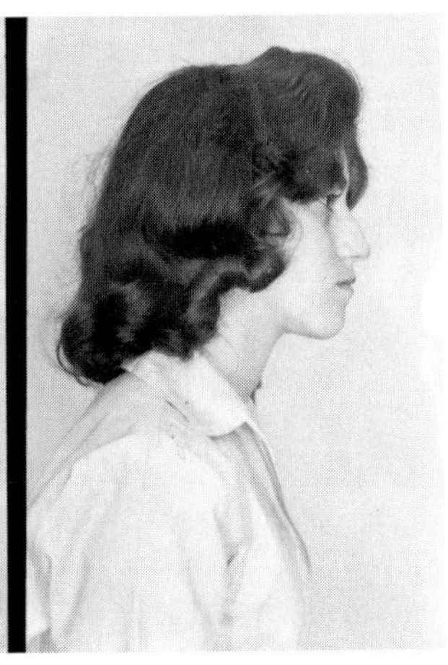

Terry Perlman shown in Jackson Police Department official photograph, front and side, with jail number, taken shortly after she was arrested on June 8, 1961, at the Illinois Central Railroad Station in Jackson, Mississippi. She was nineteen years old. Her name changed to Terry Hickerson shortly after she was released from jail, when she married Robert Hickerson, with whom she still lives in New York. Courtesy of the Mississippi Department of Archives and History.

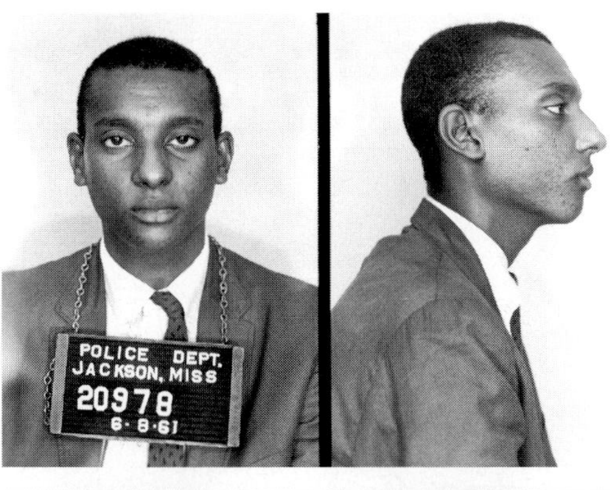

Arrested together with Terry Perlman on June 8, 1961, at the Illinois Central Railroad Station in Jackson, Mississippi, were the above, part of a group of nine Freedom Riders who had been traveling together from New Orleans, Louisiana:

- Stokely Carmichael
- Gwendolyn Greene
- Jane Rosett

Courtesy of the Mississippi Department of Archives and History.

Delta Airlines plane arriving at Hawkins Field Airport, Jackson, Mississippi, with Freedom Riders including Gwendolyn Jenkins (age twenty-one) from St. Louis, Missouri. Courtesy of the Mississippi Department of Archives and History.

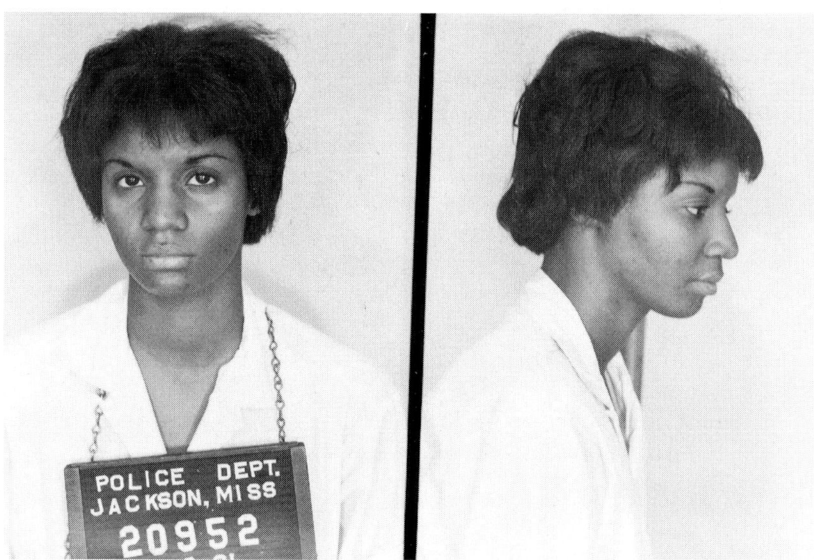

Shirley Thompson shown in Jackson Police Department official photograph, front and side, with jail number, taken shortly after she was arrested on June 6, 1961, at the Trailways bus station in Jackson, Mississippi. She was eighteen years old. Shirley passed away in 1999. Courtesy of the Mississippi Department of Archives and History.

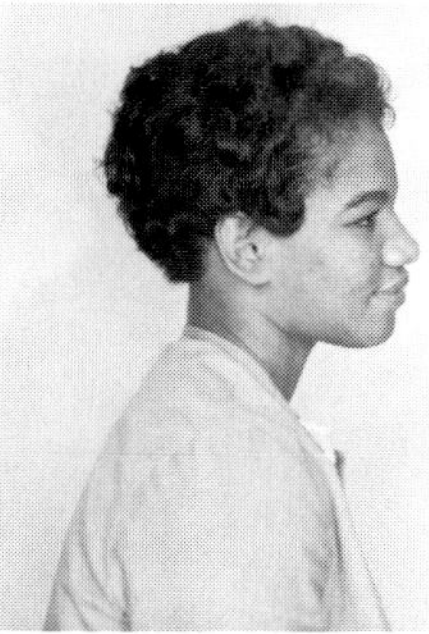
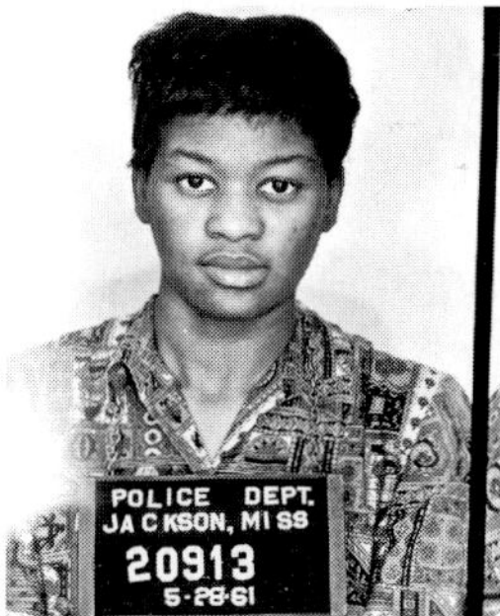

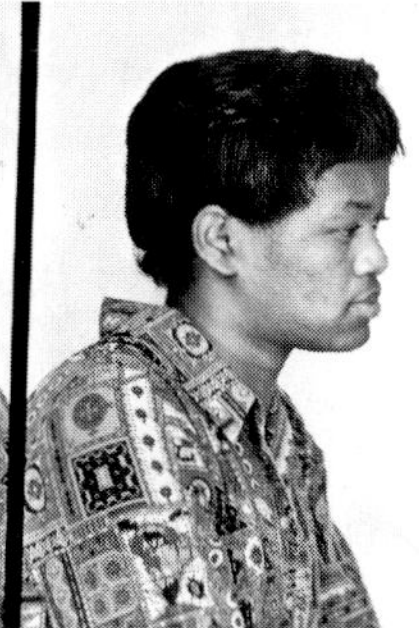

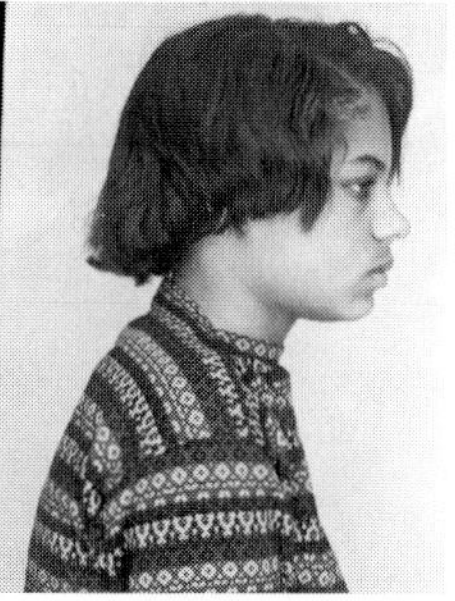

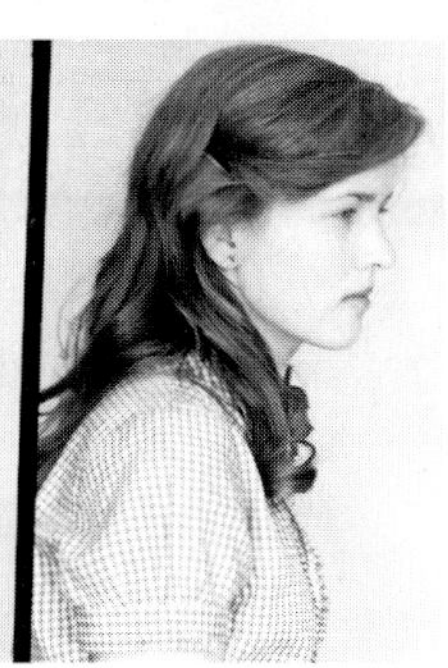
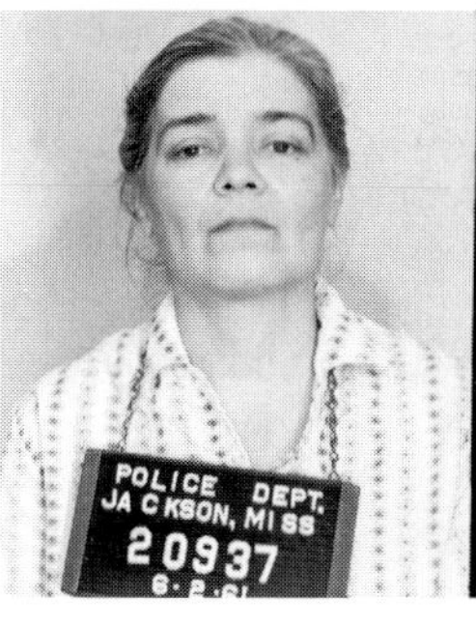

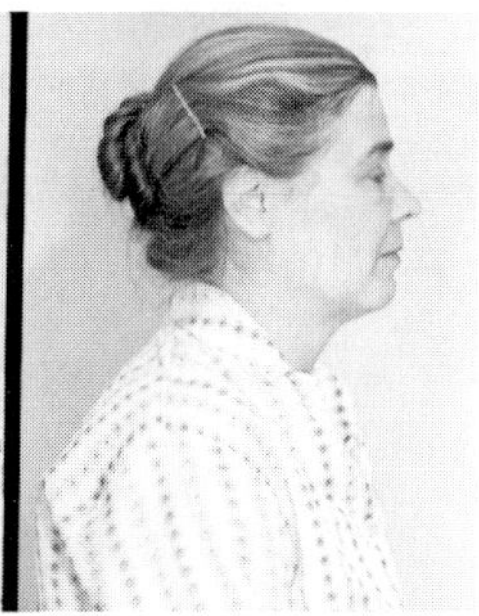

Serving time together in cells next to each other in the Maximum Security Unit of Mississippi State Penitentiary at Parchman were other female Freedom Riders, black and white. Here are a few who are mentioned in this diary:

- Ruby Doris Smith
- Pauline Knight
- Rita Carter
- Joan Trumpauer
- Elizabeth Wyckoff

Courtesy of the Mississippi Department of Archives and History.

Left to right: James Dennis from Breham, Texas, and Claude Albert Liggins from Lake Charles, Louisiana, attending a 2005 Freedom Riders reunion at Loyola Marymount University in Los Angeles, California. Both joined the Freedom Riders in Los Angeles and traveled to Jackson, Mississippi, where they were arrested and served forty days together. Both were among the group of some twenty-six African American Freedom Riders tortured in Parchman prison—they were almost asphyxiated, having been put into a six-foot by six-foot solitary punishment cell, the "hole." The Freedom Riders had refused to stop singing, and were threatened with their mattresses being taken away if they did not stop. They continued to sing, their mattresses were taken, but they kept on singing. The Freedom Riders were then pulled from their cells, some of them by brute force, by the regular prison trusties (who were also African American, but under the direction of the guards). The entire cell block of twenty-six male Freedom Riders were all dragged into the "hole," and put standing up in a cell meant to hold one person. They had almost no air ventilation, were completely in the dark, and suffered in the Mississippi heat. Photo by Bill Mitchell for Claude Albert Liggins's personal collection.

Claude Albert Liggins shown in Jackson Police Department official photograph, front and side, with jail number, taken shortly after he was arrested on June 25, 1961, at the Illinois Central Railroad Station in Jackson, Mississippi. He was twenty years old. Although born in Lake Charles, Louisiana, he has spent most of his life in Los Angeles, California, where he still lives. Courtesy of the Mississippi Department of Archives and History.

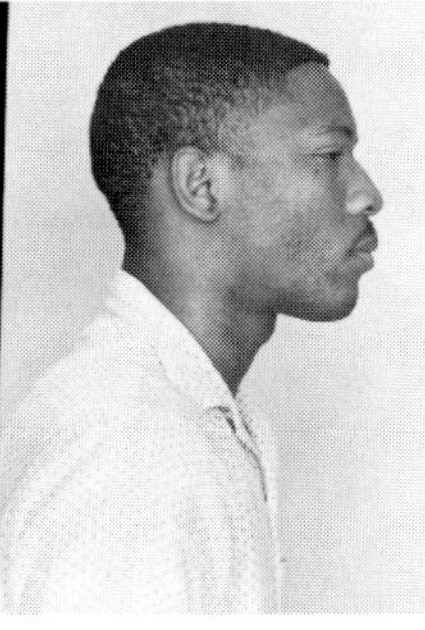

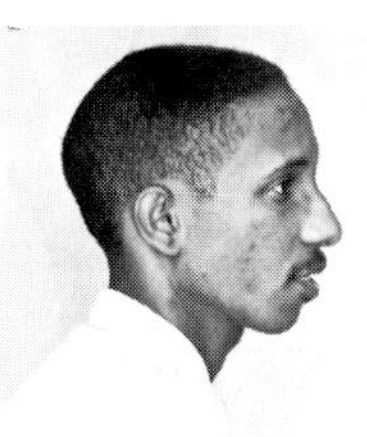

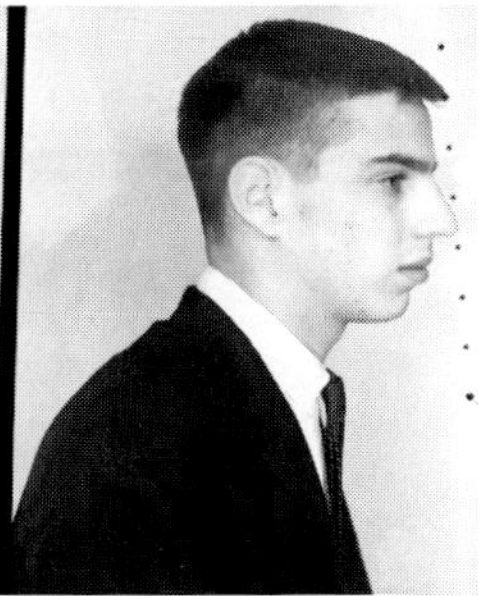

The male Freedom Riders outnumbered the females substantially. Here are a few others who were in the Mississippi State Penitentiary at Parchman at the same time as Claude Albert Liggins:

- Amos Brown
- Bernard Lafayette
- Bob Filner
- C. T. Vivian
- James Dennis

Courtesy of the Mississippi Department of Archives and History.

This photo shows the chess set which was created from white bread and spit by Carol Ruth Silver while she was incarcerated at Mississippi State Penitentiary at Parchman in 1961. The tallest pieces are only a little over half an inch in height, but they were sufficient to provide many hours of chess diversion from the monotony of life in the Maximum Security Unit at Parchman. The chess set was smuggled out of Parchman in a used letter envelope. It was placed under a protective lucite square case, and during the 40th Anniversary Reunion of the Freedom Riders, it was donated by Carol Ruth Silver to the archives of Tougaloo College, one of Mississippi's historically black colleges and universities (HBCU), located in Jackson, Mississippi. Tougaloo placed it with the Mississippi Department of Archives and History, which displayed it during the 50th Anniversary Reunion of the Freedom Riders in Jackson in 2011. Photo by Lexie Gay. Image courtesy of the Tougaloo Archives.

Who's in charge of the Mississippi State Penitentiary at Parchman now? Left, Mississippi Department of Corrections (MDOC) Commissioner Christopher Epps, shown with Claude Albert Liggins, Freedom Rider, during the 50th Anniversary Freedom Riders Reunion in Jackson, Mississippi, at a breakfast given by the governor of Mississippi in honor of the Freedom Riders, at the Governor's Mansion, on May 23, 2011. Photo by Carol Ruth Silver. All rights reserved.

Who's in charge of Mississippi highways now? Left, Mississippi Highway Patrol Chief Col. Donnell Berry, being congratulated by Claude Albert Liggins, Freedom Rider, during the 50th Anniversary Freedom Riders Reunion in Jackson, Mississippi, at a breakfast given by the governor of Mississippi in honor of the Freedom Riders, at the Governor's Mansion, on May 23, 2011. Photo by Carol Ruth Silver. All rights reserved.

James Farmer (age forty-one), from New York, arriving in Jackson, Mississippi, at the Greyhound bus station, May 24, 1961. This shows him immediately before he was arrested as a Freedom Rider. He was the national chairman of the Congress of Racial Equality (CORE), which initiated and organized the 1961 Freedom Rides. He had also been in the first group of Freedom Riders that left Washington, D.C., on May 4, 1961, but were attacked and firebombed, their bus totally destroyed, in Anniston, Alabama. Farmer had also organized and been on the predecessor Freedom Ride, called the Journey of Reconciliation, in 1947. He was an eloquent speaker and a charismatic leader. He died in 1999. Behind Farmer in this photo is Frank Holloway (age twenty-two), a Freedom Rider from Atlanta, Georgia. Courtesy of the Mississippi Department of Archives and History.

When the Freedom Rides began in May 1961, Reverend Ralph Abernathy was the pastor at First Baptist Church in Montgomery, Alabama. This church became the site of the May 21, 1961, "siege" when an angry mob of white segregationists surrounded fifteen hundred people inside the sanctuary, including a group of Freedom Riders, Dr. Martin Luther King, Jr., and Reverend Abernathy. At one point, the situation seemed so dire that Reverend Abernathy and Dr. King considered giving themselves up to the mob to save the men, women, and children in the church. Only the intervention of federal marshals sent by Attorney General Robert Kennedy averted this massacre. After Dr. King's assassination on April 4, 1968, Reverend Abernathy took up the leadership of the Southern Christian Leadership Conference (SCLC) and the Poor People's Campaign. He led the 1968 March on Washington. He is an acknowledged key figure in the Civil Rights Movement, and he and Dr. Martin Luther King, Jr., were among the leaders of the 1955–56 Montgomery bus boycott organized in response to the arrest of Rosa Parks. Reverend Abernathy died in 1990. Courtesy of the Mississippi Department of Archives and History.

William Moses Kunstler, an attorney both brilliant and controversial, was hated by the establishment. He was, however, loved and praised by the underdog. Born in New York City in 1919, he was a Civil Rights attorney who worked throughout his career against racism and injustice. When the Freedom Riders were being prosecuted in Mississippi, he volunteered to represent them, both at trial and appellate level. He devised various novel legal maneuvers, such as the use of a "removal petition" to try to move their cases from the Mississippi state courts to the federal courts. He also at various times represented the NAACP, the Chicago Seven, Malcolm X, and Stokely Carmichael (who was also a Freedom Rider). Courtesy of the Mississippi Department of Archives and History.

Roy Wilkins was the executive director of the National Association for the Advancement of Colored People (NAACP). He was born in St. Louis, Missouri, and educated at the University of Minnesota. He and the NAACP always took a cautious approach by using the court system to challenge legal segregation laws rather than the direct action that CORE, SCLC, and SNCC took and advocated. The NAACP stepped forward at a crucial time, however, to loan to CORE the money needed to post bail for the Freedom Riders from its NAACP Legal Defense and Educational Fund, Inc., as well as to help with needed legal representation. Courtesy of the Mississippi Department of Archives and History.

Left to right: David Lisker, Carol Ruth Silver, and Claude Albert Liggins, attending a 2005 Freedom Riders reunion at Loyola Marymount University in Los Angeles. In the year 2001, Carol Ruth Silver initiated a 40th anniversary reunion of the Freedom Riders, and recruited David Lisker, a historian specializing in the American Civil Rights period, who traveled to Jackson, Mississippi, to research the history of the Freedom Rides. He met and asked a police official (an African American) if there were any photos available. The response was "I don't know, let's go down to the basement and check." After moving a few boxes around they found the box with a hidden treasure of original Freedom Rider mug shots. David Lisker and Carol Ruth Silver planned, organized, sponsored, and financed the 2001 Freedom Riders 40th Anniversary Reunion at Tougaloo Colege in Jackson, Mississippi. Photo by Bill Mitchell for Claude Albert Liggins's personal collection. All rights reserved.

Carol Ruth Silver and Claude Albert Liggins, Freedom Riders, shown with a marker erected at Parchman prison by the State of Mississippi to commemorate the Freedom Rides and the incarceration of Freedom Riders, including these two, at Parchman in 1961. The photo was taken on a memorial visit to Parchman during the 50th Anniversary Reunion of the Freedom Riders at Jackson, Mississippi, in May 2011. Photo by Carol Ruth Silver.

A set of ten stamps was issued in 2005 by the United States Post Office in honor of the Civil Rights Movement, depicting some of the most well-known episodes in the Movement, including the Freedom Rides. At a ceremonial dedication during the 2005 Freedom Riders reunion at Loyola Marymount University in Los Angeles, this photo of a blowup of the stamp was accompanied by the following Freedom Riders, from left to right: Ellen Broms, Michael Grubbs, Ralph Fertig, James Dennis, Claude Albert Liggins, Steve McNichols, Max Pavesic (behind McNichols), John Taylor, Richard Stewart, Reverend James Lawson, Winston Fuller, and Carol Ruth Silver. Photo by Bill Mitchell for Claude Albert Liggins's personal collection.

the inside story of discrimination and the effects of segregation. But of all the talk, I was most impressed and moved by a young man named Pierce, who is either a cousin or another brother of the Thompsons. We were talking about the Black Muslims and the desperation which led so many young Negroes to join them. He became very intense, and leaned across the kitchen table to emphasize his point—that what the Negro must use is love, not hate, understanding, not racism.

"I believe in the American dream," he said. "That sounds sort of silly, doesn't it, coming from a Negro. But I do believe in it." And he sat back and I was very silent. I kept thinking that if I were a Negro in the South I would certainly have left long ago, and if I were a Negro in the North I would very possibly have become a Black Muslim. "Love thy neighbor" does not come easily to me. It is in terms of men like Pierce that the civil rights struggle comes home to me most vividly, until I feel so sad that I want to cry—or to go out and shoot (Mississippi Governor Ross) Barnett and (Alabama Governor John Malcolm) Patterson for trying to degrade into a "boy" and a "nigger" what they cannot accept as a man.

Wednesday, July 19, 1961

Grace pointed out to me today something which I had sort of suspected, that I am looked upon as quite a phenomenon in this all-Negro neighborhood. This is the first time that the Thompsons have had a white Freedom Rider staying with them. Every time I so much as appear on the front porch, necks are craned up and down the street. And when I walk with Shirley and her sisters, I feel even more conspicuous, since they are all a head shorter than I am. We are indeed a motley group.

I got a Western Union money order from CORE, providing me the money for my transportation to Los Angeles (the fare will be just about the same from Mexico City as it would have been from New Orleans). The delivery boy, white, rang the bell and asked Grace for Carol Ruth Silver. When I came to the door he looked, and looked, and looked again at my face, my hair, my hands, then at Grace and Shirley, and back again at me. Oblivious to his confusion, I blithely asked where I could cash the money order, and when he said about five blocks away, asked him if he could give me a lift over there. A long pause. "Yeah, I guess so." I turned tn Shirley and said gaily, "Come on, let's go." She shook her head to say "no." The delivery man, already in the car with the motor running, took off like a shot. I guess I am just not yet acclimated to the South's peculiar institution.

Chapter 10

AND OFF

Wednesday, July 19, 1961, continued

At 4:30 p.m., I left New Orleans for Houston, Laredo, and Mexico City. Shirley, Alice, Jean, and Jerome Smith came down to see me off. All of us walked into the Greyhound bus station wearing buttons which said "Freedom Ride CORE." I already had my ticket, but when I asked for a timetable, the clerk looked up, gave me the schedule, and, as I stood there for a moment with my four Negro friends checking the time for the next bus, we saw him rush to the back and start dialing the telephone. We killed about fifteen minutes having coffee at the terminal lunch counter, the only integrated restaurant in downtown New Orleans, and by the time my bus was called half a dozen policemen had drifted into the station. I finished my coffee under their attentive eyes, bid a warm farewell to the Thompsons and Jerome, and waved to them as the bus pulled out of the station. Once again I was under way.

The first thing I did, when we were barely out of New Orleans, was to remove my "Freedom Ride CORE" button. It was a cowardly act but I was feeling very much alone in enemy territory. And the second thing I did was go to sleep, because the late hours and physical exertion of the past few days had quite tired me out—I had not yet gotten reaccustomed to spending my days in activity more strenuous than lying on my stomach napping and daydreaming.

When I woke up, in the middle of the night, I had the very strong feeling that my great adventure was finally over. Even my time in New Orleans seemed long ago and far away, and Jackson, Mississippi, felt like ancient history.

Thursday, July 20, 1961

Houston, Texas: the waiting room in this fancy new bus terminal has two very distinct sections, but no signs. I suppose that Negroes are supposed to be educated enough in southern customs to figure out that the smaller, less well furbished one is, of course, for them. I did not attempt to test the rigidity of their segregation practices, and confined myself to being annoyed with Houston for its hypocrisy and with myself for my inability to do anything about it.

I had just missed a bus and so had to kill about six hours in Houston. The day was very hot but, after Louisiana, delightfully dry. I wandered around the downtown area, bought a book of tourist Spanish, almost bought a dress, and returned to the terminal restaurant to write postcards and drink coffee. When I washed up in the Greyhound bus station restroom, I noticed that in just the few days that I have been out of jail I have gained back a good deal of the weight I had lost—my face is no longer really haggard and the belt of Terry's which I borrowed from her in Jackson is beginning to be tight on its last hook. I still have my prison pallor, however, and in the cold fluorescent light I look positively sick, even though I feel extremely well.

Friday, July 21, 1961

No diary entries.

Saturday, July 22, 1961

Mexico City, finally! Second-class buses are not the most comfortable mode of transport in the world, especially since I had the great frustration of not knowing Spanish—although with my few words I did manage to communicate a little with some of the other passengers. We descended upon Mexico City, la Ciudad de México, at the ridiculous hour of 6:00 a.m., so rather than awaken my friends at that hour I wandered around downtown for a while. Eventually, I found Sanborn's, an American-style drugstore which could as easily have been located on Sunset Boulevard in LA, or 42nd Street in New York, as on the Paseo de la Reforma. I felt almost embarrassed at doing such a touristy thing, but I was thrilled to find a *New York Times* and to devour it over a cup of bad American coffee. I made up for that by eating tacos from a corner street stand, figuring that if I could have been made sick simply by a change of food and water, as everyone claims happens to Americans in Mexico, I should certainly have become sick in Mississippi.

When I did call my friends and meet them, I felt as if I had finally come home after a long trip, even though I was two thousand miles from any place I had ever been before. These friends represented my life B. J.—Before Jackson. I was delighted at the prospect of picking up the threads of my life where I had left off. A few hours, however, convinced me that that will never be possible. No one wanted to hear about the family or our old friends; the first questions and practically the whole day's conversation was about the Freedom Rides and Mississippi and segregation and what it was like to be a prisoner in a jail. And as people dropped in at my friends' home I discovered that news of my arrival had been widely spread by word of mouth on the basis of my just-completed adventure. I told my story of the Freedom Rides to so many people so many times that my words began to be set in patterns, and by the end of the day it sounded to me as if I was giving a prepared speech.

July 23, 24, 25, 1961

No diary entries.

Wednesday, July 26, 1961

What a change from Parchman I am enjoying! Here I am my own master with absolutely no restrictions. I can go for walks, I can ask to be driven here or there; I can raid the refrigerator, read, talk, sing, and write letters to my heart's content. These are all the small things which I probably would not ever have noticed except in contrast to life behind bars, but they really are the things which make life worth living. Especially letters—I have written at least a dozen since I have been here, the added joy of having a typewriter again making me write more than I even normally might.

In keeping with my promise to Marion, I wrote a long letter in our code, telling her what I had been able to find out about her habeas corpus hearing (essentially that there is as yet no information) and sending all the news I could glean from the newspapers. Then I decided that even the seemingly innocent talk, using the code we had worked out, about birthdays and mice and various individuals, might still catch the overly suspicious eyes of Sgt. Storey and Sgt.Tyson, so I retyped the whole thing with this beginning:

"Dear Sis,

"You know that what you are doing is wrong—that you are trying to impose your beliefs in the mythical equality of the races on people who do not agree with you, but people who have just as much right to their opinions as you do to yours. How can you, who have always considered individual freedom to be so basic to the Good Way of Life, now turn around and tell someone else that they have no right to their opinion? I shall write to Mother as soon as I finish this letter, although I really do not know what I shall be able to say to her. She, I am sure, feels the same way about your latest escapade as I do, and I just wonder if you will be welcome in her home when you get out."

If that one doesn't pass censorship, I really cannot imagine what will.

July 27, 28, 29, 1961
No diary entries.

Sunday, July 30, 1961
Well, eight days in Mexico and here I am flying to Los Angeles as if I were on a two-week vacation from a steady, well-paying job. My first and major project in Los Angeles, starting early tomorrow morning, is going to be getting work. My total cash resources at the moment: forty dollars in traveler's checks, seventy cents in change, and a handful of pesos worth eight cents each.

I have not felt so glad to see my family since the first time I ever left home. My mother and littlest sister Barbara (who is no longer so little; she just turned seventeen) were at the airport to greet me, and waited an extra hour while I was held up by the public health department because I had neglected to get a smallpox shot. When I was finally able to embrace them, I felt like the prodigal returned. Then we went home, and that night the whole family, my dad and my mom, my uncle Leo, sisters Jane and Barbara, and Grandma Tillie, killed the fatted calf, or at least a fatted Chinese dinner, in my honor.

In her great anxiety over my welfare, my mother had become very active in Los Angeles CORE while I was incarcerated, as well as in raising money to make sure my bail was available. She had even called and asked for help to raise my bail from her sisters Fay and Rosalie, my more financially secure aunts in Massachusetts, and suffered their criticism: "What? She's in jail? In Mississippi? I don't believe it! What's she doing there? She's crazy, your daughter!" But they came through with the money, and Mother was able to turn over to CORE enough money to cover my bail, plus some.

This evening I called Henry Hodge, the Los Angeles director of CORE, and told him who I was. I received his congratulations with equanimity but was rather shaken when practically without taking breath he asked me if I would be available to speak to a group concerning the Freedom Rides on next Thursday evening. "Well, I just got home and I don't have any plans yet, but I would be glad to do anything I can . . ."

"Fine, I'll pick you up at about seven—you'll be speaking to a group of students at UCLA." So I guess my career as a professional Freedom Rider is entering a new stage.

July 31, August 1, 2, 1961
No diary entries.

Thursday, August 3, 1961
Jobs are much more scarce this year than I have ever found them. I think that this is the first time in five years of working summers in Los Angeles that I have looked for three days and not come up with even the prospect of something. There is evidently not even a sufficiency of temporary office work, my old staple. It is most discouraging.

The UCLA student group brought back all sorts of memories of my undergraduate student politician days at the University of Chicago. It was ostensibly a meeting of the delegation to the National Student Association (NSA), but it had been expanded into, essentially, a committee for the support of the Freedom Rides, which is continuing to be major news every day as more and more Freedom Riders are packing the Mississippi jails. I gave a brief history of the Rides, and then opened to questions from the group, covering everything from prison food to my own reasons for participating. The action which one hopes will come out of this meeting is a letter to California's Governor Pat Brown expressing concern over the treatment being accorded UCLA students who are now in Parchman and asking him to send a delegation of inspection, similar to the group sent by the governor of Minnesota. Just about everyone in the meeting was overtly sympathetic, especially two women who were wives of some men included in the last group of Freedom Riders.

My escort for the evening was not Henry Hodge but Eugene Rudolph, the head of the Santa Monica chapter of CORE. He had arranged with the UCLA people that they hear me early in the meeting because he wanted me to talk to another group, the Steering Committee of the Westwood Democratic Club. We finished UCLA and got to the Democratic Club just after they had started their meeting. We listened to a little old-fashioned political talk before they got around to hearing about the Freedom Rides. This Westwood Democratic Club group was more critical and challenging than the students, and in just that proportion more interesting. I managed to answer without hesitating all of the questions thrown at me, and after the meeting one of the members of the club, Paul Alpert, told me that he felt I had made a good impression. As it was my first appearance before a nonstudent group for any reason I was quite pleased with my performance. The only thing which did bother me about it was that I had given a brief and almost flippant answer to the gentleman who tried to bait me by asking in a sarcastic way, “Do you think you did any good?” I should have been able to ignore the tone, take the question at its face value and answer it as I had many times before: with the Freedom Rides we had brought to the forefront the injustices of segregation. Although it is too early to tell whether we will be successful in the immediate future in getting rid of this evil, eventually, yes, I believe we will succeed, and our actions as Freedom Riders will be seen as a part of that future victory.

August 4, 5, 1961
No diary entries.

Sunday, August 6, 1961
Today was the big Los Angeles CORE rally in Will Rogers Park. I was very tempted not to go, since I seem not to be able to shake this miserable head cold. It annoys me especially to be sick now, after I went through jail without getting scurvy, trench mouth, or athlete’s foot, and through Mexico without getting dysentery, only to return to sunny Southern California and catch a common cold. I finally decided to go, and I am really glad I did. All of the returned Freedom Riders from LA were there, including Rita Carter, who had just gotten out of the hospital. She had just had the tumor operation which she was supposed to have had before she came to Jackson. Janice Rogers was there too—she had a miscarriage a few days after they released her from Parchman, and she feels that if they had not kept her five days after her bond was posted she might have saved the baby. I can see now how Janice looks Caucasian—no wonder that prison authorities had trouble believing she is Negro. I also met her husband, Johnnie, for the first time, and Bob Martinson, a white Freedom Rider, who is Rita’s fiancé.

Reverend Fred Shuttlesworth was the main speaker of the afternoon, and he was a very good speaker and preacher. The audience, Negro with a good sprinkling of white students and a few white adults, was very responsive. The crowd was estimated at about two thousand people, which is not so many, considering that at a Los Angeles rally for the Freedom Riders where Martin Luther King, Jr., spoke they had about fourteen thousand. Some of the Freedom Riders were presented to the rally, and everyone cheered. Then Jean Kitwell, a woman lawyer who had been at Parchman after I left, spoke for a few minutes about the conditions. Even if I were not partisan, I think I would have considered it an interesting and worthwhile afternoon, and I was glad that I had risen from my sick bed to go.

One thing which interested me especially was some people who picketed the rally with signs like "We need massive resistance, not passive resistance." I talked to a guy named Charlie Smith, who told me that they were from a group called Freedom Now. Besides being concerned with the broader aspects of the Negro problem, Freedom Now advocates the same kind of direct action as CORE—but without being committed to nonviolence and passive resistance. I cannot help but sympathize with their attitudes, although I do not think that their methods will achieve the goal of desegregation any faster than those of CORE and I do think that whatever they do achieve will be accompanied by a greater residual bitterness.

Monday, August 7, 1961

The rumors which have been abroad for the past week, that we might all have to return to Jackson on August 14 for the first part of our appeal, are now confirmed. I can think of nothing I anticipate with less pleasure. And Mother—well, she is rather disturbed. This is upsetting to all of my plans, especially since no one knows how long we might have to stay once we do get there. It is not yet quite definite that we will all have to go—evidently the lawyers are still trying to find some loophole—and the information on just why we are being required to go back anyway is very sketchy here in Los Angeles. I am still job hunting, but cannot muster up much enthusiasm, since I am probably wasting my time.

Gene Rudolph called, to ask me to appear on a TV show along with Rita, Bob, and Jorgia Siegel, who went to the SLATE conference in Berkeley after she got out of Parchman and is now back here. I reminded him about the possibility that we might have to go back to Mississippi, but he said that this would work out since the TV station will have a preliminary interview on Wednesday and the actual interview on Thursday night. If we do have to go to Mississippi, we will probably leave by bus on Friday morning. I also got a call from Hirsh Adell, the chairman of the Westwood Democrats' Political Action Committee, who wants me to come to a meeting of his committee on August 21. I explained that I would possibly be in Jackson on that date, but that if not, I would be very happy to come.

Tuesday, August 8, 1961

I really feel quite upset about the unsettled state of my immediate future. I am especially worried about the business of an indefinite stay in Jackson—I must be in Chicago at the end of September to register for law school, or else all of my plans really go up in smoke. Mother is upset about that but more especially about the fact that we are going to go back by bus, through almost two thousand miles of treacherous southern segregationist territory. She wants us at least to take a plane, if we must go, but CORE says that it cannot afford to send anyone that way. This is one battle I am staying out of, since I really think that it is as easy to bomb a plane as it is a bus and I am somewhat scared of planes anyway. The plane would be much more convenient, however, and from a selfish point of view I should certainly much prefer it because it is faster.

I have given up looking for a job, since our return to Mississippi, for however long or short a time, is now really certain, and since, anyway, I had spent a full week at it with absolutely no success. Now I am spending my last days in Los Angeles trying to see friends and relatives and attempting to transcribe the diary I kept in prison, lest I forget what my codes and abbreviations really signified. This project is very enjoyable, for each day's experiences come back quite vividly, and in retrospect they are much more amusing and interesting than they were trying and difficult while they were actually occurring.

August 9, 10, 1961

No diary entries.

Chapter 11

AND BACK

Friday, August 11, 1961

Off to Jackson, once again! Even though we have known for almost a week that we would probably, and then certainly, have to go back to Jackson, still no one seems to have any real idea about what will happen when we get there. Even on such a simple thing as housing, it seems to be a group deduction rather than any concrete information from Jackson which has made us believe we will be staying in dorms at Tougaloo College. In one letter I saw we were told we would be staying "nine miles out of the City," which is where Tougaloo College is, just barely over the border into the next county from Hinds County. The latest rumor on how long we will have to stay is from six weeks to two months, but I assured my mother with a straight face that I expected to be back in Los Angeles within two weeks. She finally, after a great deal of agitation, became resigned to my going back. But even if I talk bravely to her, I must admit that I am more frightened now than on the original trip into Mississippi—a fear born of knowledge replacing the self-confident faith of naiveté.

But I am having more fun with my traveling companions this time than I had on the first trip into Mississippi, especially since we are not under orders to segregate ourselves while we are traveling. We all decided, as a general policy, that we would travel together and eat together and together defy the segregation of the South up to the point of arrest, but that if ordered to "move on," we would. Of course, our main concern is to reach Jackson on Sunday morning, and nothing is worth failing to do that, since it would cost CORE five hundred dollars for each forfeited bail, and a big loss of prestige.

All together we are a group of seven, the girls: Jorgia Siegel, less tan but still healthy looking; Eddora Manning, a very dark, rather ample Negro girl; Marcie Rosenbaum, a bouncy white girl; Rita Carter, Negro, one of the most beautiful girls I have ever seen; and me. And then the boys: Bob Martinson, white, tall, ascetic looking; and Johnnie Rogers, our Negro prize fighter, short and muscular. We are a motley group, indeed, by any southern standards.

Johnnie is one of the most surprising members of this nonviolent movement. His whole professional life has been spent in trying to beat up some other poor joker within the rules of so-called sport, but here he is, sincerely committed to the principles of nonviolence. An enigma, yes, I suppose, but perhaps no more so than Rita. She is the type of Negro that one unfortunately finds all too rarely active in the Civil Rights Movement, a member of the northern Negro middle class who had been completely accepted by her community, whose position is far and above what any southern Negro can hope to achieve. Too often these people, and I recall examples among my friends in Chicago, do not identify with the Civil Rights Movement or with the oppressed Negro in the South. I remember very well my shock at one such character in Chicago, a light-skinned Negro born there, when we were one day discussing the degeneration of the neighborhood in which we lived (just south of the campus of the University of Chicago), saying, "It's all because of these damn niggers coming up from the South."

There are not enough of us coming from California to charter a bus, and so CORE bought us all round-trip tickets on the regular bus lines. We were told as we got to the head of the long line in the Los Angeles bus station that there were only four seats left on our bus and that the three others would have to wait for another section. We insisted that we had to stay together, and would all wait for the other bus, so we were an hour late out of Los Angeles. The FBI agents seemed rather annoyed—and I suppose it was our fault for messing up their schedule.

Saturday, August 12, 1961

We changed buses in El Paso, Texas, without incident. So far as we could see the waiting rooms and terminal restaurant were integrated, and we used the restrooms together.

In Fort Worth, Texas, we noticed that here there were two distinct but unlabeled areas, one Negro and one white, but no one stopped us from using the white restrooms together, and we did not have time to test the restaurants.

In Dallas, we had to change from Greyhound to Continental Trailways buses, which meant changing terminals, a distance of about five blocks. There was some mix-up about baggage and again, as in Los Angeles, we were at the end of the line and put on the second section of the bus. There were only six seats on that bus, but we said we would manage somehow rather than have one of us go alone on the first bus. As we were waiting for the bus to pull out, we saw FBI agents talking to the driver—this is the first time we had seen them since Los Angeles—two well-dressed men in business suits, who had been very obviously but unconcernedly observant of our little group as it moved in line. We commented to each other that they are so very conspicuous because of their ties and white shirts; most people who travel by bus dress casually. There were two agents on the platform, and a third in a straw hat who wandered in and out of the waiting room. While we were eating in the terminal restaurant (all together, Negroes and whites), we had seen the three of them come up and say something to two policemen sitting at another table.

The fact of our being on the second section means that we will have to change buses again in Shreveport, Louisiana, and also that we will be making more stops than anticipated, both of which realities rather upset me. We had been told in Los Angeles that a number of Freedom Riders had been arrested in New Orleans for "vagrancy" (they were waiting for a bus), and that the cops had also come into one of the Negro homes at which white Freedom Riders were quartered and arrested them for vagrancy, resisting arrest, and aggravated battery. Evidently, Louisiana has decided to help out her sister state Mississippi by making it difficult for the Freedom Riders to get back to Jackson on time for the hearings.

Because of the shortage of seats, the stiffest one of us volunteered to stand for the first part of the trip—poor Bob, whose legs are about three inches too long for comfortable bus travel. We were interested to note that there was not a car following us. We had expected that the federal agents would at least tail us for part of the way.

Nor was FBI or other protection for us evident when we stopped in Tyler, Texas. Here, the girls used the white restroom together without incident. But when John and Bob started to enter the restaurant, the male cashier said to Johnnie, "Hey, boy—we got a place out back for you." There was, by Bob's account, a long, slow pause of about two seconds. Then Johnnie said, "I guess they don't like Negroes here," and turned on his heel. The two of them went out onto the platform. It was about two hours before John recovered from his swallowed anger. We, Jorgia, Marcie, Rita, and I, not knowing about this, walked blithely up to the counter, sat down, and ordered Cokes. No one said anything to Rita, and the white waitress had started to serve us when Bob came up and told us that we had to go. I thought to myself, I guess a strikingly pretty Negro girl has some advantages, even in the South.

We all went out on the loading platform (accompanied by only a few scowls) and Marcie took a picture of the integrated group of the rest of us standing with arms entwined under the huge sign saying "COLORED WAITING ROOM."

In Shreveport, we changed to the first section of our Dallas bus, at about 2:00 in the morning. We did not attempt to enter the waiting room or the restaurant, even through none of us had eaten since Dallas. When they called our bus, Jorgia, then John, Marcie, and Eddora, got on and began looking around for seats. They were putting their luggage on the racks when a white woman in the front seat of the bus said angrily, "You've got to wait until the other passengers get back to their seats." In spite of the tone, this was a reasonable request, so they all got off again, including a white serviceman, who had been with us on the other bus and who had followed our group onto the new bus. As he went by her, she called out, "Oh, but I didn't mean you."

"That's OK, lady," he said, and got off.

Then we heard her call out to the rest of the bus, "They're them damn Freedom Riders!"

As we waited again on the platform, David Dennis, another Negro Freedom Rider, introduced himself to us and said that he had been waiting to join our group when it came through. Not one of us had ever met him before, although he and Johnnie had been in Parchman for a few days at the same time. David, who lives in Shreveport, told us that the whole area around the bus depot was crawling with cops, and a group of them in and out of uniform were standing near the door labeled "WHITE INTRASTATE WAITING ROOM" talking to the two men whom we had spotted as the FBI. A fat, burley man in rumpled street clothes—identified to us as the police commissioner—poked David as we were showing our tickets to the driver, and said, "Where you going, boy?"

"Jackson, Mississippi," David replied politely.

"Well, hurry up and get out of here; we know your kind."

Then he did the same to Bob, who was standing just ahead, amid many snickers from the policemen. While the cops were clustered around the

FBI men, one of them pointed to us and I, always inclined to be friendly, waved at him. They all scowled.

I was very glad that when the commissioner came up to us Johnnie was already aboard the bus. Just before he got on, he began chafing at the delay, and I reminded him to "keep cool." "Well," he said, "I'm a paying passenger, and I'm tired of being treated like a hitchhiker." That, it seems to me, is the whole Civil Rights Movement in a nutshell.

The servicemen, who transferred buses with us, had become acquainted with us on the way from Dallas. They are returning from Korea. One of them is a southerner who told us that, before he went to Korea, he had accepted unquestioningly the southern racial mores, but that now he has changed. He is planning to adopt a six-year-old Korean orphan, and Rita told him all about her sister, a Korean orphan whom the Carter family adopted some years ago. Both of the soldiers were very pleasant, and offered to share with us the pint of booze they were enjoying (in defiance of all sorts of laws). We declined, except Johnnie, who took one swig, just, he said, to be sociable.

The woman who had ordered us off the bus was unfortunately forced to share a seat with Marcie for a short while. She continued passing out John Birch Society literature and being obnoxious to the driver and everyone else nearby. When Bob went into a terminal restaurant at some small stop to bring us all coffee, she harassed the (white) waitress until the poor girl said, "Look, lady, you have to wait your turn like everyone else."

"Well, miss!" she said. "You should at least serve me before you serve that damn Freedom Rider!"

Sunday, August 13, 1961

Our last stop before Jackson was Monroe, Louisiana, at 4:30 a.m. We decided not even to get off the bus, but Bob went out again and got us coffee. He passed under the huge painted "WHITE WAITING ROOM" sign without incident. I could taste the chicory in my black, unsweetened coffee—shades of Hinds County Jail! Bob said that he didn't see any signs of the FBI or any police around—perhaps we are so far off schedule that none of the officials know where we are—now *that* is a frightening thought!

The southern dawn was like so many I remember watching through our little windows at Parchman, with innumerable strange shapes of clouds changing from dark and then to lighter gray and finally taking all the colors of the rainbow before becoming a brilliant, hot white. At 6:30 a.m. we crossed the Mississippi River, looking much more deep and majestic here than when I had seen it years ago, further upstream. (Coming to Jackson in June of this year, due south from Nashville, we did not have to cross the Mississippi.) Just over the bridge I saw a big, garish sign in red and black—"WELCOME TO MISSISSIPPI, THE MAGNOLIA STATE."

As we pulled into Jackson's Trailways bus station, the same station at which I had been arrested just a little over two months ago, the first thing I saw was the same rows of uniformed, armed police which had greeted me then. My heart began racing, from fear or just excitement, I was not sure. But then I saw, standing casually at about the middle of the platform, two pairs of legs, white and brown, sticking out from beneath two pairs of Bermuda shorts, into two pairs of rubber sandals. In great joy, we opened a bus window and waved, and hurried to debark.

Under the watchful eyes of the police, and carefully avoiding the waiting rooms (still labeled "WHITE WAITING ROOM INTRASTATE PASSENGERS" and "COLORED WAITING ROOM INTRASTATE PASSENGERS"), the two boys in Bermuda shorts led us to the parking lot next to the station where we were divided between two cars—the whites together and the Negroes together. This was because our primary objective on this visit in the city of Jackson, this time, is to avoid incidents. Some of the Freedom Riders will be staying at Coleman, a Negro college in Jackson, but we were all first driven out to meet together at Tougaloo College. As we drove under the beautiful white-painted wrought-iron gate, the white driver of our car regaled us with stories of how Negro students had been chased to the gate in years past, and how their white tormentors stopped short lest they be shot for trespassing.

The Tougaloo buildings are impressive, mostly white wood frame southern colonial style, gleaming in the already hot sun. From all the trees hung the parasitic Spanish moss which everyone keeps saying is "so lovely," although to me it only looks deadly. I cannot separate the appearance of the stuff from its nature.

As before when I arrived in Jackson, I was delighted to take a cool shower and lie down for a short nap, under decidedly more pleasant conditions. We were the first group to arrive, and so had our pick of rooms in the dormitory. The summer session of school at Tougaloo had closed only the Friday before. The kitchen staff had all left on vacation, however, and so for lunch we had to go down to the Grill, a sort of campus soda shop about a quarter of a mile down the road from the college gate. There was a sheriff's car parked on the road, and we were really apprehensive about going past it. But our rumbling stomachs got the best of us. The men, uniformed and, as always, armed, merely scowled at us.

The Grill was not adequate to feed two hundred people. As each of us finished eating, we wandered into the kitchen to ask if there was anything we could do to help feed the hoard of people still waiting for hamburgers and French fries. This, of course, only made the kitchen facilities more crowded and inadequate, and every once in a while the harried cook would shoo everyone out. I washed dishes and bussed tables (my experience as a part-time waitress in Chicago made me feel very professional).

All day, as successive groups arrived, a constant chorus of greetings rang out. People we had met briefly in a courtroom, with whom we had been closely jailed for weeks without ever meeting, were suddenly very much present, shaking hands, embracing. Of course, we were especially curious to meet the boys, with whom we had had almost no contact at all, since almost as soon as each group was arrested it had been segregated four ways. At Parchman we girls had been moved in integrated Negro and white groups together but none of us really got to see and spend time with anyone except our individual cell mates, and it was the same with the boys who had been in the Maximum Security Unit together. I was constantly hearing a very familiar voice, sometimes one to which I could even give a name, and turned toward it to find an appearance very different from the one which I had imagined to fit the voice.

As we wandered over the campus, waiting for the first scheduled event of our stay—a meeting in the chapel at 2:00 p.m.—we were besieged by reporters and photographers, each identifying himself (they were all male and all white) as friendly to our cause. We finally decided, most of us, that it was not an especially good idea to talk to them at all, rather referring them to Jim Farmer, the national director of CORE, or to one of the CORE field representatives.

The chartered bus from New York arrived just at 2:00 p.m., and so the meeting was postponed until 3:00 p.m. to allow them time to debark and unwind. Terry and I greeted each other like long-lost sisters, and she repeated the plaintive "I missed you!" as she had promised me she would, when we had finally left Parchman together. She had been working at a camp in Vermont and had been very upset at having to give up work and come trooping back to Jackson. But once there, she, and I think all of us, were delighted to have a chance to meet and be with each other again.

The meeting finally began. Guy Carawan, a folksinger who had been on the program of the Los Angeles mass meeting with Martin Luther King, Jr., and who had long been identified with liberal causes, started it off. As people began drifting into the chapel, he organized the singing which has always been the companion noise to general chatter wherever a group of us is together. Some of the boys who had been in Maximum Security Unit together at Parchman had fallen into a quartet, and they sang to his accompaniment some of our most popular "freedom" songs. One of the members was Reginald Green, one of the Negro divinity students with whom I had been arrested. I had not seen him since then, and apparently I was being inducted into Parchman at the same time that he and another group were leaving. I also saw Ed Kale and John Gager, the Yale divinity students with whom Reggie and I had been arrested. As we waited for the meeting to begin, we all swapped stories of where we had been and how we had been treated.

I finally began to get some idea of what the situation had been on the boys' side of the Maximum Security Unit. The boys had been much less cooperative with the prison staff, as a general policy, than the girls. In addition to protesting at various times, by refusing to eat or withholding their trays, some of them had answered back when provoked. The only clothes they had were tee shirts and undershorts and I expect that they were even more uncomfortable than we when their mattresses were taken away. The jailers had also used the "hole" as a constant threat, and numerous Freedom Riders were put into it.

There had also been a morale problem in that the white men especially seemed to represent much more diverse backgrounds and opinions than we girls did. Their chief occupations, evidently, were debating and fighting among themselves. They also spent much time reading the Bible and reading a copy of "Race and Reason," a segregationist pamphlet which the jailers had kindly provided. At first the Negroes and whites were in the same cell block, as the girls had been, but just about the time I was released all of the white males were transferred to a separate camp, originally intended for first offenders, outside of the Maximum Security Unit. It was much less restrictive than the Maximum Security Unit because they were all together in a sort of a dormitory and the food was much better. This unit also had its own solitary punishment cells, however, which were often used.

Finally, Reverend C. T. Vivian of Nashville called the meeting to order. The first piece of business was to ask all reporters to leave the hall—this was a private meeting. Then he introduced Mr. William Kunstler, the New York lawyer who had taken over most of the legal maneuvering. Kunstler proceeded to give us a rundown on the legal aspects of our situation, something I had tried so hard to get when we were in Los Angeles.

First, he had petitioned the judge to allow us to be represented by counsel at the arraignment (tomorrow) on the basis of all kinds of Mississippi precedents which had never before been abrogated. This had been denied—which, of course, was why we had to be here, to each appear in person. He had also begun trying to "remove" our cases over to the federal courts under the federal civil rights law, on the ground that they are civil rights cases rather than simple misdemeanors. Five cases have been entered for this transfer and if they are accepted, all our cases will be removed. The five selected were all people who could not return to Jackson for one reason or another, and the application for removal of their cases also has the effect of saving CORE from having to forfeit their bail money.

Our situation now is that we are moving not to a higher court but sideways, into a court where the only difference from our first trial will be that a full verbatim transcript, a record of the trial, including all testimony and cross examination interrogation, will be kept. On this record, the appeal will be made to the higher courts of the state and eventually to the Supreme Court of the United States. Tomorrow will be our arraignment and not a trial; all that will be done is that a date will be set at which our new trial will be held. The State of Mississippi has decided, in its judicial wisdom, that we will be tried individually, two each day, for as many days as it takes.

This whole business, Kunstler felt, is a concerted attempt by the State of Mississippi to break CORE and the Freedom Rides financially—by causing forfeit of the bail money and by requiring the Freedom Riders to make an unnecessary trip back to Jackson. They thought they could cause forfeiture of the money which CORE has posted, because Mississippi did not expect that more than a small percentage of the Freedom Riders would be able to get back to Jackson on time, or at all. Almost a hundred thousand dollars has already been put up by CORE and not only would CORE have lost that money if we did not show, but CORE as an organization has borrowed heavily on the surety of our bail money for current operations and for new bail that had to be posted. Forfeiture would have ruined CORE financially, and maybe put a real brake on the whole Civil Rights Movement. But! More Freedom Riders have already shown up in Jackson than either CORE or the State of Mississippi expected! So the forfeitures have been averted, although our transportation costs are also a financial drain on CORE.

As far as the trials themselves are concerned, the people who were arrested in the first group to reach Jackson will be given a really full-dress affair. For the rest of us, since asking us to come back for an actual trial is simple harassment anyway (since the higher court decisions will be based on the first few cases) the trials will be very much routine, so much so that Kunstler felt that Mississippi might cancel them after the first ten or twenty people had been run through (in this he was wrong, as we later found out). We can all, therefore, go back to our homes after the arraignment tomorrow (except for the first group), although still with the possibility of having to come back later in the year. It will be taking a chance, but even if we do have to come back, that will be easier than trying to keep almost two hundred people in Jackson for up to six months.

When Kunstler was finished, I for one felt terribly relieved that someone, at least, knew what the score was and could explain it so clearly. One of my greatest worries for the past week or so has been that no one seemed to know exactly what was going on. I developed a great deal of confidence in Mr. Kunstler—aside from the fact that he was both concise and precise, he looks a good deal like my father.

Then Reverend Vivian gave us a lecture on decorum, emphasizing that we are at all times under observation. This he put in the form of nine negative commandments:

No. 1. No drinking alcohol, on or off campus.

No. 2. No interracial couples—this caused quite a stir; he explained that if there was anything calculated to infuriate both the police and white citizens of Mississippi this was it, and although none of us might have any objections at all, while we were in enemy territory mixed couples should refrain from even holding hands in the presence of photographers or when off the campus.

No. 3. No shorts—again quite a stir since the majority of both boys and girls had on shorts in the hot sticky Mississippi afternoon, until he clarified that he meant this only when off the campus.

No. 4. No singing while in the city of Jackson—CORE had agreed with the police that there would be no "demonstrations," and no singing was included in the agreement.

No. 5. No boys in the girls' dorm and vice versa.

No. 6. No leaving campus at night or going into the city unescorted for any reason.

And . . . the other three I missed taking down and do not remember.

Reverend Vivian then thanked the college for sticking its neck out on our behalf, and cautioned us to be respectful of college property. He told us that the state was just looking for a chance to destroy Tougaloo, and the college had gone so far as to refuse some much-needed federal aid because accepting it would have necessitated changing their charter, which would have given Mississippi a chance to revoke the present charter. Tougaloo has long been a thorn in the side of the authorities of segregation and guardians of white supremacy.

The schedule for the rest of our stay included only two events, our court appearance tomorrow and, this evening, a mass meeting in the city of Jackson with the Negro community. The police had been very active in the planning of this meeting, and they had "arranged" that only Negroes and Freedom Riders would be allowed there, that we would come out in our chartered buses with police escort and return to the campus immediately; they had "decided" that there would be no standing room allowed in the hall, and other restrictions ostensibly for safety's sake.

I left the meeting before it was over, after my name had come up on the roll call. By the time I got back to the dorm it was raining, and by the time the meeting was over, it was pouring buckets. I decided to skip walking down for dinner, and instead took a leisurely shower (my third of the day) and tried without success to get dry in the hot, humid, oppressive Mississippi atmosphere. We all dressed for the mass meeting amidst a great deal of animated talk, and a running here and there to borrow what we had forgotten to bring. I saw Jean Kitwell and Rose Rosenberg, the two female attorneys from Los Angeles, and chatted with them about the meeting. They agreed that Kunstler seemed to be fully in control of CORE's side of our situation. Finally, the buses pulled up on the drive to take us to the mass meeting in Jackson, and we stood around on the porch deciding how best to reach them without getting soaked in the rain.

Chapter 12

EVENTS

Sunday, August 13, 1961, continued

The ride into Jackson was uneventful. It was dark and few people noticed our being sirened through all of the traffic lights by our escort of police cars. The Masonic Temple is located in the middle of downtown Jackson, on Lynch Street. When we entered, it was almost full, a sea of Negro faces (although I became aware later that there were some whites among them, even some Jackson whites, particularly from Temple Beth Israel, the Jewish congregation in Jackson). As we filed to the seats reserved for us, the people of Jackson stood up and cheered us. I felt very strange; I had never been the guest of honor at a large meeting before, and even sharing the limelight with almost two hundred others, it gave me a feeling of mixed humility and pride.

The opening invocation was given by a Freedom Rider who was a rabbi from San Francisco, Joseph Gumbiner, and I was at this point introduced to one of the strangest (to me) aspects of a southern Negro audience, their habit of responding aloud to sentiments with which they are pleased. As the rabbi repeated some of the most common and familiar (to me) phrases of Jewish ritual, I heard choruses of "That's right," "We believe," and "A-men!" At first I could not help feeling that this was impolite and inappropriate, but as it continued through the evening I began to get into the spirit too and to shed some of my northern reserve. The speeches, by Reverend C. T. Vivian, Jim Farmer, and various other leaders of the movement from all over the country, were excellent. Reverend Vivian ended his talk by pounding on the podium, saying, "We want freedom—freedom—freedom!," which the whole audience took up as a chant, to the accompaniment of hand claps and stamped feet.

But the hit of the evening (to me) was a Jackson woman by the name of Mrs. Clarie Collins Harvey, who spoke as one of five planned minor addresses complementing the main talk of the evening by Jim Farmer, national head of CORE. She had been instrumental in organizing the group of Negro women of Jackson to bring clothing and toilet articles to us girls when we were being kept in Hinds County Jail, for which we had all been so thankful. When the jailers would no longer allow such luxuries after we had been sent to Parchman, the women had arranged, at the time of our release, for the business of taking us to the hairdressers and allowing us to shower and be fed before we went off to travel to our respective homes. Mrs. Harvey reported in her remarks the establishment of the group on a permanent basis as Womanpower Unlimited. Their first project, she said, was to be education of Negroes for voter registration—and this time it was the Freedom Riders who stood up and applauded and cheered to express their great delight. Her group is also going to work on illiteracy among Negroes, and to try to get the one Negro bank in the city to become federally chartered.

Mrs. Harvey is intelligent and articulate, but the other speakers were also; she has done a lot for the Freedom Riders, but others may have done more. But to me, she represented the most exciting part of what I had come to Jackson to accomplish, the essence of the Civil Rights Movement, validating our northern participation in essentially a southern fight. She was the awakened, empowered Negro community personified, sparked by our Rides and by the knowledge that others elsewhere did care, given courage to speak out, to stand up as a member of an oppressed minority and demand her rights. I was so thrilled by her that her short speech, which was far from being the major one of the evening, became the highlight of the event for me, and all the rest of the program mere trimming.

When the meeting was over, the Freedom Riders drifted out again to the buses, still in pouring rain. We commented on the fact that so many people (the hall held about two thousand to twenty-five hundred, we estimated) had turned out in such weather—and then we found out that when Jean Kitwell had driven by at about the middle of the meeting, there were so many Negroes standing outside, on both sides of the street, that she thought that the meeting had already broken up.

The Jackson police, stationed in twos along the street near the buses, amused us greatly by telling everyone to "move on, move o-nnn." Some also said, "Get onto that bus, boy, or move on," "Y'all move o-nn now, y'hear, move on." When Johnnie Rogers came by, Captain Ray said to him, "Hey, boy, ain't you Johnnie Rogers?" "No, sir, that's my brother, I'm Don Rogers." And we all laughed and giggled.

By the time we were back on the campus, the rain had slowed to a drizzle and finally stopped, while everyone congregated in the lounge and on the porch of the girls' dormitory, discussing the mass meeting, singing and talking. At about midnight, Reverend Vivian came along and ordered all of the boys to return to their dorm, saying that the dean of the college insisted that the rules be observed, including lights-out at midnight. The boys tried to negotiate with him, saying that they felt that this was an unreasonable request, that we had barely gotten a chance to talk to our newfound and long-lost friends, and that since this was not a school situation there was no reason for making us go to bed early. Finally, the boys on the porch started saying that, under the principles of nonviolence and passive resistance, they intended to "stand in," and they did. A record player was produced; someone else brought over a guitar. Without benefit of refreshments, paper streamers, or party dresses, a good time was had by all. We sang all the freedom songs, and some of us danced little folk dances on the grass just as we had in Hinds County Jail, until we dropped exhausted on the porch to talk and joke and laugh. I finally went to bed at about 2:30 a.m., but many others seemed to be still going strong. It was a long, long day. I find it almost impossible to believe that we had arrived in Jackson only this morning.

Monday, August 14, 1961, morning

Johnnie Rogers becomes more of a phenomenon every time I talk to him. All of us spent the long, hot morning waiting until it was time to get dressed in our most respectable clothing for our court appearances in the afternoon. I had a chance to talk to John, with others, for a couple of hours. As I knew before, he is a boxer by profession. He loves the sport passionately; it is always for him one man against one man, the crowd ceasing to exist, until he has either won or been beaten. Then if he is victorious, he is suddenly the noble conquering hero and the crowd his worshiping subjects—they want to touch him, keep calling out his name. He is king of that night and that hour, and some of the doors usually closed to any Negro, of fancy restaurants and plush nightclubs, are opened in welcome. This is the life he loves and the dreams of his life are built of the fabric of these victories. Why then, I asked him, or rather how, did he ever get involved in a nonviolent movement like CORE? "Well," he said, "I've been fighting segregation all my life, and this movement has shown me a damn good way of doing it."

I asked him how he could find beating up some other poor guy in the ring consistent with being nonviolent in the hypothetical case of an angry mob. He told me rather sheepishly that he was more than a little afraid his newfound convictions were going to ruin his career. The last time he was in training, in Los Angeles just before we had to come back here to Jackson, he found that he was pulling his punches, and that he had a real aversion to trying to hurt the other boxer. "But," he went on, "this movement has given me a whole new lease on life. It's given me a purpose to live for and really given a new meaning to everything I do."

Since I had missed breakfast, I had an early lunch at the Grill. It was the first leisurely meal I have eaten since I left Los Angeles. I also got a chance to sit and talk with Pauline Knight, something I had long wanted to do. When she was our spokesman in Hinds and in Parchman, I was much intrigued by her as a person (though I never saw her, only heard her voice) and was very much annoyed at the fact that our segregation had created misunderstandings. Also in our booth were Jean Kitwell and Rose Rosenberg, the two female lawyers from Los Angeles. Both of them were less shy, although not any less curious, than I was, in asking about the thoughts and feelings of the southern Negro students. Pauline's reply (which I would have thought extremely affected if I had heard it in a Greenwich Village coffeehouse, but here knew that it was real and sincere) was that she always expressed herself best in poetry. She recited this composition of hers:

"The Way We Feel"
By: Pauline Edythe Knight
3/3/59

They are trying to stop us with a block,
But who can stop a "God seeking" Flock;
I say, "be frightened not," for our people have received a key;
And with it the doors of justice and misery we will unlock.
Our action grows not out of hate,
And though time seems near an end we don't feel
That we're too late;

There is no group using us for bait
For we are each masters of our fate;

Trouble and hardship in the air are blaring,
Yet with the tools of hope and faith, our
Way—we shall continue gently tearing
And in our hearts, minds, and on our face—
Love, peace, prosperity, faith, and good will is
What you'll see us wearing,
And with this who and what could prevent equal sharing.

To you who act with prejudice in your heart,
Sympathy and forgiveness is what we impart;
We've noticed you're fighting hard to convince
Us you're smart
But we're not worried because "God" upstairs
Is taking part.

I gratefully accepted her promise to send me the written copy of this poem, and told her that I would include it in my diary.

From Claude Liggins, a Negro guy who had been in Parchman, I heard that conditions got a lot worse after we left. He told me one really horrible story. One day Sgt. Tyson came down by the cells of the Negro males. He demanded that they stop singing or he would take their mattresses. They kept on singing. Tyson kept threatening. So they pulled the mattresses off their beds, saying, "Come and get them." So Tyson had his trusties take the mattresses. Then he ordered the Negro boys out to go into the "hole," the black, windowless, solitary cell, just six feet by six feet square, with only a grated window slot in the door for air. Some of them resisted, by hanging onto their cell bars, but Tyson's trusties finally dragged every one of them, more than twenty-three of them, and packed them all into the "hole." Tyson slammed the door and walked away. It was a hot Mississippi summer afternoon, and they were standing up against each other, in blackness, in the tiny solitary cell built for one person. The only air coming in was through the grate and a little under the door. They were sweating profusely. After a couple of hours, the heat from their bodies and lack of air made the cell really unbearable. Some of the younger boys were crying and some were close to cracking up with the strain, yelling, "Let us out, let us out!" About then Tyson came by and asked who wanted to be let out. He insisted that they had to come up to the grating, say "please," and *beg* to be let out. At first their spokesman refused to do it, but eventually the pressure of the rest of the group made him. Tyson then went away again—but finally came back to open the door and let them fall out. This incident completely broke their morale. No one is even so much as talking about protesting anything now.

Monday, August 14, 1961, afternoon

Finally, Monday afternoon, August 14, 1961: the great event, our appearance in court! We climbed into sticky nylons and our neatest hairdos and our most tidy clothes. The chartered buses were terribly hot and overcrowded, but we were all in high spirits as we rode through Jackson with our police escort. The prohibition against singing we observed, but no one had told us not to wave at passersby. We got back either surreptitious or open salutes from all of the Negroes we passed (depending on whether or not there were whites around). Most of the whites just grinned maliciously at us; a few scowled.

At the courthouse, we were greeted by our old friends, the Jackson police, and by a bevy of photographers taking stills and movies of our mass entrance into the hall of justice. The cool marble stairway was still familiar from the day less than a month ago when I signed my bond agreement in the office of the sheriff, in another section of the same building. As we passed through the foyer I saw a group of men watching us, among them Mr. Hutto, our old jailer. I waved, and he winked and smiled at me.

In the courtroom itself, we filled up all of the benches that had been designated for us, and then overflowed into the two benches customarily kept empty at the front. We were quiet and orderly. And integrated. There had been some talk yesterday about the possibility that the court would try to force us to sit in the courtroom according to southern custom, the Negroes either on one side or behind the whites, but no one attempted to separate us.

As we sat waiting for the proceedings to begin, I noticed that the two flags on either side of the judge's bench were of the United States and what looked like the old Confederate flag. Above the judge's bench, as part of the woodwork design, was a scale of justice—with one of the baskets tipped to one side. I was busy filling my notebook with such trivia when, without any fanfare, the attorneys for the prosecution filed in: six heavyset white men, among whom I recognized Mr. Travis, the interrogator at my original trial. After them came our lawyers, Mr. Young, Mr. Kunstler, Mr. Hall, and another Negro lawyer whom I did not recognize. Then came Judge Russell Moore, in his black robe, who entered so quietly, with no bailiff demanding the traditional "Order in the court, all stand," that we did not get a chance to rise in mock respect. Everyone said "shshhh," and an easy quiet settled over the room. On our left: the six prosecutors, plus about ten other people and a large case of files; in the center: the judge; on the right: our four defense attorneys; and on the far right: a full press box, including one man who was pointed out to me as being a foreign correspondent for an Italian newspaper. He had come to Jackson with the group from New York on their chartered bus.

The judge began the proceedings. "For the benefit of all of you, I am going to explain the rules of this court, and I want to see that y'all follow them. There will be no smoking while court is in session. There will be no pictures taken, and anyone whose camera was not taken by the guard at the door will please surrender it now. We will take a ten-minute break at the end of each hour of proceedings so that you can have a smoke and attend to any personal business." This seemed to me to be his stock set of instructions. I was surprised that there was not an injunction against applause or other demonstrations. Perhaps any such thing in the court was so unthinkable as to be, well, unthinkable.

The prosecutor stood up and introduced himself to the judge, and then introduced his five colleagues. Mr. Young introduced himself and did the same, introducing Mr. Kunstler as a "special counsel." After that, Kunstler did all of the talking for our side. The prosecutor then read a list of five names, of the Freedom Riders who had been in the first group arrested in Jackson. He instructed the five of them to sit on the front bench.

The first defendant is called before the judge's bench: Hank Thomas.

Mr. Travis: "Are you Henry James Thomas?"

"Yes, sir."

The man with the files (whom we all recognize as the nasty fingerprint man from the city jail) looks at one of his cards with front and profile pictures on it, turns it over, and nods.

The indictment is read by the prosecutor: ". . . did, on May 24th, 1961, at 1:00 p.m. in the afternoon, at the Trailways bus station . . . did congregate . . . the command, 'move on,' did refuse . . . arrested by Captain Ray of the Jackson police . . ."

The judge: "How do you plead?"

"Not guilty, sir."

Mr. Travis: "Your trial will be set for August 21 at 9:00 a.m."

Mr. Kunstler: "If it please Your Honor, may we ask that the date be set for August 22 instead, to accommodate one of the defense attorneys who must appear in another court?"

The judge: "Granted. August 22."

Mr. Travis: "That's all, you may return to your seat."

The names of the next two defendants are called—they file up to stand before the judge.

Mr. Travis: "Your Honor, we have agreed with the defense attorneys to dispense with the reading of the indictment for the remainder of these cases."

Mr. Kunstler: "With the understanding, Your Honor, that the indictment is identical in each case except for the dates, times, and places."

Mr. Travis: "Yes, yes, of course." He repeats the names, checks with the files man, gives the date and time of trial, and the two Freedom Riders return to their seats without having said a word.

After the first five, the rest of us were taken in alphabetical order by twos. This meant that once in a while an integrated couple stepped up before the bench of justice of the State of Mississippi, but neither the prosecutors nor the judge nor the audience deigned to take note of the fact. Someone did snicker, though, when the young Negro boy who was called up with Terry, my Parchman cell mate, politely guided her arm in mounting and descending the two stairs. The judge pointed at a perfectly silent young white boy in the second row and said sharply, "We will have order in this court!," and the bailiff came down from his station to stand over the innocent culprit repeating the order in a bellicose tone.

An hour's time took us through the M's, and then we broke for smokes and "personal affairs." So far, there had been only five people who did not answer when their names were called, including three people who we knew were in jail in New Orleans. As we had been told by Shirley Thompson and the other New Orleans people, any Freedom Rider loose in town there had suddenly, when it became known that they needed to return to Jackson or forfeit bail, become subject to arrest for "vagrancy." Louise Inghram was arrested twice, and I was told that the boys now still in jail had been eating dinner in the house of a Negro family when the police knocked at the door and arrested them for "resisting arrest," "vagrancy," and "aggravated battery."

During the recess I spoke with Mr. Kunstler about the fact that it looked as if my trial date would come at a most inconvenient date for me, that is, just about exactly in the middle of my first quarter law school exams. I wanted to know the possibility of having my trial moved either forward or backward. He assured me again that we would probably not have to come to Jackson for these trials (he was wrong), and also that he had been promised by Mr. Travis a chance to change the dates of anyone not able to appear on the date set. On the first point, I could not feel very confident, since Mr. Young had originally assured us that we would not have to appear for this arraignment and here we were. And on the second, I do not have any confidence in the good faith of the State of Mississippi to make things convenient for us.

My fears about my exams were well founded, for when we reconvened, Jorgia Siegel and I were called up together and both instructed to appear on Friday, December 15, exactly in the middle of final exams, she at 9:00 a.m. and I at 1:00 p.m.

When we had all been called, the bailiff called again the names of the nine Freedom Riders who had not appeared. Then Kunstler moved the court that the appearance of the three who were in jail in New Orleans be delayed until tomorrow morning, since, he said, they were just released and are on their way to Jackson. He asked that affidavits be accepted in lieu of the appearance of Janice Rogers, who is still sick in Los Angeles, and Alan Cason, Jr., who is in jail somewhere in Texas on a pretext similar to those with which the New Orleans group had been charged. The first motion was granted immediately, but the second motion was taken under advisement by the judge. All in all, there were only four Freedom Riders who either did not respond to CORE's request to return to Jackson or who could not be located: Mike Audain of Vancouver, B.C., Mary Magdalene Harrison, Eugene Levine, and one other. Out of a group of almost two hundred people, that is a fantastically low rate of attrition.

Our day in court was over. Our lawyers all remained to reconvene after a recess and begin the motions which will form the basis of our defense and appeals. The Freedom Riders were all dismissed to return to Tougaloo. Once again, and for the last time, our buses were escorted by the police through the streets of Jackson. At Tougaloo College, a meeting which had been scheduled never occurred, since the leaders of CORE and all of the lawyers were still in court in Jackson, and all of the Freedom Riders, the rest of us, were anxious to go our respective ways. We had a last meal in the Grill, and bid fond farewells to our friends and acquaintances.

Of the seven of us who had come from Los Angeles, I was the only one using the return portion of my round-trip bus ticket. Rita and Bob were off to a CORE Action Institute in Virginia, Jorgia and Johnnie to New York on the NY chartered bus, and Eddie and Marcie were taking the train. Some of the Berkeley people are going by bus, however, and so I rode into Jackson on the Coleman College chartered bus with Peggy Kerr and Duncan McConnell. We got off at the Trailways bus station (to the accompaniment of comments from some local taxi drivers like "Lookit, that's a nigger bus"). We entered the waiting room marked "WHITE INTRASTATE PASSENGERS." Fortunately, we were all three white, and so the police lounging in the waiting room did not find it necessary to tell us to "move on." We checked our luggage and I went to the ticket counter to request a time schedule. The clerk asked me if I wanted to buy some personal traveler's insurance. "Never can tell what will happen, riding them buses. Only fifty cents for insurance. Sure y'all don't want some insurance?" He smirked. I thanked him politely and said no, I did not feel the need of insurance. As we moved off toward the bus station coffee shop, he called after me again, "Only fifty cents—never can tell what might happen to y'all, riding them buses!"

Chapter 13

"COMES NOW THE DEFENDANT . . ."

August 15 to December 17, 1961
No Freedom Rider diary entries.

Monday, December 18, 1961
I called Tom Gaither, the CORE field secretary in Jackson, from a pay phone, as soon as I got off the plane and into the Jackson airport at 1:00 p.m. I knew full well that my plane was late and that I had missed my trial date at 9:00 a.m. that morning. (It was this same Tom Gaither, I was told, who had first proposed to James Farmer the idea of restarting the Freedom Rides in early 1961.)

"Well, well, welcome to Jackson, Mississippi!" Tom said. "I'm afraid I have some rather bad news for you," and the first-year law student in me thought, "I'll sue that airline, I will sue them!" Tom finished: "But we can talk about that when you get here. Take a cab, any one, and I'll see you soon."

In the cab, when I gave the white driver the address of the CORE office, I felt a sudden surge of hostility from him. This was the same experience which I remembered so well from Atlanta, Georgia, so many months ago. Then, when I was on my way down to Jackson for the first time, I was taken aback by the taxicab driver's reaction, and by comments like, "You know where you're going? You know that's in niggertown. . . ?" This time, I was let off without much comment at a tiny house on the business street of the Negro section of Jackson. A sign out front announced only that the office of the Something-or-other Heating and Ventilating Company was located there. After checking the number—1104 Lynch Street—I opened the flimsy door, its peeling paint matching the dislocated steps and ramshackle appearance of the whole place.

I entered a narrow, dark hall. As soon as my eyes adjusted to the dark I spotted a small sign beside a door saying, "CORE—Congress of Racial Equality." I knocked, and then entered a small, cheerful room, cluttered with kitchen chairs, an ancient filing cabinet, a desk, and about five young Negroes, one of whom was Tom. The walls were plastered with posters, newspaper clippings, the neat certificates of incarceration I recognized as souvenirs of Hinds County Jail, and the mattress-cover "samplers" the boys had sneaked out of the city jail, their fancy scroll work surrounding the awkwardly lettered names, sentences, and dates of release of their makers.

"Tom! Oh, I'm so glad to see you. I thought I'd never make it!"

"Glad you're here! Welcome to my favorite city." Tom introduced me to the other people, Helen O'Neil from Clarksdale, Mississippi, and a couple of boys from Jackson. But through these amenities my suspended anxiety kept increasing.

"Now, Tom, please—tell me what the situation is."

"Well, as you know, you missed your trial." He looked at his watch and I looked at mine; it was 1:10 p.m. My trial had been scheduled for 9:00 a.m. Originally my trial was scheduled for 1:00 p.m. on Friday, December 15, 1961, but had been switched to 9:00 a.m. today, December 18, because of my law school exam schedule.

"And with the weather so bad I could not be sure that you would get here any time today, or if so, what time. So we didn't schedule your trial for this afternoon."

"But the bond wasn't forfeited, was it? I mean, you did something about the fact that I didn't show up?"

"Oh, yes. The court gave you a continuance. Now the problem is that there are already two Freedom Rider trials scheduled for tomorrow, one in the morning and one in the afternoon. On Wednesday, the court is hearing civil cases all day. So you just may have to stay here until Thursday for your trial."

"Oh, no! No! They can't do that to me!"

"Now let me finish. There's a good chance you can be tried tomorrow morning, after the scheduled trial. I'm hoping to arrange it with the prosecutor, but he is out of town this afternoon. We'll just have to wait and see tomorrow morning."

I recovered slowly from the horrifying possibility that I would have to remain in Jackson for most of my short winter vacation from law school, while sitting with Tom and the others chatting about the current state of the Civil Rights Movement. I had been so completely involved in exams for my last three weeks in Chicago that I had only heard, and that vaguely, about the sit-ins in Albany, Georgia, where about five hundred people were arrested, and the Freedom Ride down the Baltimore highway outside of Washington, D.C.

There was real Civil Rights action and excitement in Jackson as well: a boycott of the downtown stores by the Negro community. The posters and handouts proclaimed in heavy black type: "NEGRO CITIZENS—Please Do Not Buy On Capitol Street—Until We Are Treated With Decency and Respect—REMEMBER! * Dogs! March 29, Oct. 16–31, 1961. * Police Brutality Against Negro Citizens. * Arrest of 13-year-old Negro Girl on City Bus. * Injustices in the Courts. * No Negroes Employed as Sales Clerks. * Many! Many! Many! Other Injustices.—Buy Somewhere Else—NOT DOWNTOWN—DON'T BE SECOND CLASS."

Helen, Tom's volunteer part-time secretary, told me that she had helped on an earlier boycott in Clarksdale, Mississippi, her hometown, and that it had been 90 percent effective. She said that they have hopes that this one in Jackson will be just as successful. It should impact the stores even more because December is when the sharecroppers get paid off for their year of work. Usually they come into Jackson to stock up on supplies and to replace worn-out things, as well as buying for Christmas. "But now," she said, "well, there's always mail ordering from Sears Roebuck."

A couple more boys crowded into the tiny office, very excitedly, with copies of Volume One, Number One, December 16, 1961, the *Mississippi Free Press*. They had been selling it on the street corners in the Negro section of town, and were boasting to each other about how many they had sold.

"Man, you been lying on yo' back all day. I sold a hundred and seventeen copies, just up the street."

"Yeah, but I sold fifty yesterday. I had a exam to study for, and, man, not even . . ."

"Well, man, how many you sell today?"

"Sixty-two."

Even Helen, as shy and retiring a girl as I had seen in the Movement, had been out selling on the street. I forked over my dime and duly received the four-page half-sheet. The lead story was about a Negro businessman who had just announced his candidacy for Congress in the Fourth Congressional District of Mississippi. Mr. R. L. T. Smith of Jackson, "so far as the *Free Press* can determine, will be the first Negro candidate from Mississippi for a major office in the 20th Century. . . ." Their enthusiasm was so infectious that I had to be dissuaded from playing paperboy too, by Tom's dour references to the Jackson police.

At about 2:30 Tom had to leave the office. I asked if there was a law library in town where I could do some work on a paper I had to write for my property course. He thought my request highly amusing, and informed me that the only law library in the city of Jackson is in the Hinds County Courthouse—one flight up from the room where our trials take place and two flights down from the jail where we had been incarcerated.

"Why, then," said I, "this y'here little old southern belle is jest a-gonna take herself daown to that ole county co-aut haouse, y'all jest unnerstand." Everyone in the office erupted into laughter, but Tom raised no objections and so I called a taxicab (this time from a Negro cab company). I asked if anyone else was going in the same direction. Tom just grinned and reminded me that it was bad enough that the cab driver was Negro.

It was with some trepidation, I must admit, that I walked into the Hinds County Courthouse and found the law library: a room about the size of a large living room lined on all sides with familiarly legal-looking sets of books and with a heavy oak table in the center of the room. The printing on the door gave the name of the circuit judge, and through a door on the other side of the room I saw a secretary busy at a desk. Wearing my most confident smile I walked up to her and said, "Excuse me, ma'am," with just the faintest trace of a southern drawl, "but would y'all mind if I used your law library this afternoon?"

"Why, no. Certainly, go right ahead."

"Thank you, ma'am."

And so I put my notebook on the table, pulled a copy of the *Mississippi Probate Code* off the shelf, and worked busily all afternoon. The crowning glory of my subterfuge came at about 4:30 p.m, when the judge was leaving for the day (his secretary had already departed without my noticing). Across the table the judge said to me, "I'm going now for the day, ma'am, but that's all right, you can stay right there. When you leave, you just close the door and turn out the lights."

"Why, thank you, Judge," I said. About half an hour later I gathered my things, carefully replaced the books I had been using, and closed up the Hinds County Law Library for the night.

Emerging from the marble coolness of the Hinds County Courthouse into the balmy late afternoon sunshine, I decided to walk the couple of miles from downtown Jackson to the CORE office on Lynch Street. This was the first walk I had ever taken in Jackson, and I reveled in my incognito freedom. I asked directions twice, once from a white man who looked at me very strangely when I inquired how to get to Lynch Street but who, with great courtesy, gave me elaborate (but incorrect) directions.

The second time I stopped a Negro matron, saying, "Excuse me, ma'am . . ." Her face, at that greeting, registered great surprise, and did so again when, after being told that I was approximately where I thought I should be, I finished by saying, "Thank you, ma'am." She stood still watching me until I turned a corner. And I recalled clearly the surprise, last summer, one of the Negro girls in our party felt when a white waitress in a Texas bus station addressed her with that "ma'am" which connotes only the most minimal courtesy—to anyone other than a Negro woman in the South.

Tom had arranged for me to stay with a Mrs. Noel, and so after he and I had dinner (in a Negro restaurant) he called a cab. When it came he said to me, "Wait a minute—I'll ask the driver. I think it should be all right for me to ride with you." After a rather long conference (it was now almost dark) he finally came back to the office, saying, "Come on, he says it'll be OK now."

Mrs. Noel lives in a small, neat white frame house on a residential street not far away. I stopped for a moment to look at some flowers which were in bloom in the front garden, but Tom said nervously, "Come on, you can't stay out here." He introduced me to Mrs. Noel, and then left, warning me to be in the courtroom at 9:00 the next morning.

Mrs. Noel is an ample, grandmotherly lady with Negro features and skin lighter in color than mine. I followed her through the old-fashioned living room, with a worn green velvet sofa and polished dark wood tables exuding comfort and warmth, across the formal lace-curtained dining room, to the back of the house where I was shown to a large, light bedroom with a huge four-poster bed, a dressing table, and a picture of the Virgin Mary on the wall. She lit the small open-flame gas heater, apologizing that she had not known when I would be coming and so had not put on the heat beforehand.

"Poor thing, you look plain tired out," she said, giving me a towel and showing me the bathroom. She was right! It had been a long day.

But by the time I finished my bath, a heavenly odor of baking had permeated the house. I wandered into the big, old-fashioned kitchen "just to say goodnight." By the time I had finished a slice of delicious fruitcake and a glass of milk, I had been coaxed into telling my favorite jail anecdotes and been informed in turn about the current state of the nonstudent Civil Rights Movement in Jackson. Mrs. Noel was shelling a huge bowl of pecans which had come from the tree in the front yard, carefully separating the shells from the meat and the whole from the broken nuts. The big, heavy, round table was half covered with potted plants and cooling fruitcakes.

Mrs. Noel told me how her own children had all left Jackson and vowed never to return: they were constantly trying to get her to move north. "But," she said, "Pappy and me, we built this house ourselves, for us to live here and for them to be born in. He's dead now, but I get along. And I reckon I'll stay." In her soft drawl, she told me how her husband and she had come to Jackson when they were about to have their first child because, she said, "we wanted to give the kids a chance.

"We done the best we could—never saved no money, but we managed to see the kids to college. We thought the best thing we could do was to move to Jackson. Seems sort of funny, now, that they don't never want to come back here."

Tuesday, December 19, 1961

I woke with a start. Late? No, no, only 7:00, plenty of time to get to court by 9:00 a.m. Wash, dress, court-appropriate outfit, mustn't be late. Collect my things—only 7:30 now, I should do some work on my law school course, some reading for that paper. No, real property conveyances couldn't possibly hold my attention this morning.

Mrs. Noel insisted on making breakfast for me although (much as I would have denied it) my stomach was feeling fluttery. At 8:15 I was done, and after fidgeting for ten minutes, sitting in a big comfortable chair in the living room and watching Mrs. Noel rock placidly back and forth as she read the morning paper, I decided I would be better off calming my nerves by walking to the court.

In fifteen minutes I was again at the Hinds County Courthouse. When I got up to the second floor I looked around for Tom but he was not there yet (it was only ten of nine). Sitting on the benches in the hall outside the courtroom were a large number of casually dressed white men. Even though I was a little tired by my walk, I went right by them and over to the window by the elevator. I stood there waiting for something to happen. The men kept staring at me. Finally Tom arrived, accompanied by Leon Smith, the Negro boy whose trial was already scheduled for that morning. We greeted each other warmly, shook hands, and then walked between the two benches of white men and into the courtroom. I sat down in the front row of the spectators' gallery and waited for Tom and Leon to do the same, but they continued instead to the other side of the room and sat down on one of the back benches. So I picked myself up and walked over to them. There was no one else in the room. "What's the matter," I said to Tom, "have I got bad breath or something?"

He laughed and answered, "No. It's just better this way."

"Why?" I asked with vehemence.

"Because if the judge comes in and sees us all sitting together, and if he is in a bad mood—well, he might just cite me up for contempt of court. Then he slaps on a fine and it's pay up or go to jail."

"You're kidding."

"Don't you wish it."

I went quietly back to my seat on the other side of the courtroom and sat down.

At exactly 9:00 a.m. the room began to be busy with all sorts of people. Mr. Brown, the lawyer who will represent both Leon and me, is one of only five Negroes who have been admitted to the bar in the state of Mississippi; he seemed prosperous and self-confident. The same prosecutor as at my first trial, Jack Travis, is a huge man with a red face who looks to me more like the stereotype of a bartender than an attorney. The stenographer took her place with a great deal of bustling efficiency. The men who had been sitting outside were called in. They sat down on the benches behind me. Then in came the famous Captain Ray, who had arrested more than three hundred Freedom Riders in the course of the last summer. He struck me as looking more like a distinguished professor or doctor than a cop. His neat crew cut seems very prematurely gray on his tall, athletic form. In the midst of all this activity, the judge in whose library I had spent yesterday afternoon walked into the courtroom from the judge's chambers. "Oh, no," I thought, as he came up to me with a big smile.

"Well, young lady," he said, "are you going to see a real live trial this morning?"

And in my best New England accent I answered, "No, sir. I'm the defendant."

"Well," he said, as he quite literally took a step back, "I wish you luck." And he turned and went out of the courtroom.

The clerk of the court called the names of the jury. Twelve of the perhaps thirty white men from the benches filed in to the jury box and sat down. Then Judge Russell Moore entered. He had presided over the arraignment in August. At that time, I seem to remember, Judge Moore entered in imposing black robes. This time he came in inconspicuously, in street clothes, with a lit pipe clenched in his mouth. He knocked out the ashes and nodded to the clerk. Leon and Mr. Brown had moved to one of the tables inside the railing of the courtroom.

Tom got up at this point and started walking out. As he passed me he whispered, "Everything's OK. You go on after Leon; the prosecutor said it would be all right. And I'll be back in about an hour."

So I settled back to enjoy the spectacle. With my notebook on my lap, I amused myself writing comments about the trial, Mississippi justice, the judge, the all-male jury, and the like. I was scribbling busily—I had just written, "Engraved three inches high on the front of the judge's desk, cut deep into the wood and shining with bright gold, the letters J-U-S-T-I-C-E stare out at me across this Mississippi courtroom . . ."—when the bailiff came up to me. In a belligerent tone he whispered, "The judge wants to know if you're writing in shorthand." I assured him I was not, although I did not offer to show him what I had written. He went back and whispered to Judge Moore.

Leon never took the stand (nor would I), since the strategy of our defense is to have the trials as identical as possible. This will help preclude hitches in the anticipated mass reversal of our convictions after the first cases are reversed (we hope) by the U.S. Supreme Court. Captain Ray offered the only testimony.

Finally, the jury filed out to "deliberate" in Leon's case. They were soon back, and Leon Smith was found "guilty as charged." A few more formalities, and—now my case.

During the ten-minute recess between Leon's case and mine, I moved my notebook and purse up to the table in front of Judge Moore's bench and chatted for a few minutes with my lawyer. He was rather amused to find that I was a law student, female law students and lawyers being only a little less scarce than Negro law students and lawyers. Then, and somewhat to my discomfort, when Judge Moore walked past our table, Mr. Brown told him that I was a law student and a "future lawyer." Judge Moore smiled (the first time I had seen him do so), and said, "Well, well. Perhaps you'll be a lawyer in time to argue your own case before the Supreme Court."

"I hope so," said I, and we exchanged a few pleasantries about law schools.

A fresh jury was called and, to my astonishment, there was a Negro among the men. I registered my surprise with Mr. Brown, and he nodded, saying, "They'll excuse him, of course. They always do. Negroes, Jews, Catholics, Orientals—they always get excused."

"Always? Or just for our cases?"

"Well, if it's a case of a Negro against a Negro, they sometimes let a Negro sit on the jury. In the Civil Rights cases, they strike off anyone who might be even the slightest bit 'uncommitted.' Nobody ever sits on the jury who isn't a Baptist or Methodist."

By this time the jury was all seated. The lone Negro—a very tall, very black man wearing a rather uncomfortable grin—was in the middle of the back row. Judge Moore then addressed the jury (as he had in Leon's case): "Gentlemen, this is a case of the State of Mississippi versus Carol Ruth Silver. Do any of you have any knowledge of the defendant or of the case?" Each juror shook his head negatively. "Mr. Travis, you may proceed."

The prosecutor picked up his long yellow legal pad and went up to the front of the jury box. "Gentlemen, the State of Mississippi is going to prove . . . (and he went through and described the "crime" and the evidence which he would present). Do all of you understand that?" Positive nods from the jurors, including from the Negro juror. Travis listed the three elements of his case.

All the while I corrected and augmented the notes I had taken at Leon's trial. The argument was, of course, identical, although the factual circumstances had been somewhat different.

Mr. Travis asked if each of the jurors was sure he could be impartial and fair. Again positive nods, some vigorous. Mr. Travis then asked each juror to state his full name, which he wrote down. With the list he walked over to the judge's desk and conferred briefly with Judge Moore, referring to the pad.

"Chris Harris is excused," said the judge, and the tall Negro man rose self-consciously and left the jury box. "You are excused until Thursday at nine, Chris," the judge continued, and I fumed in silence at the discourtesy of the judge's failure to address him as "mister," as every other juror had been. We waited while another man was called from the group of white men still sitting in the visitors' gallery.

I whispered to Mr. Brown, "Why does he have to come back Thursday? That's another Freedom Rider trial, isn't it?"

"Yes, of course. But they are playing it cool, doing everything strictly by the rules. They'll just keep excusing him. He's on the voting register, so they have to call him as a juror. They don't get too many that way, you know."

And, I noted angrily to myself, it is a form of intimidation to prevent Negroes from registering to vote, if they must give up a day or days of work to show up for jury duty, only to be insulted by being excused for being Negro.

When the new juror was seated, the prosecutor went briefly through the same speech for him alone, finally announcing, "Your Honor, we accept this jury."

Now Mr. Brown picked up *his* long yellow legal pad and walked up to the jury box. "Gentlemen, you have heard Mr. Travis. But you must also be ready to bring in a verdict of innocent if the state fails to prove its case beyond a reasonable doubt. Now do each of you understand that?" A few nods. "Is there any one of you who believes he could not give the defendant a fair trial because of her race?" Brown pointed to each of the jurors in turn with the corner of his legal pad, receiving a few more nods. "Or because of the race of her lawyer?" All but two give very slight nods; the two sit unblinkingly still even as he points to each juror one by one. A few more questions then, with a slight shrug, he turns to the judge: "We accept this jury, Your Honor."

A Lieutenant Wilson was the prosecution's witness this time, since it was he who arrested my group (the ubiquitous Captain Ray had been busy at the airport that afternoon arresting visiting dignitaries, New York Assemblyman Mark Lane and Manhattan Borough President Percy Sutton). Wilson is not as smooth as Captain Ray, and fumbles more for words. But as with Ray, Travis leans heavily on the witness's many years of experience on the Jackson police force. "Now please tell the jury, Lt. Wilson, whether in your judgment, the situation at the Trailways bus station, in the east waiting room, was such that the defendant's refusal to obey the order to 'move on' created a situation which in your judgment might have been about to lead to a breach of the peace. Please tell the jury in your own words, Lt. Wilson." And Lt. Wilson told the jury, more or less parroting the exact words of the prosecutor.

Now it was Mr. Brown's turn to cross-examine the prosecution witness, Lt. Wilson. Mr. Brown, in his line of questioning, tried to show that the defendant (me) had not been the cause of whatever situation had existed at the time of her arrest, even if there was the danger of an imminent breach of the peace, and that if such a situation had actually existed the proper procedure for police would have been to give the order "move on" to whoever was actually about to breach the peace. Lt. Wilson stuck to his position, that it was me, the defendant, who was the "cause" of the disturbance, and not the crowd who, in his judgment, might possibly be about to attack the defendant and her party if the defendant did not obey the order to "move on." Twice, Mr. Travis objected to a line of questioning on the grounds that it was repetitive. The judge overruled the objection and allowed the questioning by Mr. Brown to continue.

Then Mr. Brown got to the race questions. In Leon Smith's trial, Mr. Brown, as the defense attorney, asked three questions involving race. After each question, Mr. Travis had said, "I object, Your Honor. This is not a race issue." "Objection sustained," ruled the judge, and Mr. Brown moved on to the next question. He had explained to me that the point of these questions and objections was to put into the record the fact that the State denied race was a factor in our arrests. This issue could then be raised on appeal, with the defense laying out what it would have shown if it had been allowed to ask the question.

Mr. Brown asked the first of his three standard questions in my case: "Officer, were the waiting rooms at the Trailways bus terminal designated as to race?"

He paused expectantly. The witness paused. The judge was not listening. And neither was the prosecutor—he was busy reading my prison record, his whole head moving from side to side of the page. "Uh, uh, yes," said the witness, "I mean. . . ." The stenographer cleared her throat loudly.

Mr. Brown, with a disgusted look, put his hands on his hips and said, "Hey, Jack—don't y'all want to object?"

Travis: "Oh, yeah, yes. I object, Your Honor. I object. . . . This is not a race case."

"Objection sustained."

"Your Honor," said the stenographer, "I'll eliminate the witness's answer from the record."

"Yes, of course. Thank you. Counsel, you may proceed."

The remainder of the questioning went along smoothly. When Mr. Brown was finished, he came over and sat down next to me. Mr. Travis summed up for the prosecution, then Mr. Brown summed up for the defense. Then Mr. Travis got one last shot in rebuttal, addressing the all-white, all-male Mississippi jury: "There are three links to the chain of law enforcement, gentlemen. The police, the prosecution, and you. The police have done their job. The prosecution has done its job. We have proved the guilt of this defendant beyond a reasonable doubt. It is your responsibility to bring in a verdict of guilty."

And finally, the presentation of the instructions to the jury. The instructions were so standard that they had been prepared on mimeographed sheets, respectively by the defense and by the prosecution, approved by the judge by the application of a special red stamp. They were now read to the jury by the two attorneys. The State's jury instructions consisted of two, one of procedure (on the exact form of words in which to return a verdict of guilty) and only one of substance (Mr. Brown gave me a blank one from his supply):

"The Court instructs the Jury for the State of Mississippi that if you believe from the evidence beyond a reasonable doubt that the defendant, ______________________________, did, on the date charged in the affidavit, willfully and unlawfully congregate with other persons in a place of business engaged in selling or serving members of the public under circumstances such that a breach of the peace may have been occasioned thereby, and if you further believe from the evidence beyond a reasonable doubt that the defendant, ____________________________, after having congregated with others, under such circumstances, did willfully and unlawfully fail or refuse to disperse and move on, when ordered so to do by a law enforcement officer of the City of Jackson, Mississippi, then you should find the defendant guilty."

The instructions approved by the court for the defense were about ten in number, among them:

"The Court instructs the jury for the defendant that if you find that the arresting police officer arrested defendant in order to preserve separation or segregation of the White and Negro races in the Trailways Bus Station then you cannot find the defendant guilty."

And then:

"The Court instructs the jury for the defendant that if you find that the defendant committed no act other than the refusal to remove himself when ordered by the arresting police officer from the location where his arrest took place, then you cannot find the defendant guilty."

After the jury had marched out to deliberate, I mentioned to Mr. Brown my surprise at the approval of such clear instructions to the jury in favor of the defendant. But he just smiled and shrugged. And I remembered one of my law school lectures on the overimportance usually given to jury instructions by the plaintiff's attorney, the judge, and the defendant's attorney—everybody, that is, except the jury.

Mr. Brown was busy filling out some additional sets of mimeographed sheets, and when he was done he showed them to me. They were two motions which would be the basis of the appeal of my case. One was "Motion for a New Trial," and I had a sinking feeling of horror about the possibility (however remote) that it might be granted. The other was

"Motion for a Directed Verdict," which began, "Comes now the defendant and moves this honorable court to exclude the state's evidence and direct the jury to bring in a verdict of acquittal on the following grounds: (a) The state has failed to prove the offense charged in the affidavit, (b) To convict this defendant on such a record barren of evidence of guilt would deny to him rights secured by the due process clause of the Fourteenth Amendment to the United States Constitution . . ."

After exactly eight minutes of "deliberation" the jury returned to the court. The bailiff received from one of them a sheet of paper, which he showed to Judge Moore and then read to the court. "We the jury find the defendant guilty as charged."

And that, so far as I was concerned, was the end of the matter. I sat back in my chair and smiled prettily at all of the jurors. But that was not quite the end, for Mr. Brown leaned over and whispered, "Say, you have to be sentenced. They found you guilty. Go on up to the judge."

When I was standing in front of him, the judge leaned over his bench and, speaking in a conversational tone, said to me, "You are guilty as charged. I hereby sentence you to four months in jail and a two-hundred-dollar fine." I must have looked distressed, for he smiled, and said, "I take it you want to appeal."

"Yes, sir," I said, and returned the smile. I could hardly keep from laughing, both from a release of tension, that the whole affair was done with—and from the farcical nature of the proceedings. Mr. Brown handed over the forms for the appeal of my conviction, the ones he had been filling out during the jury's brief deliberation, and a certified check for a thousand dollars (provided by the NAACP through a loan to CORE). For about fifteen minutes, until my appeal bond was registered and various papers filed, I was technically a convict, a prisoner of the State of Mississippi. (Note: this conviction was reversed in 1965 by the U.S. Supreme Court, *Thomas v. Mississippi*, 380 U.S. 524.)

I thanked Mr. Brown and shook his hand firmly. And then I was free to go.

AFTERWORD

—Cherie A. Gaines—

I was both flattered and honored when Carol Ruth Silver asked me to prepare an afterword for the diary of her experiences as an arrested, prosecuted, and then imprisoned Freedom Rider. I felt honored because Carol Ruth is an extraordinary person who has "kept the faith" and sought to correct injustices well beyond the years this book encompasses. Her asking anything of me was and is an honor.

I felt flattered because Carol Ruth is such an extraordinary person, and it is nice to think she values me almost as much as I value her. But realistically I understood that Carol Ruth wanted to have someone give you, the reader, a bit of perspective about the atmosphere of the years involved in her diary. She wanted to call upon someone who would tell it like it was—and indeed that is me.

Following in the tradition Carol Ruth established for her diary by giving you her autobiography to help you understand and evaluate the perspective and possible biases from which she wrote, I will introduce myself and give you the same opportunity to evaluate my vision.

My name is Cherie A. Gaines. I am an attorney, now retired. I am a light-skinned black American. I am using "black" herein because it has become an acceptable term and because it is the equivalent of "white," which has always been acceptable. I note, however, that in the days relevant to this diary, "Negro" was the proper and the polite term for me and mine.

My father was proud of his heritage as a respected descendant of the freed slave who settled in Marquette, Michigan, before the American Civil War. He found less respect once he left Marquette. My mother was a properly intimidated black woman from Lexington, Kentucky. She was treated kindly in New York by the Quaker and Jewish families for whom she worked as a maid but she never overcame her ingrained fear and awe of "white folks" and warned me that you can never trust them when the chips are down. Actually they both gave me that warning.

I grew up in a black slum, Bedford Stuyvesant, in Brooklyn, New York, during the 1930s and '40s. Nobody trusted white folks and particularly not white policemen—which, of course, was the only variety available. One slogan was: If you're white, all right, if you're black, step back. In fact, my community felt amazement and gratitude when President Lyndon Baines Johnson did not bomb Detroit during the black riots there—that is just how deep was our distrust.

Because I was light-skinned, my neighbors, schoolmates, and others believed I had an unfair advantage which helped me get along with "white folks." This attitude often alienated me from them. But, of course, they were right.

Over all of the years of my life many white people have assumed I was one of them and treated me accordingly, i.e., better than they treated the brown-skinned person next to me. They were relaxed and comfortable in my presence—which is to tell you I could clearly see they were less comfortable with obviously black people. In fact white people often said bigoted things in front of me because they forgot I was one of those they were slurring. "Oh, but you're different. You're not like the others," etc., were expressions I heard when I chose to push the point. These issues have never gone completely away. As recently as the 1980s a white "colleague" asserted I had no right to the views I had expressed because the Jew sitting next to me was darker than I was. Others at the meeting were relieved when I laughed out loud and conceded he was right because I wore all over my skin the mark of my family's years on the plantation (and the masters' standard operating procedure rapes of their female slaves).

I resisted the subtle psychological and often direct pressures of white America to "pass" and get the advantages of being "white." I remained "black" despite an appearance which confused so many white (but rarely black) Americans, because my father had taught me to be proud of my black heritage. My father, not the public schools of my day, taught me about Crispus Attucks, the first man shot by the British in the Boston Massacre which kicked off the American Revolution, and other black heroes.

The point is that, due to my skin color and the American tradition that one drop of black blood made you black (a standard which helped preserve and multiply slave property on the plantations), I grew up on the cusp between the two dominant cultures of my era. In fact I learned to recognize flaws in each, but my greatest hostility was to the hypocrisy of the white folks.

I grew up when lynchings took place regularly in Mississippi and nobody white cared after the newspapers were sold. I grew up in a neighborhood where one dodged the cops because they brained you with nightsticks whenever they could and you were better off handling the gangs by yourself. Short, puny, and female, I learned to protect myself with street smarts, a loud mouth, and quick rhetoric.

I grew up coached to be aware of the hypocrisy of the American dream—the so-called ideals "they" lie about and never mean to be real for you (me). I grew up knowing I would have to fight every inch of the way to preserve personal self-respect despite a culture and people who would put me down whenever it or they could. Carol Ruth has expressed surprise that I did not grow up hating "whitey." That answer is simple: I was reared in the black church—the church which provided the moral basis and led the Civil Rights Movement. I was ingrained with the "hate the sin not the sinner" tradition. This is an energy I have not found to exist to the same extent in white congregations.

I grew up trained to distrust the white systems—which I admit I sought to change from within as a lawyer—and fully convinced that survival in white-dominated America required great discretion about when, where, and how you asserted yourself. Because I wanted to emerge alive I did not go south.

I grew up where white Freedom Riders were considered naive daydreaming fools who didn't know what they were getting into, and black Freedom Riders were considered Negroes seeking martyrdom.

I did not go south. I did fight against segregation but not on the Freedom Rides. OK, I did do some restaurant testing in New York City. Yes, I sued to get an apartment in Berkeley, California, and yes, I was the first OEO-funded "poverty lawyer" west of the Mississippi. Yes, I fought a few significant legal battles in Oakland, California. But I never put my body on the line. That required a courage and a faith in American ideals which I did not have.

Carol Ruth had the advantage of a single vision of the world as it should be and of her duty regarding it. She had, and she has kept, the faith. I am proud of the manner in which she used her vision. I admire her and I admire those who joined her. But I saw the world differently. I did not believe in any of the ideals Americans espoused before the Civil Rights Movement.

And now we get to the main event:

DID THE FREEDOM RIDERS MAKE A DIFFERENCE?

YES!! THEY DID!!!

The Freedom Riders shattered white America's rationalization that legally enforced segregation was simply a quaint regional custom.

The Freedom Rides, the sit-ins, the march on Selma, the black and white deaths which did occur during the Civil Rights Movement demonstrated to white America that the self-deception, the denials and hypocrisy of the past, could no longer survive. White America did not really care what had been happening to black America but it had to face what was then happening to its own youth: young white victims who were putting their bodies on the line, risking and sometimes losing their lives and their futures, in order to correct injustices that those idealistic white youths recognized were contrary to everything America claimed to be about. White America could not ignore what was happening to its own.

Black Americans bore the brunt of the challenges, most of them. They suffered bombs at their homes and their churches. They lost children in Sunday school. They, black people, young and old, paid dearly, as sheriffs and others took special pains to "enforce the law" quite forcefully. Black people—idealistic "Negroes," not the cynical ones like me—were the bulk of the heroes. They provided the majority of the bodies. They provided the religious base which set and maintained the moral tone (a moral tone Carol Ruth's diary acknowledges had an impact on her) for change. Black people's unrelenting rejection of the status quo, their willingness to continue the struggle despite bombings, murders of their children at church, etc., their determination—signaled that the days of rationalization had to end.

But white Americans had ignored what was happening to black Americans for two hundred years. The presence of idealistic young white Americans like Carol Ruth Silver, together with white clergy, finally awakened to the moral issues involved—those were the presences which made the difference.

Carol Ruth Silver, and those who joined her putting their lives on the line on Freedom Rides, going to jail, risking their futures, making the point that America had to be the same for everybody, young white people who became murder victims for registering black voters, conscience-stricken white religious leaders, ministers marching with their black colleagues, risking broken heads and bodies—these were people white America did care about. They made the difference for the great majority of Americans—the white Americans.

These were the people white America could not ignore. The white Americans who for so many years had simply looked the other way and pretended that no real problems existed—white people who actually said, "After all, it's their fault if they don't take advantage of the American dream" and "They're just lazy/dumb . . ."—those white people could no longer deny and ignore what was happening to their own peaceful young people who were provoking nobody, just putting their lives on the line for equal treatment of everyone. White Freedom Riders, and those who joined them in confronting the South, were the people who forced the white majority in America to acknowledge the reality of the black experience and to accept the need for change.

Specific changes can be noted in many different areas. I will list only those changes of which I have personal experience and knowledge, and since I was in the West we know that even more dramatic changes occurred in the South and elsewhere in our country. Formal historians can provide details for those readers who wish to look them up. This is a list of just a few which stand out in my mind.

Before confrontations like the Freedom Rides forced white Americans to open their eyes to the reality of my community, in the minds of most white Americans significant numbers of blacks simply did not exist. It is impossible to communicate how lily white America's image of itself was. "The melting pot" meant all "immigrants" (and to this day white Americans forget some of us were imports who did not come voluntarily) were expected to become indistinguishable from the dominant white Anglo-Saxon Protestants, otherwise known as WASPS. Therein was a kernel of the anti-Catholic bias, the anti-Jewish bias, and several other attitudes. "Tolerance" was the byword for coexistence with the non-WASPS—"tolerance," not "acceptance." But in fairness white America considered tolerating the difference the proper form of acceptance. That is why the plight of black America was ignored so long.

Modern viewers can not begin to imagine how lily white television was before the Civil Rights uproars. It wasn't just *Father Knows Best*—it was as if all America was lily white and WASP. Period. The same was true of movies and other media of those days. You could count the blacks on the fingers of one hand. True, an exceptional "Negro" might appear on rare occasions on Ed Sullivan's popular variety show. But TV programming was nothing like the present, which depicts people working together in mixed teams: black and white, yellow, red and brown, male and female, good characters and bad.

The Freedom Rides, other parts of the Civil Rights Movement, and a president who did not bomb Detroit caused legislative changes which benefit all Americans to this day—even as some people do try to undo a few of them. The women's movement, for example, owes some of its progress to the recognitions America now acknowledges because of the Freedom Rides and the entire Civil Rights Movement. The War on Poverty, which is where I met Carol Ruth, was an effort to bring about true equality of opportunity as a result of the new awareness which arose from the Freedom Rides and the Civil Rights Movement. That particular effort did achieve some changes in the economic conditions which had helped trap in poverty the black community of my youth. So there have been some concrete and positive accomplishments to which I pray we will hold on.

However, the biggest and most important "change" was spiritual—for all Americans.

Many white people ceased their self-deception and began to acknowledge truths about a few flaws in our country, and many blacks began to believe there might be hope of access to the American dream for them. Other "minorities" dared to come forward and speak up for recognition of their heritages and access to the American dream. Today even a black child can aspire to become president of the United States. We have had the first. What a profound change that was!

Other specific changes:

In the years 1958–1960 I was the only black student in my law school at the University of Pennsylvania in Philadelphia. There is a now a Black Student Association there and a program honoring the school's first black woman graduate, Sadie Pace Alexander. In one of those years there were only two black law school students at Boalt Hall in Berkeley, California. When my daughter attended that law school twenty years after the Civil Rights Movement that number had also changed.

In fact during 1970–1973 five colleges and Golden Gate Law School in San Francisco came together to develop and implement a curriculum designed to help minority (primarily black and Latino) college students qualify for and succeed in law school. Nobody sought to create lawyers from minority groups before the Freedom Rides and Civil Rights Movement. (The program did succeed with as much as 40 percentile improvements in LSAT scores.)

When I began practicing law in the San Francisco Bay Area of California in 1961, a black woman entering the courtroom—regardless of how she was dressed—was presumed to be a prostitute and ordered to go into that group to await arraignment. Believe me, that had changed by 1965. We black women attorneys (few as we were in those days) were vocal, and national events like the Freedom Rides helped speak up for us.

Before the Freedom Rides, the sit-ins, etc., a white licensed realtor, Arlene Slaughter, in Oakland, California, had to sue to get standard multiple listings of houses for sale delivered to her office, because she dared to show properties in white neighborhoods to black clients. When she died in 1980 over seven hundred people, including the very people who had opposed her initial efforts, attended the memorial service to honor her many contributions to interracial relations in that community.

In 1960 when I arrived in the San Francisco Bay Area, apartments available to me during the day were unavailable when I returned with my brown-skinned husband after he got home from work. The experience was so consistent we started looking only in the evenings when we could go together. Finally we sued over a unit we especially wanted. The white professor who taught the case to my daughter's law school class twenty-four years later called it an example of a "test" case which had changed the law. When my daughter tried to tell him at the end of the class session that her parents had really just wanted that apartment, he dismissed the idea, telling her "it teaches better this way." Clearly he preferred to keep racial discrimination abstract rather than acknowledge it is a reality which hurts actual human beings. So there are throwbacks to the pre–Freedom Rides mentality but at least the law was changed, and that legal victory came about in part because of the climate Freedom Riders had created by the time our case went up on appeal.

In the 1940s and '50s I was asked to stay away from the YWCA summer program in Queens, New York, on Tuesdays because that was the day they used a swimming pool which did not admit blacks. In those years I was allowed in the "white" YWCA in Detroit only because I was traveling with a white member of the YWCA national board. And in around 1953 I was allowed to stay in the whites-only YWCA in Washington, D.C., because I was traveling with a group of girls from my college—of course, I was the only nonwhite among them.

In the late 1960s my children, a nanny, and I dined in the elegant Skylight Dining Room of a Washington, D.C., hotel overlooking the White House. We were recognized as a black family. We were welcomed by the all-black serving staff and accepted by the other (all-white) diners. So simple. So ordinary. But a direct change which resulted from Freedom Ride–induced legislation.

In 1969–1970 even President Richard Nixon had to deal with residual segregation. He decided to make his move regarding the construction trade unions by calling for local communities to work out "Home Town Plans" to integrate the unionized construction trades in their areas. Black and brown (mostly Mexican) men in Oakland used a black woman attorney to represent them. Before the Freedom Rides that assortment would never have come together. (We negotiated a "Home Town Plan" with "goals" for the various trades and an arbitration clause (!) so we could locally enforce things with or without federal intervention.)

Today there are black elected officials all over America—even black sheriffs, FBI agents, state legislators and governors, congressmen and other national officials, including our president—not to mention the black appointed people of recent years such as Colin Powell and Condoleezza Rice. Every one of these people represents a change from the pre–Freedom Rides era.

The Freedom Rides impacted the "soul" of America. If the American dream of equal opportunity for one's future lives on, it is because of the Carol Ruth Silvers, who believed the dream could become real and who risked their lives here at home to make it true. Read her diary with that thought in mind.

CLAUDE ALBERT LIGGINS, FREEDOM RIDER

From Lake Charles to Los Angeles to Jackson, Mississippi

Claude Albert Liggins was born in Lake Charles, Louisiana, to parents Theo Liggins and Earlie Vee Thomas, and he grew up there.

Claude remembers that his mother had very strong feelings about the racial injustices experienced by black people in Lake Charles. Also, his third-grade schoolteacher, Mrs. Carether Pork-Roy, and his eighth-grade teacher, Miss Rupert Florence Richardson (who later became a member of the national board of the NAACP), taught him to be proud of himself and to be proud of the great black men and women who worked to advance the race.

One of his first lessons about segregation occurred when he was about six years old. His grandmother, Ora Thomas, took him with her to a doctor's appointment in downtown Lake Charles. While sitting in the doctor's office he told his grandmother that he was hungry. She gave him "two bits" (a twenty-five-cent coin) and told him to go get himself a candy bar that cost a nickel.

Instead of buying a candy bar, Claude decided he wanted a hamburger, which cost twenty-five cents. He walked into a café in the building where the doctor's office was and sat down on one of the empty counter stools. The white man behind the counter accepted his order, took his two bits, and proceeded to cook the hamburger. Another white man walked in and saw this little black boy sitting at the counter.

He asked the man who was cooking the hamburger what this boy was doing sitting there. The cook told him that he was waiting for his

Claude Albert Liggins. Courtesy of Skirball Cultural Center | Photo by Peter Turman.

hamburger. The second man told the cook that Claude had no business sitting there. The cook told Claude to get up and stand by the wall.

Claude knew that something was wrong. There he was standing next to the wall, neatly dressed in his green britches, feeling humiliated and hurt. He wanted to leave but didn't because he had paid for his hamburger.

He did not realize it at the time but this was his first sit-in, and it is what later inspired him to become a Freedom Rider and to be active in the Civil Rights Movement.

Claude attended Second Ward Colored School. As a young boy in the second grade he loved to pick up a neighbor's newspaper so he could see the pictures of the Korean War soldiers. He wanted to be a soldier. Later he joined an all black troop of the Boy Scouts and proudly wore the uniform in parades and at other special events.

He always had an interest in current events, civics, and history. He loved going to the Palace Theater on Saturdays or Sundays to watch the film clips of MovieTone news of the world.

Claude attended W. O. Boston High School in Lake Charles where he was very active. He joined the school band and became one of the drum majors doing dance routines during halftime at his high school football games and in parades.

Everything was segregated in Lake Charles—the schools, stores, movie theaters, food counters. Colored/white signs hung over water fountains and restrooms. The Greyhound bus depot, Trailways bus station, and train station waiting rooms, as well as the city buses, were all segregated. Even when there were no signs he knew where he was not welcome.

Claude was tired of the colored and white signs, and resented the discrimination and segregation in his hometown. When he was about sixteen years old he got on a city bus and sat down in the white section. There were black people standing behind the colored/white sign. The white section was empty except for one middle-aged white lady who was sitting directly across from him.

When he sat down in the front section, the bus driver told him to move. Claude refused. The driver left the bus to call the police. While the bus driver was gone, people in the colored section told him that he should move. They said that he was going to get hurt, get his family in trouble. Then the unexpected happened: the only white person on the bus, the woman sitting across from Claude, stood up, faced those in the colored section, and told them that he had a right to sit there.

Claude was scared and tears began to roll down his face. He said later that he tried with all his might to remain in his seat. When he did not move, the people in the back of the bus kept yelling at him to come to the back of the bus or get off.

Finally he could not take it any more. He left the bus and cried all the way home. Claude said that he was not afraid to go to jail; he just could not take the criticism. He had not prepared himself for or expected criticism from other black people.

It was a painful lesson. He told his mother that he regretted leaving that bus. He told himself that he would never move again. It was a lesson that gave him the strength to join the Freedom Riders, the courage to participate in the Civil Rights Movement, and the fortitude to handle the criticism.

Because Claude wanted to become a dancer, in August 1959 he took the train to Los Angeles. Arriving with just $116 in his pocket, all the money he had in the world, Claude made friends immediately, and was able to find an uncle whom he had never before met. He finished his last year of high school and graduated from Fremont High School in Los Angeles in June 1960. He had just begun to take dance lessons when the Freedom Rides started. He believed that the Freedom Riders movement was more important than being a dancer.

In September 1960 Claude enrolled at Los Angeles City College while working full time at night. On May 5, 1961, at about 1:00 a.m., he was on his way home from work when he heard a radio news report that an interracial group of men and women had left Washington, D.C., on a Greyhound bus to test the segregated facilities in the southern states. He said to himself, "I should have been on that bus."

About two weeks later he was on his way home from work when he heard that the bus had been bombed and set afire. "Damn," he said to himself, "I knew I should have been on that bus." The thought that he could possibly have been beaten, jailed, or killed did not bother him. What bothered him was that he had missed an opportunity to strike out against segregation.

In early June 1961 Martin Luther King, Jr., was scheduled to be in Los Angeles for a rally. Claude arrived at the L.A. Sports Arena about 10:00 a.m., even though the rally would not start until 4:00 p.m.

It was about 11:00 p.m. when they asked for volunteers for the Freedom Rides. At first Mr. Earl Walters, who was chairman of the Congress of Racial Equality (CORE) in Los Angeles, told Claude that he could not let him go because he was only twenty years old and needed his parents' permission. Claude was so determined to be a Freedom Rider that he told Mr. Walters he was going even if he had to buy his own bus ticket and follow them. Mr. Walters must have seen how committed he was, because he changed his mind and allowed Claude to sign up to be a Freedom Rider.

That was a good thing for Claude, because following them would have been impossible, for the Los Angeles group did not take the bus. On June 19, 1961, Claude quit school, his job, and his dance class. A few days later he left Los Angeles on a plane going to New Orleans for nonviolence training. On June 25, 1961, he was in an interracial group of nineteen men and women who left New Orleans by train for Jackson, Mississippi.

As the train pulled up to the Jackson station there were policemen lined up on both sides. When the group got off the train the black Freedom Riders went into the waiting room labeled for whites, and the white Freedom Riders went into the one labeled for colored. All were immediately arrested and taken to the Jackson jail. A few days later they were in a Mississippi court and were found guilty of breach of peace. They were taken to the Mississippi State Penitentiary at Parchman, the state's maximum security prison. Their sentences were four months and two-hundred-dollar fines.

When Claude arrived at the prison he was put in a six-by-nine-foot cell built for two men. In it were two bunk beds, a face bowl, and a toilet. A mattress had been placed on the floor for a third person, because there were two other Freedom Riders already there. Claude slept on the mattress.

One of the Freedom Riders was Henry Thomas, who had been on the bus that was firebombed in Anniston, Alabama. Claude thought that was fantastic, to be in the company of someone who had just been in the national and international news. (Thirty years later he met Janie McKinney, a white girl whose father owned a store across the street from the burned bus. She had been only twelve years old, but she got a bucket of water and dragged it across the street to the Freedom Riders who were choking from the smoke of the burning bus.)

At Parchman the Freedom Riders sang freedom songs. The deputies did not like the singing. Prison was meant to punish and break your spirit, whereas the Freedom Riders sang as if they were happy to be there.

The deputies kept threatening to take their mattresses if they did not stop singing. One day the Freedom Riders took their mattresses off their bunk beds and told the deputies to come get them. The guards did not know that some of the Freedom Riders wanted to stop singing, because of the echo in the cell block and because their voices were tired. But because the Freedom Riders knew that the deputies hated their singing, they sang all day and into the middle of the night.

The deputies came and took the mattresses after this direct challenge to their authority. Then the Freedom Riders started singing even louder. The deputies opened up the cell gates one by one and had the black trusties drag them from their cells. The trusties put them in the "hole," a six-by-six-foot punishment cell designed to hold one man. Some of the Freedom Riders resisted and held onto the beds or bars and had to be pulled from the cells. The guards had the trusties jam about thirty Freedom Riders into the small "hole."

With so many in the hole the air was sucked up, the Freedom Riders were dripping with sweat, and some were yelling, "Let us out." Claude was the spokesman for the group. The deputies said that if Claude asked to let them out they would. But the deputies wanted Claude not only to ask them; they wanted him to say "please." That was something that he did not want to do. The other Freedom Riders began yelling, "Say please, say please." Someone yelled, "It's so hot I'm going to pass out." Claude was hesitant but decided to say it. "Please let us out," he said to the deputy. The deputy smiled.

After getting out of the hole the Freedom Riders had to sleep on the bare steel bunk beds because the mattresses had not been returned. It got colder when the guards deliberately turned up the cooling fans. The Freedom Riders did not have any shoes on and they were only wearing boxer shorts and tee shirts that did not fit. They were not given any sheets or blankets. The cement floor and the steel bunks were so cold that they felt like their bones were frozen.

A few days later the Freedom Riders were still without mattresses. Along came the guards and opened a couple of cell doors. They told Stokely Carmichael, Henry Thomas, Lawrence Triss, and Claude to step out of the cells, and then led them to a van. They did not know why they were being separated from the other Freedom Riders.

The van went down a narrow dirt road deeper and deeper into the woods. They saw black prisoners in their black-and-white striped pants and shirts working in the ditches next to the road. There were white prisoners who were trusties, dressed in the same black-and-white striped uniforms, but they were holding shotguns, guarding the black prisoners.

The four Freedom Riders thought that they were being taken to some remote area to be killed. Instead they ended up at a prison camp where there was a big building. As they got out of the van, there was a white prisoner aiming a shotgun at them. They thought, "This is it, this is the end, they are going to kill us right here." Instead, they were led into the building. It had a lot of empty twin-style cells. The Freedom Riders were locked up and left in two of the jail cells in the back of the building.

There were no lights and it was very dark. Claude described their feelings: "We thought they would come in the middle of the night and kill us. We were all very scared. We kept thinking that we were so far into the woods, no one would ever have found our bodies."

They were kept there about three days, after which they were taken back to the main prison site. Most of the Freedom Riders were gone by the time they got back. But the mattresses had been returned to the cells. The Freedom Riders who were left said that there had been inspectors going through the cell block to check up on the conditions.

Claude spent forty-three days in Parchman prison and was then released on bail.

After he got out of prison Claude worked in the city of Jackson, Mississippi, for CORE, where he met many of the most prominent people in the Civil Rights Movement. One particularly striking in his intelligence and speaking ability was Medgar Evers, a representative of the NAACP, who was later assassinated in the driveway of his own home.

After a couple of years working in the Civil Rights Movement in Jackson and other places in the South, Claude returned to Los Angeles. He was very active with CORE and became its financial and fund-raising chairman. He marched, picketed, staged sit-in demonstrations, and was arrested at the L.A. Federal Building for supporting the Civil Rights Act. He spent six months in jail. He was also arrested for sitting in at the Real Estate Association in support of the California Fair Housing Law. He spent two weeks in jail.

In Los Angeles, Claude started his own business, manufacturing certificate and menu covers, DVD boxes, game boards, and a wide variety of custom-made paper products. He is still active in the community.

Until recently very little recognition was given to the Freedom Riders. The year 2011 marked the fiftieth anniversary of this great movement. Claude Albert Liggins is proud that he, along with others, has been telling this story across the nation.

AUTOBIOGRAPHICAL NOTES

—Carol Ruth Silver—

The question I am most commonly asked is: Why? Why did you go on the Freedom Rides?

This question asks who I was, and how I had become who I was, in May 1961, when I made the decision to join the Freedom Rides.

The answer goes all the way back to my earliest memory—corresponding with the United States Department of Agriculture about how to grow pearls in an oyster farm, which I proposed to locate in the bathtub of my family's modest apartment in Revere, Massachusetts.

That my parents, Mildred and Nathan Silver, were supportive of me in this absurd oyster farm idea is demonstrative of the level of nurturing, encouragement, and moral certitude which I received from them from my very earliest years.

My story is their story. My decision to "get on the bus"—to put on the line all of their aspirations for me and the sacrifices they had made for me, as well as my dreams of a future career as a lawyer, and, indeed, my very life—was the direct product of who they were and who they had caused me to be.

In this I was not so very different from many of the African American students at Fisk and Jackson State and others of what are now called the HBCU, Historically Black Colleges and Universities, throughout the South. Their parents had sacrificed greatly to create the opportunity for them to get an education and a better life, all of which they were putting at risk by joining the Freedom Rides.

My story is not their story, however, for I was not black, not African American, not subjected on a daily basis to the evils of discrimination and segregation.

Even this diary, written over fifty years ago, poses the question to myself: Why me?

And this was also the question posed to me over and over in the scratchy long distance telephone calls, when I told my mother and father that I intended to travel through the South, in an integrated group of Negroes and whites, on a Greyhound bus like the one which had been firebombed just days before in Anniston, Alabama.

My story starts with their story, and cannot be understood without telling their story.

My father had, he told us, been born in a Jewish bakery in the West End of Boston, where his mother, Tillie Silver, a widow with six children, toiled six days a week, from before dawn to late evening.

My father worked when I was very young for the federal government in the WPA, the Work Projects Administration. He took this job when he was unable, after graduating from law school, to find an entry-level job as a lawyer, at the height of the Depression which followed the 1929 stock market crash. Things were so bad that he wound up hanging his shingle, "Nathan Silver, Attorney at Law," on the bakery wall.

My middle sister, Jane Maxine Silver, was born in 1941 in Eastport, Maine, where the WPA sent my dad. Far from family, friends, and her urban roots, my beautiful and elegant mother gamely followed him to the rural seacoast of Maine. She afterward regaled us with descriptions of her tea with First Lady Mrs. Franklin Delano Roosevelt, at the Roosevelts' summer home on Campobello Island, near Passamaquoddy, Maine. After we returned to the Boston area and rented a little apartment in Revere (a beach resort for Boston which had cheap rents because it had fallen on hard times) my youngest sister, Barbara Ellen Silver, completed our family in 1944.

My father had, along with his brothers and sister, been educated in the hard-knocks school of upbringing by my grandmother, Tillie, who had been widowed with six children when the youngest was only about ten. For over six decades, she supported the family and ran the Silver Bakery with an iron hand. As a woman-owned business, it was an unusual phenomenon for the times, and it was possible only, my father told us, because Boston was a more liberal place than almost anywhere else.

All of Tillie's six children were given the opportunity for education. Their dinnertime conversations, around the huge dining room table in Tillie's Boston brownstone, were legendary for feeding the intellectual appetites as well as the need for chicken soup and hot bagels and knishes and kasha varnishkas. These traditional foods were to remind everyone of the Old Country, Eastern Europe, Vilna, Lithuania, and Poland, which Tillie had fled to escape one of the many deadly waves of anti-Semitism (dramatized in sanitized fashion in the popular musical *Fiddler on the Roof*). Socialism and Marxism, ideas and idealism, Jewish orthodoxy and reform, piety and atheism, were served up with relish and passion, as well as fears about the impending dark cloud of Nazism sweeping across Europe. Relatives and friends were wistfully talked about, most still stuck in the Old Country. (When my uncle Leo traveled there after the defeat of Nazi Germany in the Second World War, they were all gone, even their graves unknown.)

When I was old enough to know things but not yet old enough to understand them, I watched as my father struggled into a number of businesses after we returned to Boston from his stint in Maine for the WPA. He attempted to create a wholly new business out of an amazing new technology: household plastic. It is ubiquitous today, but at that time sales techniques of explanation and demonstration were required to sell it to hesitant housewives, who would eventually use plastic to replace linen tablecloths, cotton shower curtains, clay-fired and metal containers, and just about everything else.

His entrepreneurial energies drove him to a door-to-door sales model, selling this amazing new substance in its many household forms, particularly tablecloths, to people of limited means in the urban areas around Boston. He would trudge up and down old apartment buildings, carrying his heavy bundle of samples and wares, to collect one dollar from each housewife toward the plastics she had already purchased and attempt to sell her additional items.

This was labor intensive, extremely hard work and not particularly lucrative, as retail competition exploded with rapid acceptance of plastic in its infinite varieties.

My mother took a job at a retail department store in Boston, exercising her artistic and fashion sense to bring in additional income. Unlike my father, who had finished not only high school at the prestigious Boston Latin School and then gone on to law school, my mother had dropped out of school in the eighth grade to work, to help feed her five younger half-siblings and her beloved mother, Dora, trapped in an abusive marriage to a chronic gambler.

My parents were grateful when our economic lives intertwined with my uncle Harry Schneider, my mother's brother-in-law, who had married my aunt Fay. Uncle Harry was building a successful business in another new technology of the day, the refrigerated truck, which allowed ice cream to become a manufactured commodity instead of being prepared on-site, a home kitchen concoction. Uncle Harry hired my father to drive the truck delivering ice cream to retail outlets and restaurants. My father had no experience whatsoever, and probably did not even initially have a driver's license. But he was family, our need was great, and my father brought to my uncle's business the intangibles of reliability and trustworthiness, literacy, and honesty. So to support his family, my mother and his three girls, my father gave up his dream of a professional career as a lawyer and shelved his lawyer shingle, still hanging at the premises of the old Silver Bakery in the West End of Boston, to accept the job delivering ice cream on a suburban route.

I remember riding with my father on one of those delivery days, in the middle of a Boston winter, when the snow was accumulating on the windshield of the large truck that he was driving. It had no windshield wipers, so my father's side window was kept open and he would periodically wipe the outside of the front windshield with his mittened hand.

Decades later, I can still feel the chill of the wind and the fear for our lives of that bitter cold day. I was cold, and I was frightened, as we drove at what seemed like excessive speeds—probably at least thirty-five miles an hour—with impaired visibility from the snow, my dad squinting through his thick glasses, and the truck occasionally skidding on its worn tires.

I remember also waiting up for my father to come home. He would arrive in the dark, late, after my sisters and my mother were asleep. He and I would sit at the kitchen table while he had the milk and crackers my mother had set out for him. I would read to him, or he would read to me, from his store of books of the great literature of the world. I remember particularly Edgar Allan Poe, and the lilting phrases in which my father would impart to me the poetry that I didn't yet know was within him, coming out at that time only as he read to his ten-year-old eldest daughter in the late evening of the cold New England winter night.

From our low-rent apartment in the Boston suburb of Revere, my mother enrolled me in Boston's smorgasbord of free or low-cost cultural offerings. I went for years to Saturday art classes at the Boston Museum of Art, and both my middle sister and I went to music classes at the Boston Conservatory of Music in the West End. We studied piano and solfeggio (music theory).

To get there we needed to walk from home half a mile to the streetcar, transfer in the Boston subway to another train, and emerge at the Scollay

Square station on Boston's skid row (this whole area has now been torn down for redevelopment). We held each other's hand, I, just three years older, being at ten or eleven the leader and the protector of my sister Jane. Even today, sixty-some years past, she tells the story of how on one occasion I pushed her, alone, terrified, onto an overcrowded trolley with the admonition to get off at the next stop.

At some point my father was offered a real opportunity by my uncle Harry: if he would move the family from Boston to a place called Worcester in central Massachusetts, my father could become the head of ice cream distribution for the area, with financing for trucks and freezers, allowing him an independent business in Worcester (pronounced WUH-sta by New Englanders), while allowing Uncle Harry to grow his wholesale ice cream empire.

Worcester was the second-largest city in Massachusetts, a vibrant industrial city but a long fifty miles from Boston before freeways, about a two-hour drive. It separated my parents, particularly my mother, from the warmth of her extended family, her large network of friends, and the established Jewish community. But opportunity called, and again leaving behind family, friends, and support, my mother and father, this time with us three girls, packed and moved.

We stayed in Worcester for seven years. I graduated in 1956 from Worcester's Classical High School, the excellent public high school for college-bound students. I graduated with six years of French, four years of Latin, and a grounding in history, social studies, math, and physical science that still stands me in good stead. (I can read the algebra equations in my grandson's homework although I may not remember how to solve them. I still remember from science class learning how electricity flows through copper wires, and not to touch them together.)

In Worcester, the ice cream and associated frozen food business prospered. Both my dad and my mother worked in it. My father drove the big ice cream trucks and hired other drivers as well. My mother, attractive and vibrant, drove around to small retail stores to sell them on the idea of frozen foods. This involved the open top display freezer, another new technology. That display and the flash freezing of vegetables and fruits began to allow housewives to serve vegetables and fruit throughout the winter without their having been dried or salted, pickled or canned, the traditional food preservation technologies of centuries past.

If the grocer agreed to try a freezer, Uncle Harry would finance the purchase, and Mother would contract to have frozen foods delivered to the store for sale along with, of course, ice cream, all delivered by my dad and his trucks.

Frozen foods, including ice cream, were an expanding business model, and one that was able, finally, to generate a modest middle-class living for our family. We moved from a rented apartment in the Irish section of town (where I had been pushed around, derided, and cursed by other kids for being Jewish) to the purchase of a small house in Worcester at Number 7 Westview Road.

The house was on a hill, with trees and a yard. But, most important to my mother, it was in the small Jewish section of town, which she felt would protect us children from the worst manifestations of the fairly pervasive anti-Semitism of the day. Actually, the even more important thing for her was that it was the culmination of the American dream, a home that, for the first time in her life, she owned (even with a large mortgage), and where she could paint the walls, put nails up to hang her paintings, consider having a pet, all without needing to ask the permission of a landlord. Yes!

As my mother was fond of remarking, my parents were second-generation Jewish atheists, following after my grandmother Tillie.

The term which more correctly describes her and their beliefs, and mine, is really, however, agnostic. Grandma Tillie, for example, while expounding on the irrationality of religion, all religions, continued to keep her home and kitchen strictly kosher, including a double set of dishes to maintain the Jewish separation of meat and milk, until the day she died—because, she said, "You can never tell for certain."

My parents, trying to figure out how to convey to their children the Jewish half of the Jewish-agnostic equation, joined a reform Jewish congregation in Worcester where, although they never attended religious services except once or twice a year on the Jewish high holidays, we three girls were enrolled in after-school activities.

The ethical traditions of the Jewish religion, however, were imparted to us by my parents by example and precept. It was only much later that I identified the fundamental legacy of my parents, and that it had a name—as summarized by the Hebrew phrase Tikkun Olam (pronounced tee-KOON oh-LAM), meaning the commandment to "repair the world." Later Jewish scholars have defined this as synonymous with the notion of social action and the pursuit of social justice, including in particular the responsibility for active participation in creating justice and righteousness.

I received and internalized this precept as the responsibility to fix whatever is wrong in the world, or at least to fix whatever it is in your power to fix, in whatever is your part of the world.

Later, I was one of those Girl Scouts who did not complain about the rule that we must bring home from a hike in the woods more trash than we created, using our presence and energy to make the paths easier and cleaner and better for those, unknown to us, who would come later. But with the religious nonbelief of my parents excusing us from formal after-school religious training, I also had time for fun: I joined a Jewish girls' social club, sang in the chorus of a local Gilbert and Sullivan production with the Worcester Light Opera troupe, and joined the community chorus annually dedicated to putting on George Frideric Handel's Christian masterpiece, *The Messiah*.

At Classical High School, I maintained good grades, in a trio at the top of my class. I participated in girls' chorus and the chess club and befriended Felicia, the one and only African American student in the school. I wrote for the school magazine, and I wrote well enough that the faculty advisor paid me the compliment of accusing me of plagiarizing something, although she admitted, when challenged by my mother, that she could not identify the source.

Among my after-school jobs in Worcester were some which, even today, I still find useful experiences: they included a stint at bookkeeping, in which I learned the importance of double-entry bookkeeping (long before computers, of course), and one behind the counter at a soda shop, where I studied the most efficient ways to wash and dry dishes.

In Worcester, the ice cream business was seasonal, robust in the summer, dead in the winter. So one winter my mother convinced my father that instead of almost literally hibernating in the winter, that is, spending most of each day in bed reading (this was before bedroom or any other television), he should, she suggested, travel to California and visit with his mother and brother, my grandma Tillie and my Uncle Leo. They had moved there upon my grandmother's retiring from the bakery in Boston.

Los Angeles was exciting and new, and my father thoroughly enjoyed his experience there, staying in the spacious though a bit shabby art deco apartment of my grandmother and Uncle Leo. (Leo was the youngest of the brothers and very dear to my father. He had never married, but spent his entire life living with my grandmother, until she passed away later on at age ninety-five.)

So my father was in Los Angeles for the winter, and scheduled a routine eye examination just, he thought, to change his eyeglass prescription. The examining doctor, however, diagnosed him as having cataracts and recommended immediate surgery on both eyes.

To the great distress of my mother, who was convinced that Boston offered much better medical practice than Los Angeles (she was right), my father decided to have the operations in California.

The operations on both of his cataracts were successful. However, both eyes became seriously infected while he was in the hospital. One eye was lost entirely. At the end of two years of recuperation, he had recovered approximately 20 percent vision in the other eye. He was, from the day of the operation, legally and essentially blind.

My mother, back in Massachusetts as these traumatic events were happening to my father in California, tried desperately to run the business without him. As the winter season turned into spring and then summer, she hired a man to drive the big truck, and others to do the physical work that my father had always done. But the income from the business could not support these additional expenditures. In short order, she became acutely aware that the business debts were in excess of any chance of her being able to pay them, and that they were continuing to increase. With my father totally disabled, blind, and gone, she was alone with three children, no business background except her years of working at outside sales in my father's enterprise. She was under unbelievable pressure from creditors and at the same time was trying to support us children and figure out what to do. She decided that there was nothing else she could do except to close the business.

Today, she would have comfortably made a trip to a bankruptcy lawyer and filed for Chapter 11 protection, for at least an orderly winding up and to shield herself and the family from the business debts and aggressive creditors. But in those days bankruptcy was still considered, at least by her, to be so shameful that, instead, she allowed her stress levels to go off the charts as she apologized to all the creditors and promised to pay them as soon as she could.

My father urged her to come to California, where my grandmother and uncle would provide a place to stay and minimal support until she could find a job. The two younger children, Jane and Barbara, would go to high school and junior high, while I, the eldest, would, as planned, go off to college at the University of Chicago where, in a series of serendipitous events, I had been accepted with a full scholarship.

And so it came to pass. She decided that she had no option but to move to Los Angeles. Before that, however, to finance the move and pay at least some of the debts, my mother decided she had to sell the little house in Worcester, the first house she had ever owned, where she had expected to live for the rest of her life. My sisters and I, now teenagers, applied a coat of paint to the front and sides, weeded the rock garden, swept, cleaned, and prettied it as best we could.

As soon as escrow closed, we packed up the old Studebaker, and, at age seventeen, I started driving us west. My mother, the only other driver, was ill most of the way, physically as well as depressed, beaten down by stress and the distress she felt at the disintegration of our economic situation, while at the same time trying to put on a happy face to protect us children from the panic which was engulfing her.

The car broke down in Ohio and again in Amarillo, Texas, but was put back on the road and finally brought us to California. I will never forget my mother's reaction as she lay in the backseat of the car and looked at the royal palm trees that lined the freeway. "Ugly," she said, "they are ugly! I want to go back home."

But that was the problem: this was her new home, and there was no place to go back to. She cried softly for a few minutes, then shook herself as if to remember that she could not show such weakness in front of the children who relied on her. She smiled and said, "I guess we'll get used to them."

My father spent about two years recuperating before he was able to get around with his 20 percent eyesight in one eye. But that was not the end of his story, nor even of his working life. With the help of my uncle Leo, he was able to find a retail job in the Los Angeles Watts area ghetto, where his trustworthiness and willingness to work at whatever had to be done, whatever he was able to do, served his employer well enough to compensate for his poor vision. He was hired into an army surplus retail store, and there he worked every day, until late at night in the Christmas season, faithfully putting in long hours plus his long commute, until he eventually retired onto Social Security at age sixty-five.

But that's also not the end of his story. As a retired senior with time on his hands, he and his brother, my uncle Leo, took advantage of being able to enroll without paying tuition in a variety of Los Angeles Community College courses. My father found himself in a creative writing class in poetry, and his long-suppressed or ignored talents began to bubble up. For the last twenty years of his life, he devoted himself to writing poetry, and regaled the family, his friends, and eventually his nursing home harem of senior ladies, with poetic free verse and haiku, poetic political commentary, holiday and birthday cards. He passed away peacefully at age ninety-one, and was buried, as he wished, next to my mother, who had preceded him by thirty years.

When he was in his eighties, we, his three girls, collected and published first one, and then a second small volume of his poems. Here is one about me, written for my birthday in about 1985:

First Seed
Nathan Silver

Sturdy stem
Colorful bright blossom
I saw you when
You first took seed

Precocious
Early independence
Wild cub in throes
Of new adventure
Ready to right
The world at twenty
Fashioned to
Civic causes
Provocative voice
Rowing upstream
Head high
In struggle
For justice

Glowing
Prime flower
In my garden
Proudly
You prolong the breed.

The hospital where my father's eyesight was destroyed was one of the best in Los Angeles, Cedars-Sinai, but, as with most hospitals until the present day, standards of infection control were not adequate. Also not adequate was my reaction as a young, about-to-be lawyer. It would have been very appropriate for a lawsuit to have been brought, or at least a claim against the hospital, for the negligence which caused my father to lose his eyes and the last half of his working life. None of that happened, however, something which I still deeply regret.

Because of our financial problems, I had taken part-time jobs while I was going to high school in Worcester. So my daily routine had been to rise early and race out of the house to catch the bus to my school, which was near downtown. After school I would go to the public library, to do my homework and wait until my evening job as a soda jerk and dishwasher. Then I would take the bus home.

One day, I saw a poster in the Worcester Public Library advertising a ten-week adult education class on international relations, offered by the Great Books of the Western World, a community education project created by the University of Chicago. At this point—I was a junior in high school, age about fifteen—I was intrigued and very interested in the subject matter.

So I, with my pocket money from working, said to the librarian that I wished to undertake this class. The librarian looked at me disdainfully, as if I was doing something outrageous, and told me that I could not register for the class because I was not an adult.

Even then, to forbid me something in what seemed an unjust manner only stimulated my resolve. So I took this rejection home that evening and asked my mother to register for the class. I will pay for it, I proposed; you will attend with me in tow, and I will participate as much as I am able. My sainted mother, perhaps rolling her eyes at yet another harebrained scheme of her eldest daughter, as always, complied. And so she and I began attending these classes.

In the hallmark of the College of the University of Chicago, there was no text for these classes, but rather a set of readings of original materials. We read the United Nations Charter. We read excerpts from Marx and Lenin, and the treaty agreements between the countries which would later be the Allies, aligned against Nazi Germany, and we discussed how Poland was sacrificed on the altar of Chamberlain's appeasement strategy. We read contemporaneous newspaper and other accounts of the systematic murder of Jews, gypsies, gays, and the mentally ill by the Nazi Germans as the Holocaust began, and we tried to figure out why no one seemed to care.

One of the exciting things to me about these classes was that they provided an opportunity for me to hear and talk on par to people of significant education and intelligence. Most of the other fifteen or so people who attended the sessions were PhD students at Worcester Polytechnic Institute or Clark University, also in Worcester, or they were academics, already teaching at these institutions. And I, a fifteen-year-old high school girl, found that I was able to keep up with them by dint of nothing more magical than hard work—that is, more so than anybody else in the group, I had read and carefully annotated all the readings as they were assigned. This was in and of itself a marvelously useful lesson.

Toward the end of this series of ten sessions, one of the topics was about Africa, particularly the British colonies in Africa. We read original materials (although I cannot now recall their titles). The year was 1954. At some point I reacted to a statement by somebody about how the British were operating in their African colonies. I said to the group, "Why do the British continue to have colonies? Why don't they just give these countries back to the people that they belong to?"

Question from across the table: "Are you saying—Africa for the Africans?"

Me: "Well, yes, the African countries should belong to the Africans. Yes, Africa for the Africans."

The whole group exploded in good-natured laughter. What a marvelously funny thing had been proposed by this fifteen-year-old girl (who was in the group somewhat on sufferance anyway). The group leader called for a break to be taken before the group resumed its deliberations.

Well, as we all know, that fifteen-year-old girl was right, and not just morally right but politically as well. Within a very few years, every colony in Africa had either ejected the British or another European master or was in the process of doing so.

The effect on me, as I read the news over these next months and years, was enormous. I could not then restrain myself from the certitude that when I experienced something as right, it was right, and that when I experienced something as wrong, it was wrong. That certainty, that knowledge drawn from this experience, has been a burden and an opportunity, a responsibility and a source of accomplishment, for the rest of my life.

The University of Chicago alumna who had brought the Great Books sessions to Worcester was instrumental in convincing me to apply to the University of Chicago, although my family's financial limitations dictated a much less prestigious institution. But lo and behold, with her recommendation, I was accepted and provided scholarships which, with a continuation of my high school career in dishwashing, enabled me to attend.

When the Freedom Rides started in 1961, given my education, my background, my experiences, my support from this wonderful mother and wonderful father, and my personal sense of certitude, I found myself experiencing a sense of personal and universal responsibility. My education at the College of the University of Chicago had fostered in me a commitment to criticism and analysis, what is today called critical thinking, as well as cementing my opinions about rightness and wrongness.

The obligation of what we today call Tikkun Olam is always limited by the practical, by the possible. One must repair the world within one's capabilities. And the answer for me was shaped also by another Jewish saying, from two centuries ago, of Rabbi Hillel: "If I am not for myself, who will be for me? If I am only for myself, what am I? And if not now, when?" So there was no escaping it. The time, the opportunity, the responsibility had come together. It was time for me to "get on the bus."

The time from the spring of 1961 when I decided to become a Freedom Rider to the time when I was released from Parchman prison in Mississippi is the subject of my diary for those days. It is amazing that I was able to walk out of Parchman penitentiary with a handful of scribbled scraps of paper.

I was then able to read and interpret these writings in a marathon typing session when I got home to my family in Los Angeles, enlisting my sisters, Jane and Barbara, my mother, and other friends. The diary was typed with one or two carbons on the little pink manual portable typewriter which I had used all through my college years.

In addition to my journal, I also walked out with a crumpled, rather lumpy envelope, just a regular, ordinary-looking, business-sized envelope, which, however, had in it my amazing chess set. This chess set had been made out of the soft white bread which we were served and which was of little gastronomic interest to me. Combining the inside of the bread with spit and kneading it gently, I was able to mold it into very recognizable little chess pieces, which hardened as they dried. And in order to color the ones that represented the black pieces, we used menstrual blood. One does what one must.

In the fall of 1961, still out on appeal bond from my Mississippi Freedom Rider conviction, I started law school at the University of Chicago, putting behind me the excitement of the Freedom Rides. But the lessons learned and experiences shared have stayed with me for the rest of my life, particularly the deep understanding and commitment that while one person is unfree, so am I, so are we all.

During law school, 1961–1964, I organized the University of Chicago Law School chapter of the Law Students Civil Rights Research Council (LSCRRC), sending interns to the South during the summer and producing research during the school year for Civil Rights lawyers in the South.

In the summer of 1962, however, I took a break from political organizing. Instead, I organized a group of students to deliver a new automobile from Detroit to Anchorage, Alaska, and spent an idyllic summer camping out in the parks a few miles from Anchorage. My neighbors in the woods were brown bears and feral juvenile delinquents. My experiences included bathing in rushing cold streams and learning to shoot a gun for defense against critters, both four-legged and two. I found a job in a law office by offering to use my quite considerable secretarial skills, which offices in Alaska found in even shorter supply than lawyers' skills, if they would give me a chance to prove my worth as a law clerk. I won the bet, and clerked all though the summer, enjoying the long days of twenty-hour sunlight.

For the next summer, 1963, I decided to find a law firm to employ me as a law clerk—in Africa. At the law library in Chicago I wrote to every English-speaking law firm listed in Butterworth's Empire Law List, asking for a job.

Amazingly, I received an offer from a law firm in Kampala, Uganda, and although I had to pay my own air fare there, which totaled more than the modest salary I received, it was an enormous thrill. I worked there for two months, and still have great memories of the cases that I handled: the most dramatic of these was a complaint by a local co-op against a farmer whose farm was at the edge of the jungle. Does the farm at the edge of the jungle have an obligation to protect the farther-in farmers from rampaging elephants? This case involved not only property law but tort law, all of which, fortunately, was very familiar to me from my University of Chicago law school course work, since both the United States and former English areas of Africa rely on the ancient English common law.

In 1964, I became the first full-time intern for Law Students Civil Rights Research Council (LSCRRC) in the law offices of African American Civil Rights Attorney Floyd Bixler McKissick, McKissick & Burke, in Durham, North Carolina.

In the year that I spent there, 1964–1965, I learned from Floyd McKissick what lawyers need to know but law schools do not teach. He was a true master at the craft of practicing law, from file maintenance to billing records to client confidentiality to client management and much more. At the same time, I was learning from the Durham black community the true measures of charity, piety, warmth, and love. With Jocelyn McKissick, Floyd's daughter, I sang in the gospel choir of Third Baptist Church of Durham, Reverend Grady Davis, Pastor. The songs we sang, the rhythms we clapped out, are with me still.

I helped Floyd with research and memos in the defense of criminal cases of Civil Rights activists arrested all over North Carolina, but only very occasionally did I make appearances in those courts. Floyd was afraid a white woman traveling by car through rural areas, to appear in an up-country courthouse with him or another African American attorney, would be a dangerous provocation against local customs.

And female attorneys were such a rarity at that time anyway, they required additional special consideration of when and where to have them appear in court.

I also learned enormously from the civil litigation in which Floyd involved me. I learned that there are no sacred cows. And so I prepared and filed a Petition to the National Labor Relations Board to decertify the all-white and segregationist Tobacco Workers' Union of Durham. This was filed despite the fact that organized union financial support was still crucial to the Civil Rights Movement, and despite the death threats that were received by Floyd, by the Black Tobacco Workers' Union leadership, and everybody else in town—except me, probably because I was kept as much as possible out of sight, hidden in Floyd's office far from the courthouse and the offices of other lawyers, churning out legal memos, motions, and that audacious Petition.

To give me a little relief from the tensions of being on the front lines of the Civil Rights Movement in Durham, Floyd sent me a few times on the Greyhound bus up to Washington, D.C., to lobby for passage of President Lyndon Johnson's Economic Opportunity Act of 1964, which was the economic companion piece to the landmark Civil Rights Act of 1964. The passage of the Economic Opportunity Act was, as Floyd described it, the effort finally to provide freed slaves with the "40 acres and a mule" included in their dreams of freedom.

The legislation passed, and included a provision to provide civil attorneys to the poor, with emphasis on high-impact cases. In 1965 and for the next five years or so, I worked in federally funded Office of Economic Opportunity (OEO) programs for Legal Services for the Poor, first in Oakland, California, and then for California Rural Legal Assistance (CRLA) in Delano, California (in parallel with Cesar Chavez's efforts at organizing farmworkers), and elsewhere.

My research, in an article giving practical advice on how OEO Legal Services attorneys could challenge local county welfare department decisions, was published and reprinted in thousands of copies by the Social Workers' Union. I was very proud that for the first time we were giving a voice to the poor for whose benefit the welfare departments were supposed to have been established. I also worked with Don B. Kates, Jr., on the appellate brief to challenge the vicious "man in the house" rule, by which the children of female welfare recipients were dropped from federal welfare benefits if a man was perceived by the county welfare department to have stayed overnight in the home, on the fantastical theory that he had by so doing somehow undertaken to support the children.

Being early in a new field creates instant expertise, and I found myself much in demand to help new Legal Services for the Poor offices all around the country set up and develop their new law practices. In Alaska, I developed a forms package to allow adoptions by grandparents to legalize the Inuit and Native American custom of parents leaving children with their elders while they went off on sometimes deadly hunts for seals and whales. In California I helped develop the routine forms (on mimeograph machines, before computers) which preceded the court-mandated family law practice forms which are now ubiquitous. In other offices I helped organize ways of managing the excess numbers of people asking for services, including creation of a forms-based system to allow one attorney to supervise numerous law students or interns doing interviewing and research.

During these years, I spent part of each summer pursuing the unfinished business of the Civil Rights Movement in the South, either Mississippi or Louisiana, with the Lawyers' Constitutional Defense Committee (LCDC).

My personal life at this time was the common fate of young lawyers, a sixty-hour week devoted to the important work at hand. Rebelling against this standard custom of law practice, and being an early advocate of the value of exercise, I demanded that the half-dozen young lawyers under my supervision, all male and all showing the beginnings of expanding waistlines, join me in undertaking some kind of sport, whatever they wanted to choose. I chose, and they chose to follow me, karate—the Shotokan hard-style version of the Japanese sport which was then becoming newly popular in California. So with our sensei, John Egan, an American who had trained in Japan, our little group of young lawyers, Ed Wilson, Don Kates, myself, and a few others, huffed and puffed, kicked and punched at each other, ran for miles, and, to cool down, did yoga. For three hours. Three or four times a week. For three years.

At the end of this period of time, I took my exam and got my brown belt, as did the others who had stuck with the program. The belt itself I wore until it shredded, but the certificate for this accomplishment I framed and hung with great pride, right beside my Certificate of Admission to the Bar of the Supreme Court of the United States.

Around 1971, I was invited to teach at San Francisco's Golden Gate University Law School by Roger Bernhardt and Lani Bader, new faculty member and new dean respectively, recruited from the University of Chicago. They needed someone to teach evidence, and I conditioned my agreement to teach this very dry, very traditional course on being able to teach also a new and never-before-taught course which I would create, on the civil legal rights of prisoners.

Students flocked to this exotic new class. I felt that there was an opportunity here, so I picked up the phone and dialed the newly elected sheriff of San Francisco, Richard D. Hongisto. I asked him to allow law students to offer to his San Francisco county jail inmates legal aid–type civil legal services. He and I both believed this to be the first such initiative in the country, if not in the world. He agreed, despite the opposition of every one of his subordinates, his jail deputies, and the civilian staff. The program was a great success. Eventually, even the deputy sheriffs on the main cell block began referring inmates they felt had been unjustly dealt with and needed civil legal help.

This collaboration with the sheriff's department led me after about a year to be engaged by the sheriff as his legal counsel, which brought me to my first San Francisco job under the dome of the architectural marvel that is the San Francisco City Hall.

At the same time I was working for the sheriff, I was also involved in a number of other organizing efforts. One of these was to create First Women's Savings and Loan, the first bank or savings and loan in California which offered as its primary objective to serve the special financial needs of women. Today that seems not very special, but women were at that time only fitfully emerging from the control of the husbands or other men who had for centuries legally ruled over the property of their female partners and family members.

I worked not only in the women's movement, but for the rights of gays (later the rights of all of lesbian, bisexual, gay, and transgender persons), as well as of Native Americans, the disabled, seniors, immigrants, and jail inmates. "The Movement" morphed during these years into a general view, consistent with what I personally believed, that every individual is precious, has a right to live and be educated and to be an economic participant in society, and that all laws and government impediments based on irrelevant categories, of which race and sex and age are only the most general, are fair game to be attacked.

In 1973, I traveled to Taiwan to adopt a child, my first son, a Chinese orphan whom I named Steven Chou Silver. Three years later, I was surprised and delighted to find myself pregnant, and bore my second son, Jefferson Chou Frensley Silver. I raised both while being a single working mother. I still adore them, and also my two grandsons, Destin and Reeves.

As a result of my adoption of Steven, I returned to San Francisco with a personal commitment to make sure that his birthright of Chinese culture was not lost to him. I turned to my Chinese friends in San Francisco and asked where I would find a Mandarin-speaking school for my newly adopted child. The answer: there is none. There were Cantonese schools. But neither Steven nor his birth siblings had ever even heard spoken Cantonese. I wanted for him the opportunity to be able to be in touch with them, and also to learn and speak the official language of both Taiwan and the People's Republic of China, which is Mandarin, not Cantonese.

And so, I announced, there being no such school, "Well, we will just have to create one." And so we did.

With the help of many of my San Francisco friends, both Chinese American and not, I organized a preliminary board of directors committed to creating a private elementary school in San Francisco, teaching half in Mandarin Chinese and half in English (what today is called an "immersion" program). The reason that it was to be a private school was the unfortunate experience I had in trying to involve the San Francisco public schools: something new seemed to be too much of a challenge to their existing programs. As I myself am a product of the public schools and as a public official committed to the public schools, I certainly wanted this new school to be part of the public system. I even entertained the hope that the school board would later change their collective mind. And they did, but not until some twenty-five years later, when the public schools in San Francisco created their first Mandarin-English bilingual classes, just like the first classes of the school which I caused to be created. That school, now called the Chinese American International School (CAIS), is still in existence, still flourishing. Celebrating its thirtieth anniversary in 2012, Chinese American International School is now over five hundred students with a large campus in the Civic Center of San Francisco, right near the San Francisco City Hall where I spent so much of my time planning for it.

Actually, CAIS was the second Mandarin-English elementary school I helped create for my son Steven in San Francisco. The first, in conjunction with the nuns of the Gold Mountain Buddhist Monastery, was called the Instilling Virtue Elementary School. It operated for two years in San Francisco and taught Steven not only in Mandarin and English but also a bit of Sanskrit. But the monastery and the school then moved about 110 miles north of San Francisco, to near Ukiah, California, to found the City of Ten Thousand Buddhas. The little Instilling Virtue Elementary School has also continued on there, and grown large and successful.

In 1975 at the urging of my boss, Sheriff Richard D. Hongisto, I began my political career by challenging the incumbent district attorney of San Francisco. My biggest handicap was being female, because (as I was constantly told by the regular SF political contributors) there had never been a woman district attorney, and, although they were at pains to admit that I was much more qualified, as well as smart, knowledgeable, and politically correct, there never would be a female DA because a woman could never raise the funds—from them!—to run a successful campaign.

I did not win that race. But it did make me realize that I had outgrown my job as the sheriff's half-time legal counsel, and the time had come to open my own law office. Based on my experience and inclinations, I decided on civil law practice, including litigation, of contracts, personal injury, and real estate. Later I would find myself branching out, into trusts and family law and government relations (no criminal defense, no probate, no appeals).

For thirty years I maintained my civil legal practice, sometimes with an associate, Sister Barbara Dawson (a Catholic nun who was also an attorney), or a partner, Arthur Siegel, but mostly as a solo practitioner. Along the way I took the California real estate broker's examination and enjoyed a comfortable combination of legal and real estate brokerage practice.

In 1977, I again ran for political office, and this time I did win! I was elected to a seat on the Board of Supervisors of the City and County of

San Francisco. For almost twelve years, from 1977 to 1989, for three terms, I served in San Francisco City Hall.

While I was a San Francisco elected official and legislator, my career and accomplishments were substantial, but they were overshadowed by the assassination, in my first year in office, of the mayor of San Francisco, George Moscone, and my close friend, political ally, and colleague, Supervisor Harvey Milk. Harvey was the first-in-the-nation out-of-the-closet acknowledged homosexual to be elected by a general electorate to serve in public office. Information garnered later indicated that his murderer, who was a fellow elected official, had been gunning also for me, and as well the speaker of the assembly, because we also were colleagues and partisans of the mayor. The martyrdom of Supervisor Harvey Milk energized the gay rights movement, and Harvey has continued to be one of its major heroes. (He was commemorated by actor Sean Penn in the movie *Milk* in 2010, in which I was both portrayed by an actress, Wendy King, and was given a small acting part as the grandmotherly volunteer who opens Harvey's hate mail.)

My legislative record, before and after the assassinations, is still a source of pride to me. Rent control and limitations on conversion of rental apartments to condominiums were a part of the legislative legacy of both myself and Harvey Milk. Throughout my three terms, I continued to support legislation and other efforts to empower the disenfranchised and follow the mandate to think globally and act locally. I supported the boycott of South Africa because of apartheid and supported the farmworkers in California. I called for a bill of rights for children, for ending the death penalty because of its distortion of the criminal justice system, and repeal of ancient sodomy laws which criminalized actions of consenting homosexual adults in private. I also began then, as so often in my life, far and away ahead of the times, to call for reducing or eliminating the draconian penalties for marijuana and other drugs.

I was also appointed to numerous regional boards by my fellow members of the board of supervisors, and rose to be president of two of those boards, the Golden Gate Bridge, Highway and Transportation District and the Bay Area Air Quality Management District. In this latter capacity, I supported the staff proposals for adding reduction of airborne toxins to our original mandate to reduce smog, riling up major opposition from Big Oil. Despite Big Bucks lobbying of our otherwise low visibility agency, I prevailed, and those regulations became the model for air quality control boards all over the country.

Many of my activities during my years on the board of supervisors involved not legislation but using my elective office as a bully pulpit. As a feminist and in support of the newly won rights of women, for example, during this time I organized support for the availability of RU-486, the morning-after birth control pill. In spite of a campaign of lies and smears and half-data, ultimately we won that fight, and it or a similar medication is generally now available.

My career as a member of the San Francisco Board of Supervisors came to an end when I had the hubris to run for a fourth term in a public atmosphere where term limits on politicians, usually two terms, were becoming more and more popular. Losing my seat was devastating, in particular because I had no alternative plans at hand. I retired to lick my wounds, practice law, and sell real estate.

About four years later, between an economic downturn and some bad decisions, I found myself greatly in debt. My children were already gone off to school elsewhere, and I was an empty nester who could no longer afford the nest. Bankruptcy was strongly recommended by my financial advisors and lawyer friends, particularly those who specialized in bankruptcy.

But I made an alternative decision. My house I rented out so that the rents could carry the mortgage and contribute to paying down my debts. I put everything I owned in storage in the basement except what fit in my car. To reduce my living expenses to almost nothing, I went to live in a twenty-eight-foot sailboat belonging to my old friend Jack Martin, moored at a dock in Emeryville, California, near Oakland. The dock had one plug for electric power (my light or my microwave but not both) and a hose for water (cold), no shower, no toilet. So every morning I carried my porta potty to be emptied at the shoreside public bathroom, took my shower and performed my toilette, then whisked myself away to my law and real estate office in the little convertible which had been one of the extravagances of my prior life.

For two years, I lived first in that sailboat and then on another sailboat of about the same size, moored at the prestigious St. Francis Yacht Club in San Francisco. I was circumspect and stayed on, because that allowed me to continue working while I had reduced my expenses to bare subsistence—to my car, health insurance, professional expenses, and a bit of food.

And so I was ready, my financial health restored, when, in 1996, a friend visited me on my sailboat and urged me to enter the Democratic primary for the U.S. Congress, in what was then the First Congressional

District of California. It stretched from the Oregon border south to the town of Winston, just north of Santa Rosa in Sonoma County, California, some fifty miles north of my law office in San Francisco. We found me an apartment in Healdsburg, in Sonoma County, within the district (although to my surprise there was no requirement that candidates for Congress live in their district).

The campaign was hard fought, but money which I did not have and was not able to raise was the deciding factor. The candidate who did win spent vastly more than I did, because she had it to spend. My campaign consisted primarily of driving a large recreational vehicle, painted with my name and message in five-foot-tall letters, from one community meeting to another, up and down the main highway through the mostly rural district. In the end, however, the winner in the Democratic primary lost to the Republican incumbent in the general election.

The campaign, however, was the occasion for me to get to know and spend time in a little town in the California redwoods called Myers Flat, where, in addition to other activities, I began to publish the only newspaper which had ever existed in Myers Flat.

Every two weeks, on my new and wonderful IBM laptop computer, technology's highest flowering at that time, I published two pages, three columns, of articles, commentaries, even advertisements and jokes. For six years, I continued publishing the *Myers Flat News*, and am delighted that the history department in the Main Library of the County of Humboldt, in Eureka, California, has given shelf space to a complete set of all of those little newspapers. They are a snapshot not only of an otherwise forgotten rural community but of my own philosophical musings (in the era before the Internet, before blogging).

In 2001, with the help of historian David Lisker, a teacher at San Francisco State University, I organized a 40th Anniversary Reunion in Jackson, Mississippi, of the 1961 Freedom Riders. It was the first-ever effort to bring together all of the over four hundred people who comprised the Freedom Riders of 1961. About half of those still alive came to the reunion, held at Tougaloo College in Jackson, Mississippi.

After the 9/11/2001 airplane attacks by terrorists based in Afghanistan on New York's World Trade Center and other American targets, the United States attacked Afghanistan. Less than a year later, I flew to Afghanistan on a citizens' diplomacy mission I had created, mindful of the Marshall plan in Europe and McArthur's plan in Japan, by which after World War II, America had revitalized our enemies into democratic, peaceful states. As citizen diplomats, we wanted to ask one question: What can we as Americans best do to help the people of Afghanistan? In talks with local Afghans, I became convinced that education, particularly of women and girls, was (and is) the answer to that question.

And so education of women and girls in Afghanistan has been my focus since that mission. I created or cocreated three organizations: Afghan Friends Network, which supports girls on scholarship at Kabul University who graduate from our supplemental high-school-level school in Ghazni; the Hayward-Ghazni Sister City Committee, which supports a widows' literacy class in Ghazni and various exchanges; and an organization which is supporting the introduction of educational technology, including One Laptop Per Child (OLPC), into Afghanistan. In five trips to Afghanistan (so far), to the cities of Kabul, Kandahar, and Ghazni, I have tried my best to do my part to Repair the World.

Despite these other interests, I have continued my focus on the unfinished Civil Rights Movement issues of America's South, including the 40th Anniversary Memorial Service, in Neshoba County, Mississippi, for the three civil rights workers slain in 1963, Chaney, Goodman, and Schwerner. In their memory, I contributed to the local public library a set of books about the civil rights movement. I wonder if there is an empty place on the library's shelves, to mark the place where those books should have resided. Or are the books I contributed still there? I wonder.

In 2008, some thirty-five years after I first brought law students into the San Francisco County Jail to help prisoners with their civil legal problems, I was appointed by Sheriff Michael Hennessey, who followed Richard D. Hongisto as sheriff of San Francisco, to serve as Director of Prisoner Legal Services. This arm of the City and County of San Francisco today provides San Francisco jail prisoners with legal aid to attempt to remedy inmates' civil legal problems (often the very problems obstructing their ability to stay out of jail after they are released, such as lack of a driver's license needed to get a job or an erroneous credit report).

Most of these prisoners are minority, black or brown, and most are incarcerated for drugs. By 2009, my work in the jails had caused me to recognize and acknowledge just how bad, how cruel, how absurd are the drug prohibition laws of California and of the United States. I notified the sheriff that I could no longer in conscience participate in the criminal justice system as it applied to drug offenders, particularly African Americans—who were (and are) the vast majority of the prisoners in the San Francisco County Jail.

So I quit and took retirement from my job as Director of Prisoner Legal Services. And having retired from the sheriff's department, I found an appropriate vehicle for my absolute revulsion against the current state of the drug laws in the United States: LEAP, Law Enforcement Against Prohibition. It is an organization of ex-policemen, ex-narcotics officers, ex-sheriff's department officials, ex-prosecutors and defense attorneys, judges and ex-judges, anyone who has been engaged in the criminal justice law enforcement system. Except for one or two judges who came to the view that drug prohibition is wrong while securely in office, all the rest of us at LEAP are ex-something, for to understand the problem makes participating in continuing it well nigh impossible for anyone with any kind of moral compass.

The drug prohibition laws have given a vastly profitable monopoly on the sale of drugs to criminal elements. By greatly magnifying residual discrimination in law enforcement, these laws have also created a prison system filled with African American men and women, suffering from a revived form of the discrimination which I fought as a Freedom Rider. In a recent book by Prof. Michelle Alexander, she details how "The New Jim Crow" has taken the advances of the Civil Rights Movement back, in an even more pernicious form, to the days of slavery. I have signed on to be a speaker for LEAP, and have spoken out to every group that will agree to listen, about the sad, sad situation to which our drug prohibition laws have brought us.

All good things must end, including the lives and the stories of Freedom Riders. In 2011, I participated in the two 50th anniversary reunions of the 1961 Freedom Riders, including sitting on the dais with Oprah Winfrey at her show in Chicago honoring the Freedom Riders, and returning to visit Parchman penitentiary during the 50th Anniversary Reunion in Jackson, Mississippi.

With the publication of this book, my diary of fifty years ago, which I kept while in jail and prison as a Freedom Rider, I am perhaps embarking on yet another new career, as a writer, as did my father at about the same time in his life. As did he, I hope that by my words I can inspire and bring joy to those who come upon them.

CHAPTER NOTES

Chapter 1

1. Jim Crow, laws and customs of rigid discrimination against nonwhite races.
2. The city of Jackson, Mississippi, was named for Andrew Jackson when he was a general, prior to his becoming president of the United States.
3. Klansman, member of the Ku Klux Klan, a white supremacist terrorist organization.
4. Edward H. Levi, dean of the University of Chicago Law School.
5. Leslie (Les) Rosen, New York artist, student of Raphael Sawyer.
6. Muslims, Black Muslims, Nation of Islam, an American religious and racist organization of African Americans.
7. Professor Abram Lincoln Harris, Jr., PhD, my fourth-year undergraduate tutorial professor, University of Chicago College, the leading African American economist of his generation.
8. Pullman Palace Car Company, subject of an 1894 strike which expanded nationwide.
9. *The Magic Mountain*, a novel by Thomas Mann.
10. Dana White, one of my New York roommates, from Chicago.
11. Joan Doe, another roommate, from New York.
12. Gordon Carey, CORE New York Freedom Rider coordinator.
13. Carol Ruth Silver, the author: use of Carol Ruth as a first name, in the southern style, was first adopted in the course of the author's experiences in the southern Civil Rights Movement, and then retained throughout her career and life.
14. James L. Spencer, Jackson municipal judge.
15. Woolworth's, F. W. Woolworth Company, chain of five-and-dime stores with lunch counters.
16. Governor of Mississippi, Ross Barnett.
17. Rockefeller Institute, a vaccine research institute in New York.

Chapter 2

1. William Barbee, a Negro Freedom Rider.
2. Continental Trailways, a nationwide bus company, later bought out by Greyhound.

Chapter 4

1. Hinds County was named for General Thomas Hinds, a hero of the Battle of New Orleans in the fight against the invasion by the British in the War of 1812.
2. Captain J. L. Ray, Jackson police captain.
3. The prosecutor, Jackson District Attorney Jack Travis.
4. A trusty (plural: trusties) is a regular jail inmate who is trusted with tasks working for the jailers in exchange for privileges.

Chapter 5

1. U.S. Attorney General Robert Kennedy.
2. Mississippi County Farm, a low-security jail facility.
3. The Mississippi State Penitentiary at Parchman.

Chapter 6

1. Gwendolyn (Gwen) Greene, Negro Freedom Rider, from Washington, D.C.
2. Patricia (Pat) Elaine Bryant, Negro Freedom Rider, from Elmira, New York.
3. Dion Tyrone Diamond, Negro Freedom Rider, from Howard University.
4. Lowell A. Woods, Jr., Negro Freedom Rider, from Chicago.

Chapter 7

1. Plasticine is a soft material used for making sculptures.

Chapter 8

1. Elmer L. Anderson, governor of Minnesota.
2. Elaine May and Mike Nichols, a popular comedy team.

Chapter 12

1. Poem by Pauline Edythe Knight, reprinted by permission of Durrette Ofosu for the estate of Pauline Knight-Ofosu.

Autobiographical Notes

1. Quoted from MyJewishLearning.Active.com.

SUGGESTED ADDITIONAL READINGS AND DOCUMENTARY FILMS

Adler, Mortimer J. 1969. *The Negro in American History*. Chicago: Encyclopedia Britannica.

Alexander, Michelle. 2010. *The New Jim Crow: Mass Incarceration in the Age of Colorblindness*. New York: New Press.

American Experience, Freedom Riders. 2010. Directed by Stanley Nelson. Produced by Laurens Grant. PBS. Available.

Arsenault, Raymond. 2006. *Freedom Riders: 1961 and the Struggle for Racial Justice*. New York: Oxford University Press.

Bausum, Ann. 2006. *Freedom Riders: John Lewis and Jim Zwerg on the Front Lines of the Civil Rights Movement*. Washington, D.C.: National Geographic.

Blackmon, Douglas A. 2008. *Slavery by Another Name: The Re-Enslavement of Black People in America from the Civil War to World War II*. New York: Doubleday.

Cobb, Charles E., Jr. 2008. *On the Road to Freedom: A Guided Tour of the Civil Rights Trail*. Chapel Hill: Algonquin Books of Chapel Hill–Workman Publishing.

Dickoff, Micki, and Tony Pagano. 2010. *Neshoba: The Price of Freedom*. New York: First Run Features.

Etheridge, Eric, Roger Wilkins, and Diane McWhorter. 2008. *Breach of Peace: Portraits of the 1961 Mississippi Freedom Riders*. New York: Atlas & Co.

"Facing History and Ourselves." 2006. *Eyes on the Prize: America's Civil Rights Movement, 1954–1985; A Study Guide Written by Facing History and Ourselves*. Boston: Blackside.

Holsaert, F. S., M. P. N. Noonan, J. Richardson, B. G. Robinson, J. S. Young, and D. M. Zellner, eds. 2010. *Hands on the Freedom Plow: Personal Accounts by Women in SNCC*. Urbana: University of Illinois Press.

Kunstler, Emily, Sarah Kunstler, Jesse Moss, Susan Korda, and Shahzad Ismaily. 2010. *William Kunstler: Disturbing the Universe*. [United States]: Arthouse Films.

Sanfield, Steve, and John Ward. 1989. *The Adventures of High John the Conqueror*. New York: Orchard Books.

Zellner, Bob. 2008. *The Wrong Side of Murder Creek: A White Southerner in the Freedom Movement*. Montgomery: NewSouth Books.

INDEX

Page numbers in **bold** indicate illustrations.